MW01258482

Creating a Confederate Kentucky

CIVIL WAR AMERICA · Gary W. Gallagher, editor

CREATING A

Confederate Kentucky

THE LOST CAUSE AND CIVIL WAR
MEMORY IN A BORDER STATE

Anne E. Marshall

The University of North Carolina Press · CHAPEL HILL

© 2010 The University of North Carolina Press

All rights reserved. Designed by Courtney Leigh Baker and Set in
Arnhem with American Scribe Display by Achorn International, Inc.
Manufactured in the United States of America. The paper in this book
meets the guidelines for permanence and durability of the Committee on Production Guidelines for Book Longevity of the Council on
Library Resources. The University of North Carolina Press has been
a member of the Green Press Initiative since 2003.

Library of Congress Cataloging-in-Publication Data
Marshall, Anne E. (Anne Elizabeth), 1975–
Creating a Confederate Kentucky : the lost cause and Civil War
memory in a border state / Anne E. Marshall. — 1st ed.
p. cm. — (Civil War America)
Includes bibliographical references and index.
ISBN 978-0-8078-3436-7 (cloth : alk. paper)
ISBN 978-1-4696-0983-5 (pbk. : alk. paper)
1. Kentucky—History—Civil War, 1861–1865—Social aspects.
2. Collective memory—Kentucky. 3. Memory—Social aspects—
Kentucky. 4. Kentucky—History—Civil War, 1861–1865—Influence.
5. United States—History—Civil War, 1861–1865—Social aspects.
6. United States—History—Civil War, 1861–1865—Influence.   I. Title.
E509.M37 2010
976.9'03—dc22
2010020419

cloth   14 13 12 11 10   5 4 3 2 1

paper   17 16 15 14 13   5 4 3 2 1

THIS BOOK WAS DIGITALLY PRINTED.

For my parents,

WILLIAM AND JANET MARSHALL

Contents

Acknowledgments · xi   *Introduction* · 1

⬦⬦⬦⬦⬦⬦⬦⬦⬦ 1 ⬦⬦⬦⬦⬦⬦⬦⬦⬦

A MARKED CHANGE IN THE SENTIMENTS OF THE PEOPLE
Slavery, Civil War, and Emancipation in Kentucky, 1792–1865 · 9

⬦⬦⬦⬦⬦⬦⬦⬦⬦ 2 ⬦⬦⬦⬦⬦⬦⬦⬦⬦

THE REBEL SPIRIT IN KENTUCKY
The Politics of Readjustment, 1865–1877 · 32

⬦⬦⬦⬦⬦⬦⬦⬦⬦ 3 ⬦⬦⬦⬦⬦⬦⬦⬦⬦

WICKED AND LAWLESS MEN
Violence and Confederate Identity, 1865–1885 · 55

⬦⬦⬦⬦⬦⬦⬦⬦⬦ 4 ⬦⬦⬦⬦⬦⬦⬦⬦⬦

WHAT SHALL BE THE MORAL TO YOUNG KENTUCKIANS?
Civil War Memorial Activity in the Commonwealth, 1865–1895 · 81

⬦⬦⬦⬦⬦⬦⬦⬦⬦ 5 ⬦⬦⬦⬦⬦⬦⬦⬦⬦

TWO KENTUCKYS
Civil War Identity in Appalachian Kentucky, 1865–1915 · 111

⬦⬦⬦⬦⬦⬦⬦⬦⬦ 6 ⬦⬦⬦⬦⬦⬦⬦⬦⬦

A PLACE FULL OF COLORED PEOPLE,
PRETTY GIRLS, AND POLITE MEN
Literature, Confederate Identity, and Kentucky's
Reputation, 1890–1915 · 133

⬦⬦⬦⬦⬦⬦⬦⬦⬦ 7 ⬦⬦⬦⬦⬦⬦⬦⬦⬦

A MANIFEST AVERSION TO THE UNION CAUSE
War Memory in Kentucky, 1895–1935 · 155

Afterword · 183   *Notes* · 189   *Bibliography* · 209   *Index* · 225

Illustrations

Scene from "Confedrit X Roads" · 50

Henry Watterson, as portrayed in *Harper's Weekly* · 74

State seal of Kentucky as revised after
Goebel assassination, 1900 · 135

Annie Fellows Johnston and Hattie Cochran · 139

Photograph of Rebecca Porter, model for Annie
Fellows Johnston's Mom Beck · 142

Paul Laurence Dunbar's "Nelse Hatton,"
in *Folks from Dixie* · 152

John Hunt Morgan monument unveiling,
Lexington, 1911 · 173

Abraham Lincoln's birthplace cabin,
Louisville, 1906 · 178

Monument to African American refugees,
Camp Nelson, Kentucky · 186

Acknowledgments

Though the experience of writing a history book is meant to be a solitary one, mine has been anything but. Since I began to conceive of this project over ten years ago, I feel as though I have been in constant conversation with mentors, professors, colleagues, academic observers, history buffs, thinkers, and well-wishers. I offer many thanks to Centre College professors Milton Reigelman, Mark Lucas, Elizabeth Perkins, Clarence Wyatt, and Michael Hamm, whose passionate sense of inquiry and wonderful teaching made me want to pursue this line of work in the first place.

I am greatly beholden to the archivists who aided me in unearthing all of the scattered clues and slippery ways that helped me define the strange ways in which Kentuckians remembered the Civil War: the staff at repositories around the state, including the staff at the Kentucky Heritage Council State Historic Preservation Office; Gordon Hogg and Frank Stanger at University of Kentucky Special Collections; Betsy Morelock at Kentucky State University; and Shannon Wilson at Berea College. I would especially like to thank the good folks at the Filson Historical Society: Mark Wetherington, Jim Holmberg, and Shirley Harmon, who made my Filson Fellowship experience so productive and rewarding. I also want to thank all those who were at the Kentucky Historical Society at the time I conducted research there: Lynne Hollingsworth, Ken Williams, Beth Van Allen, Stuart Sanders, Nelson Dawson, Marilyn Zoidis, Diane Bundy, Darrel Meadows, and Tony Curtis all generously shared their ideas and insights and offered many kinds of support.

I have also been lucky to have wonderful role models in the historians of Kentucky who have preceded me. The late Thomas D. Clark, William Freehling, and James Klotter have been generous with their inspiration and encouragement. I am fortunate to be working at a time in which there is burgeoning scholarship on post–Civil War Kentucky. Thanks to Helen Lacroix, Aaron Astor, and Luke Harlow for their camaraderie and wonderful insights.

Much of this project germinated during the time I was a graduate student at the University of Georgia, where I had great friends, colleagues, and mentors. Tammy Ingram, Bruce Stewart, Alex Macaulay, Jennifer Gross, Judkin Browning, Robby Luckett, Laura Mason, Steven Soper, Susan Rosenbaum, and Kathleen Clark all helped to shape this project with their support and ideas. John Inscoe was particularly generous with his time and support, and I am grateful for his infectious enthusiasm and advice as the work was beginning to take shape.

It goes without saying that anyone interested in probing questions of southern regional identity and historical memory could not have a better example to follow than James C. Cobb. I have always appreciated his willingness to mentor me and his insistence that questions like the ones I was asking were as much about spending time "chewing on the end of my pencil" as they were about time spent in archives. Last but not least, I thank him for providing living proof that great intellectual measure does not have to be accompanied by pretension.

My life has also been made profoundly better by my friendship with Bryant Simon and his family. I will be forever grateful for the time he spent teaching me to be a better scholar and writer, and even more thankful for the way that he, Ann Marie, Benjamin, and Eli have included me in their lives over the years.

In the past few years at Mississippi State University, I have been privileged to have wonderfully engaged colleagues like Jason Phillips, Kathryn Barbier, and Alan Marcus, who have provided me with the encouragement and impetus to complete this project.

I am so very fortunate to have had a loving and supporting family throughout this long endeavor. My parents-in-law, Barb Giesen and Phil Giesen, have offered continual interest and encouragement. My sister, Jennifer, an accountant, has offered moral support and assurance that one day I too might become "financially solvent." Most of all, my parents, Jan and Bill Marshall, have supported me in more ways than I can count. As historians, librarians, research assistants, proofreaders, and providers of financial assistance, they have selflessly given me more assistance than anyone could ever deserve. Through countless educational "vacation" excursions, which I resisted in my youth, they planted an appreciation of and respect for history upon which I continually draw. For this, and because I will be eternally grateful for all they have done for me, I dedicate this book to them.

Though I started this project long before they arrived on this earth, my children have provided much inspiration. Many thanks to Walt, my sweet, funny boy, who is constantly reminding me to get my head out of the past and into the present, and to Eleanor, whose impending birth was at once the most beautiful and the most frightening push that I needed to finish this book.

That brings me to Jim Giesen. As a fellow historian, best friend, supportive colleague, and spouse extraordinaire, he inspires me everyday. No one could ask for more.

Creating a Confederate Kentucky

Introduction

Standing before an immense crowd at the opening of the 1895 Grand Army of the Republic (GAR) encampment in Louisville, Kentucky, *Louisville Courier-Journal* editor Henry Watterson delivered words of welcome, proclaiming, "It is . . . with a kind of exultation that I fling open the gateway to the South!" Many in attendance noted the irony of an ex-Confederate soldier and eminent New South spokesman offering his greetings to Union veterans. What many listeners may not have noticed, however, was the manner in which Watterson cast Kentucky's wartime position, even as he extended his wishes for sectional reconciliation. "You came, and we resisted you," he said of Kentucky's wartime response to men in blue; "you come and we greet you; for times change and men change with them. You will find here no sign of the battle; not a reminiscence of its passion. Grim-visaged war has smoothed his wrinkled front."[1]

Along with many of his fellow white Kentuckians, Watterson seemed to overlook the fact that his home city stood with the Union during the Civil War and had served as a major supply center for the Union army. Furthermore, Union veterans would have had to wander only a few blocks to the intersection of Louisville's Third and Shipp Streets to see an unmistakable "reminiscence of passion," a towering Confederate monument erected just a few months earlier. In fact, the GAR reunion of 1895 fell amid a late nineteenth-century swarm of Lost Cause activity that led many people, both inside and outside of the commonwealth, to forget that Kentuckians had never fully been part of the mythic past they celebrated so fervently. Theirs, it seemed, was a cause they had not actually lost.

In the thirty years between the end of the Civil War and Watterson's speech, Kentucky developed a Confederate identity that was seemingly at odds with its historical past. From the first rumblings of sectional tension early in the nineteenth century, Kentucky lay at both a geographical and an ideological crossroads. The commonwealth shared in that most defining characteristic of southern society—slavery. Yet a vested interest in the peculiar institution proved insufficient reason for most white Kentuckians to leave the Union. In 1860, white Kentuckians had voted overwhelmingly for John Bell, the presidential candidate whose platform was dedicated to maintaining the Union. When Governor Beriah Magoffin's pledge to keep Kentucky a neutral state proved untenable early in the war, Kentuckians famously divided against themselves, brother against brother, father against son, neighbor against neighbor. Eventually, between 90,000 and 100,000 men chose to fight for the Union, while only 25,000 to 40,000 pledged themselves to the Confederate war effort.[2]

One might have guessed that the way Kentuckians would remember the war would have approximated the divisive manner in which they fought it. By the 1870s, however, the contrast between Kentuckians' wartime sympathies and postbellum sympathies was marked. In the decades following the conflict, with amazing accord, white Kentuckians elected five governors who had sympathized with or fought for the Confederacy. They cheered in the streets in 1877 when the last Federal troops left the South, removing the final vestiges of Reconstruction. They built Confederate monuments, published sectional periodicals, participated in veterans' organizations and historical societies, and produced literature that portrayed Kentucky as Confederate, while seemingly leaving the Union cause and the feats of its soldiers largely uncelebrated.[3]

This outward incongruity between the way that white Kentuckians entered and participated in the Civil War and the way that they remembered it has become one of the great paradoxes of Civil War history. Kentucky's postwar identity shift is a phenomenon that has captured the interest of many scholars who have studied the state's political behavior during the Reconstruction period, even before E. Merton Coulter enshrined the popular notion that Kentuckians "waited until after the war was over to secede from the Union." The prevailing thought among historians who have answered Coulter has been that Kentuckians' seemingly Confederate behavior simply masked concerns that had little to do with southern war aims. Some scholars downplay Kentuckians' supposed embrace of the Lost Cause as a "grandfather's myth" or at most a mistaken assumption on the part of national observers who equated Kentucky's antifederal sentiments as Confederate sympathies.[4]

Other historians have attributed the postwar southward turn to the efforts of various "power groups," or economic and geographic factions, to seize control of the "power vacuum" that existed after the war. Viewing pro-Confederate rhetoric as a self-contained effort by Kentuckians in various areas of the state to control railroad, coal, and other commercial interests, they have concluded that "neo-Confederatism was only a weapon" in postwar economic and political competition within the state.[5]

Another trend among historians has been to blame Kentucky's shifting loyalties on the supposed distinctiveness of its citizens. According to this line of thinking, residents of the Bluegrass State shared a "Kentucky Mind," which was "conditioned to individuality" and which combined love for Union with resentment of interference in state affairs. Other historians, drawing upon the theories of Maurice Halbwachs, have asserted that Kentuckians held a unique "collective consciousness," which made them think differently about the Civil War than citizens of any other state. E. Merton Coulter summed up this rationale when he wrote, "Unquestionably Kentuckians were simply different. They got into the war in their own way, fought it their own way, and came out of it in their own way. If they should wait until after the war to secede whose right was it but their own. . . . Kentuckians were not like their neighbors, and of this they were duly proud." The implicit assumption in this line of reasoning is that the collective distinctiveness belonged to *white* Kentuckians, and only they remembered or had influence over the memory of the war.[6]

These theories are rather shortsighted and oversimplistic, in many cases obscuring more than they reveal. Furthermore, by confining their studies to the ten or so years that followed the war, these scholars, I argue, miss the locus of the long-lasting Confederate identity of the state. Although Kentucky earned its rebellious reputation through the electoral politics and racial and political violence of the immediate postwar period, by the late nineteenth century expressions of Confederate identity were largely cultural. This book traces the long and varied development of Confederate identity in Kentucky between 1865 and 1935 and argues that it is because the latter-day rebellion accumulated in myriad forms for such an extended period of time that it holds so much power in the interpretation of the state's history.

Rather than focusing exclusively on the short-term political and economic factors, this book looks at the long-term political culture, or the cultural practices of Kentuckians through which they recalled the Civil War. Toward this end, I have utilized a body of evidence that historians of Kentucky have yet to apply to this subject. In addition to traditional sources such as manuscript collections, diaries, memoirs, and newspaper accounts, I have used travel accounts, fiction, and songs and periodicals both from and about Kentucky. Other evidence includes public celebrations such as parades, monument construction, veterans' meetings, and other memorial and organizational activities.[7]

Rather than revealing the existence of a "Kentucky Mind," a single shared consciousness among Kentuckians, these activities reveal that there was no *one* memory of the war in Kentucky but rather divergent memories belonging to many Kentuckians, which competed with one another over time for cultural primacy. While white Confederate memory dominated the historical landscape of postwar Kentucky on the surface, a closer look reveals an active political and cultural dialogue that included white Unionist and Confederate Kentuckians, as well as the state's African Americans, who from the last days of the war drew on the Union victory and their part in winning it to lay claim to the fruits of freedom and citizenship. This book will look at how and to what end these groups employed their memories of the Civil War in the sixty years following the conflict. Moreover, it will examine how Kentuckians' efforts to remember sectional conflict affected the state's identity in the eyes of outsiders.

Here it is necessary that I insert a point of clarification: it is important to understand that Kentucky was, before, during, and after the Civil War, a southern state. In this book, I do *not* argue that Kentucky became a southern state after the Civil War, but rather that the efforts of white Kentuckians to celebrate the Confederacy played a major role in cementing and embellishing Kentucky's already-existing southern identity, in effect making it more southern.

The first chapter roots Kentuckians' postwar behavior in their antebellum and Civil War experiences, focusing on the state's relationship to slavery, as well as on how and why most Kentuckians chose to remain in the Union and why they began to reject that decision during the war. The next two chapters examine Kentuckians' postwar allegiance to the Democratic Party and the rampant political and racial violence that helped create the idea that it was a "rebellious" state. Chapter 4 looks at public memorial activity between 1865 and 1895 and traces how and why Confederate historical work began to overshadow Unionist memory.

Chapter 5 moves to the eastern portion of the state to look at how Appalachian Kentucky became a Unionist counterpoint to a Confederate Kentucky, and chapter 6 looks at popular literature produced by Kentuckians around the turn of the century that influenced public perception of the state's Civil War experience. Chapter 7 returns to the subject of memorial activity in the state, focusing on the years between 1895 and 1935. In this period of time, Confederate culture took over the public face of the state, masking a remarkable level of historical conversation regarding the interpretation of the war. Finally, the afterword examines Kentuckians' continually evolving conceptions of the Civil War.

KENTUCKY NATIVE ROBERT PENN WARREN, himself the grandson of a Confederate veteran, wrote of the way Americans remember the Civil War: "When one is happy in forgetfulness, facts get forgotten." In the case of Kentuckians, and all Americans, it is less important to ask what facts were disregarded than to reveal *why* they were forgotten. The conservative racial, social, political, and gender values inherent in Confederate symbols and the Lost Cause greatly appealed to many white Kentuckians, who despite their devotion to the Union had never entered the war in order to free slaves. In a postwar world where racial boundaries were in flux, the Lost Cause and the conservative politics that went with it seemed not only a comforting reminder of a past free of late nineteenth-century insecurities but also a way to reinforce contemporary efforts to maintain white supremacy.[8]

Most scholars of the subject have imagined the contest for the Civil War identity of Kentucky as a battle between white Unionists and white Confederates, assuming that white Kentuckians alone had the cultural power to shape postwar memory. Even before the war ended, however, Kentucky African Americans sought to appropriate war memory to further their own aspirations. In Emancipation Day celebrations, Fourth of July parades, and political gatherings, they infused the Union victory so effectively with their own meanings and aims that conservative whites found little in Union victory that was associated with their own racially conservative values. Essentially, this study reveals that Union memory in Kentucky became too closely associated with emancipation and African American progress for white Unionists to accept it as their own.

IN RECENT DECADES, scholars of historical memory have shown how societies are defined by the stories they tell about their past. Historical pasts, they have revealed, are not simply immutable, transhistorical narratives, but dynamic human constructions. Scholarship on the subject has increasingly focused on the role humans play in the production of their own history. Historical narratives do not simply construct themselves, but are, as W. Fitzhugh Brundage states, the products of "the active labor of selecting, structuring, and imposing meaning on the past." Furthermore, people often construct the past in ways that serve their current needs, choosing to remember some events and versions of history, while downplaying and willfully forgetting others. Historians of memory are particularly interested in the intrinsic power that lies within history and its interpretation and the broad political and cultural authority it carries in buttressing contemporary social, political, and economic objectives.[9]

Taking this scholarship into account, a major theme of this book is the malleability of historical memory and its change over time. Rather than generalizing Kentuckians' apparent Confederate turn as wholesale, my work seeks to highlight the temporal and geographical inconsistencies in the state's postwar identity. It also reveals how outsiders' perceptions of Kentucky's latter-day rebelliousness changed over time. In the years immediately following the war, northerners viewed Kentuckians' "rebel" behavior as betrayal, but by the twentieth century, they viewed vestiges of the Confederacy more nostalgically. This was due in part to the changes in the ways that northerners viewed southerners and their Civil War cause as well as the national growth of reunionist sentiment. It also has much to do with developments inside Kentucky, such as feuding and other violence, political corruption, and the postwar decline of the state's overall reputation.

These findings also bear implications for recent scholarship in national war memory, in particular, that of David Blight, who has garnered much-deserved praise for his masterful interpretation of shifting national sentiment. Blight has suggested that by the end of the war there was in the North at least the possibility for a postwar emancipationist consensus among whites and African Americans. Between 1865 and 1915, he argues, this chance eroded as "sentimental remembrance won over ideological memory." In the end, the white impetus for national reunion ultimately came at the expense of a northern "emancipationist" vision and black political aims. What Blight overlooks, however, is that vast numbers of loyal citizens never embraced an "emancipationist" version of Unionism, and, as Kentucky's path shows, in the border South and likely in many other loyal states, the "emancipationist" narrative was never in viable contention for white memory.[10]

In their apparent uniqueness, Kentuckians' efforts to find meaning in the Civil War have something to tell us about the way many Americans remembered the brutal conflict. Their example suggests that in many places and over time the way people interpreted the war often had little to do with their wartime loyalties. In this sense, the study of postwar memory in the Bluegrass State complicates simple distinctions in sectional war memory and generalizations between North and South, "Confederate" and "Yankee." Focusing on this border state reveals that, although few Americans went as far as white Kentuckians in actually trading a Union group identity for a Confederate one, Civil War memory was not always geographically defined, and that it was pluralistic and subject to myriad nuanced interpretations, and, most important, it was, and still is, greatly contested.

1

A Marked Change in
the Sentiments of the People

SLAVERY, CIVIL WAR, AND EMANCIPATION

IN KENTUCKY, 1792–1865

On a spring day in 1865, Maria Hawes traveled by boat up the Mississippi River toward her home in Kentucky. The daughter-in-law of Kentucky's short-term Confederate provisional governor, Richard Hawes, Maria and her family were banished from the state because of their high-profile disloyalty. She had spent much of the Civil War following her husband's Confederate regiment from battle to battle around the South, and now, as she traveled from New Orleans, sadness filled her. The war had been full of physical and fiscal hardship, a fact underscored by her recollection that the bonnet she wore now had adorned her head ever since she left Kentucky years earlier. For the Hawes's traveling companion, however, the trip back to Kentucky was a homecoming of a different sort. Her Kentucky owner had sold the elderly black woman, known to the Hawes family as "Mammy," to someone in Texas years before. Acting upon her newly gained freedom, she was returning home in search of friends and loved ones left behind. In exchange for traveling expenses, Mammy agreed to serve as the family's nurse and was, according to Maria Hawes, "very glad of the opportunity." Hawes and Mammy, two strangers who negotiated a working relationship starkly unlike any they would have known prior to the war, returned home to Kentucky together to face a new and uncertain future.[1]

Like Maria Hawes and Mammy, no matter what their sectional loyalties or their feelings about the war's outcome Kentuckians faced a postwar social order that bore little resemblance to the world they had known before.

As Kentucky Confederate Basil Duke wrote decades later in his memoirs, "No such metamorphosis, perhaps, has been produced in so brief a period," with the exception of the French Revolution. "The life of the post-bellum South," he concluded, "no more resembled that of the [antebellum] than the life of the early settlers of this continent was like [that] they had left on the other side of the ocean." Kentucky at the war's close was a world of disorder. Fields, farms, and infrastructure lay in ruins, as did the social and familial relationships of families and neighbors. There was the human cost as well. Nearly 30,000, or one in five, Kentuckians who fought had lost their lives. Neighbors had sided against one another, churches had split over the morality of slavery and questions of secession, and the war had destroyed the slave-based labor system and jeopardized the racial hierarchy. Most whites lamented the uncertainty of black freedom; formerly enslaved African Americans joyously celebrated it even as they faced new worries about subsisting on their own.[2]

Issues unique to Kentucky, a border slave state that had remained within the Union, complicated the universal agonies of war. Kentuckians had to make sense of a war that had vastly different ramifications from those many had expected when they chose sides five years earlier. The Civil War had many consequences, but none more profound than releasing from bondage 4 million enslaved African Americans. This radical action on the part of the Lincoln administration, designed to provide more manpower and moral impetus to the Union at a crucial juncture in the war, changed the nature of the conflict as well as its meaning. Americans would come to remember the war as not only a conflict over states' rights and the meaning of nationhood but as an event that ended slavery, making it a "second American Revolution." It is easy to forget that black freedom was not an original war aim and that many border southerners offered their loyalty to the Union with the expectation that the United States government, instead of destroying slavery, would be the best *protector* of the institution. Although this assumption seems unlikely, if not foolish, in retrospect, their perceived betrayal by the Federal government became key to the way white Kentuckians would remember, define, and assign significance to their wartime experience in the coming decades.[3]

BY THE TIME questions of slavery erupted into war in 1861, white Kentuckians had been wrestling with the institution for decades. Slavery existed in Kentucky well before statehood, and African Americans were among the earliest explorers of the state. Kentuckians inherited slavery from Virginia, and slave labor helped white settlers from the mother state and from North Carolina transform Kentucky from "a good poor man's land" into a good rich man's land, as settlers with means established hemp and tobacco plantations in the image of those they left behind in the old commonwealth. Slaves composed 6.2 percent of the state's population in 1790, and they made up 24 percent in 1830, a rate of increase that eclipsed white population growth during the same period. Most of these slaves inhabited the Bluegrass region and the corridor between Lexington and Louisville. But as settlers claimed land in the less fertile, less desirable Pennyroyal and Jackson Purchase regions in the western portion of the state, they established slavery in those areas as well.[4]

From the time of statehood, white Kentuckians shared an ambivalent relationship with slavery. Written in 1792, the state's first constitution protected the right to own slaves, demonstrating the influence of native Virginians, who hoped to cast Kentucky in the mold of her mother state. Nevertheless, a sizable contingent of white laborers and men without property opposed slavery because of the competition it posed. White Kentuckians actively debated the drawbacks of slavery during the first decade of statehood, but as many of the more zealous antislavery citizens relocated to the Northwest Territory and the remaining citizens gained an ever-increasing stake in the system, the institution became the accepted status quo.[5]

Patterns of slavery in Kentucky varied as much as the state's disparate geographical and topographical regions. Within the central Bluegrass region, a lush and fertile expanse stretching between the foothills of the Appalachian Mountains in the south and east, beyond the Green River in the west, and just shy of the Ohio River to the north, slavery came the closest to the plantation form it took in the Deep South. In the Pennyroyal and Jackson Purchase regions that form an isosceles triangle in the western part of the state, slavery was more diffuse but still essential for the tobacco production that dominated the area. Louisville, Kentucky's largest urban area, quickly grew to be a major center of urban trade, while Covington and Newport, tucked just south of the Ohio River, served as commercial outposts to Cincinnati, the bustling "porkopolis" across the river. Slavery in these cities was widespread. The institution was much less prevalent in the ruggedly mountainous eastern portion of the state but not uncommon in valley areas. Appalachian scholars have argued in recent years that even counties that recorded no slaves in the census were touched by the institution, as slaves, owners, and traders moved through the mountains on their way to central Kentucky slave markets. Thus, patterns of slavery varied within Kentucky, but the institution touched every corner of the commonwealth.[6]

By 1800, slave labor fueled both Kentucky's large-scale hemp economy, which gave rise to the landed aristocracy of the Bluegrass region, and the tobacco economy in the central and western portions of the state. The early nineteenth-century Bluegrass economy, centered in Lexington, was based on hemp culture and its manufacture into rope and the bags in which the cotton from the Deep South cotton was packaged. As cotton production grew during the 1840s, so did the demand for hemp production, which remained strong until the Union army cut off Kentucky trade with the South during the Civil War and the region turned elsewhere for its rope and bagging needs. The labor-intensive tobacco and hemp industries necessitated large-scale slave use, but they also featured short growing seasons. Even when farmers applied their slave labor to their secondary crops, such as corn and wheat, Kentucky's agricultural cycle resulted in much "idle" time for slaves and less profit for slave owners and created the state's long-held reputation for having a particularly benign form of the institution.[7]

This agricultural pattern also meant that Kentucky remained a state of small slaveholders. According to the 1850 census, 38,385 Kentuckians, 28 percent of the white families, owned slaves. Yet the average slaveholder owned only 5.4 slaves, the lowest average per owner in the South, with the exception of Missouri. By 1860, the number of slaveholders in Kentucky had increased slightly, with only Virginia and Georgia having more. Unlike their counterparts further South, however, they owned relatively few bondsmen and women. Of Kentucky slave owners, 57 percent held fewer than five slaves, and many had as few as one. Only seventy slaveholders owned fifty or more slaves, and just seven claimed over one hundred. No Kentucky families owned over three hundred slaves. Slave ownership was thus a widespread practice shared by small farmers and large-scale planters alike.[8]

Beyond ownership, the state's flourishing slave trade ensured that slavery touched many Kentuckians. By 1820, white settlers of the Deep South states of Mississippi, Alabama, Louisiana, and later Texas needed a massive amount of slave labor to transform densely wooded land into acres of cotton and sugarcane. Slaves consequently became more valuable in these labor-intensive areas than they had ever been in places like Kentucky, and white Kentuckians began to sell their slaves "down the river" to Natchez and New Orleans at a steady pace. The beginnings of the commonwealth's southbound slave trade are difficult to pinpoint, but English observer Henry Fearon noted its appearance as early as 1818, when he noted fourteen flatboats full of Kentucky slaves on their way down the Mississippi.[9]

Thus, although Kentucky whites comforted themselves with the notion that slavery was more benign in the commonwealth than in any other southern state, they simultaneously participated heavily in what was perhaps the worst aspect of the peculiar institution. Throughout the first half of the nineteenth century, coffles of slaves traveled across the state, through the mountains from Virginia, from towns and rural areas north, south, east, and west, toward Lexington's bustling slave market. There traders assigned their value and sent them to Louisville, where they boarded boats that would take them down the Ohio and Mississippi Rivers to the cotton and sugar plantations of the Deep South. As both demand for and prices of slaves rose in the 1840s and 1850s, more white Kentuckians realized the profit to be made from selling their slaves.

Along with the immediate economic benefit, the ever-proximate Ohio River and chance of escape compelled many Kentucky slaveholders to sell. Seven hundred miles of the commonwealth bordered freedom, and along with other border states Kentucky was the point of departure for many of the more than 5,000 slaves who escaped north annually. In the 1850s alone, traders sold approximately 15 percent of the state's slaves southward. The net effect of the declining usefulness of slavery and the increasing trade in human flesh created what William Freehling has referred to as the "slave drain," which helped to lessen the state's commitment to the institution, something about which Deep South slaveholders fretted.[10]

This weaker economic dependence on slave labor in Kentucky accommodated a growing public debate regarding slavery that would have been unthinkable further south. White Kentuckians tended to tolerate antislavery sentiment to a point. The state boasted several nationally prominent abolitionists, including John Fee, the Methodist minister who founded Berea College in the name of biracial education. Fee's abolitionism was rooted in intense religious conviction. In 1859, an angry proslavery mob eventually drove him out of Kentucky after he gave a speech in New York in which he called for "more John Browns." Most Kentucky abolitionists, however, made their pitches with less religious fervor, arguing against slavery because they thought the institution was bad for white citizens. The state's best-known and most colorful antislavery activist was Cassius Clay. The author of the antislavery publication *The True American*, Clay defended his Lexington press office with a small cannon and his person with a bowie knife. Along with other emancipationists, he envisioned a Kentucky developed along northern industrial lines and argued that slavery was a hindrance to the growth of manufacturing and the state's ability to attract white labor.[11]

Robert J. Breckinridge's brand of emancipationist thought illustrates the contradictory ideals held by many white Kentuckians. The politician-turned-Presbyterian-minister was, himself, the owner of many slaves, but he argued in favor of gradual, compensated emancipation. Like Clay, Breckinridge's antislavery conviction was primarily based on his interest in increasing economic opportunities for whites. As he explained in 1849, "one of the leading motives" of his work was "the hope of substituting the race of negro slaves with the race of free whites." Moreover, Breckinridge harbored aspirations for a lily-white Kentucky. He clearly stated his position in December 1848, when he wrote in the *Lexington Observer and Reporter* that "emancipation is not the main thing—not even *a* main thing as it may aid an object more important than itself, *Unity of race, and that the white race for Kentucky*." Other antislavery quarters echoed the thinking of Clay and Breckinridge. The editor of the northern Kentucky Newport-based abolitionist paper, the *Free South*, appealed to this line of argument in 1853 when he implored: "Workingmen of Kentucky, think of yourselves! See you not that the system of slavery enslaves all who labor for an honest living. You, white men, are the best slave property South, and it is your votes that makes you so."[12]

For most white Kentuckians, however, racial anxiety dominated the discussion of slavery. Many slaveholders and nonslaveholders alike believed that slavery was a necessary evil. Historian Harold Tallant explains that before the 1850s "the existence of slavery was tolerated only out of deference to the property rights of slaveholders and out of concern for the alleged necessity of controlling the black race of Kentucky." Viewing "the races" as inexorably different, white Kentuckians believed it was impossible to peacefully coexist with African Americans outside of slavery and that racial hatred and competition were inevitable by-products of a society where the two races cohabited. Many whites believed that African Americans, freed from shackles but not from resentments, would retaliate against them. In 1860, free African Americans in Kentucky numbered fewer than 11,000, less than 1 percent of the state's population, but their specter loomed larger than their actual numbers. They were, as E. Merton Coulter described, "pariahs of the land and despised by all."[13]

Despite their own ambivalence about the institution, abolitionist pressure generally made white Kentuckians more defensive of slavery. In the

1830s, the majority of voters favored some variation of gradual emancipation; but the idea lessened in popularity in the 1840s because of what Kentuckians perceived as the persistent "interference" of radical northern abolitionists who were inundating the state with what seemed to be incendiary propaganda. White Kentuckians feared that this material would provoke slaves into violence and rebellion or, more likely, escape. Even more abhorrent to white Kentuckians was the widespread practice of the most aggressive abolitionists, who kidnapped slaves and carried them to freedom. Even nonslaveholders disagreed with what they saw as a blatant violation of property rights. So threatening and insulting was the perceived interference of northern abolitionists that by the late 1840s most Kentucky whites were unwilling to back gradual emancipation.

Even as some Kentuckians grew more convinced of slavery's imminent demise within the state, others tried to secure their grasp on the institution. At the state constitutional convention of 1849, proslavery whites saw an opportunity to strengthen their hold on the institution. By effectively preventing an antislavery presence at the convention, they were able to include a proslavery article in the new constitution that ensured the ownership of slaves as an "absolute property right." In addition, the delegates instructed the General Assembly to draw up new legislation that required free and manumitted African Americans to leave the state under threat of imprisonment. The 1849 convention became the last major state political forum in which Kentuckians discussed slavery before the Civil War.[14]

TWO WORKS OF popular culture served to familiarize most Americans with the distinctive form of the peculiar institution in the commonwealth. By far the most famous account of Kentucky slavery appeared in 1852 with the publication of Harriet Beecher Stowe's *Uncle Tom's Cabin*. In her monumental critique of slavery, Stowe set much of her story in the Bluegrass State, where, as she explained, "perhaps the mildest form of the system . . . [was] to be seen." Stowe, who lived in Cincinnati at the time, visited Kentucky several times, traveling to a number of locales, including Paint Lick, Mason County, and Garrard County.[15]

She set her story in Kentucky not only because of the ample material and observations collected during her travels, but also because the state served a greater allegorical purpose. Kentucky proved that even in its most benign form, slavery was fundamentally evil. "Whoever visits some estates there, and witnesses the good-humored indulgence of some masters and mistresses and the affectionate loyalty of some slaves, might be tempted to dream the oft-fable poetic legend of a patriarchal institution, and all that," Stowe wrote of Bluegrass slavery, "but over and above the scene there broods a portentous shadow—the shadow of the *law*." For the book's millions of readers, the kind-hearted but financially strapped Shelbys came to represent slavery's unavoidable tragedy: that economic value of human bondage "could cause [owners] any day to exchange the life of kind protection for hopeless misery and toil." The lesson Kentucky offered for Stowe's millions of readers around the world was that it was "impossible to make anything beautiful or desirable in the best regulated administration of slavery."[16]

In 1853, Stephen Foster also drew upon the tragedy of slave families torn apart by sale, when he wrote the world-famous ballad "My Old Kentucky Home." The song enjoyed immediate national popularity—Christy's Minstrels performed it all over the country—and achieved even greater vogue after the war, as it invoked white nostalgia for the antebellum days of "young folks roll[ing] on the little cabin floor, all merry, all happy, and bright." Conveniently forgotten and unsung by many Kentuckians were the more ominous second and third verses, which told of a Kentucky slave family torn apart by the southward sale of one of its members. Verse three ends with these lines:

> The head must bow and the back will have to bend,
> Wherever the darky may go;
> A few more days and the trouble all will end,
> In the fields where the sugar-canes grow;
> A few more days for to tote the weary load,
> No matter, 'twill never be light;
> A few more days till we totter on the road,
> Then, my old Kentucky home, good night![17]

It is no surprise, considering the border state's internal debate and its national reputation, that Kentucky found itself in the center of national political issues in 1860. The election that year pitted two native Kentuckians, Democrat John C. Breckinridge and Republican Abraham Lincoln, against Constitutional Union candidate John Bell. Bell, whose party's platform focused almost exclusively upon preserving the Union, dominated central and southwestern Kentucky, where slaveholding and commercial interests were strongest, as well as urban Louisville. Although they would later become unionist strongholds, the state's Appalachian counties showed their continued loyalty to the Democratic Party and voted overwhelmingly in favor of Breckinridge. Lincoln, Kentucky's other native son, received less than 1 percent of the state's popular vote, and Bell carried the state by 13,000 votes.[18]

Despite the indications of the 1860 election, Kentucky's commitment to the Union was not a foregone conclusion. Governor Beriah Magoffin was a southern sympathizer, and after the attack on Fort Sumter in April 1861 many Kentuckians quickly formed a States' Rights faction. Magoffin, however, had no wish to secede, but when Lincoln requested that the state organize militia units he replied that Kentucky would "furnish no troops for the wicked purpose of subduing her sister Southern States." Ultimately, the state declared neutrality, pledging to remain independent of both sides and demanding that troops from neither side enter Kentucky borders. Hundreds of men and the State Guard stood armed and ready to back up that pledge.[19]

Both the Federal government and the Confederacy complied with these demands for several months, each side fearing that violation would mean Kentucky's defection to the other. Neither northern nor southern troops, however, could stay out of Kentucky's strategically important territory indefinitely. By September 1861, the state's policy of neutrality became moot as Confederate troops entered the state, with Union troops fast on their heels. Meanwhile, the state's secession faction, based in the heavily proslavery western portion of the state, formed a provisional Confederate government in Russellville, near the Tennessee border. The secessionists set up a capitol in nearby Bowling Green and became the twelfth state admitted to the Confederacy in 1861. Their venture was short-lived, however, as they were forced to evacuate the city in February 1862, along with Kentucky's rebel troops. After their retreat, the secessionists were reduced to using an army tent as their capitol.[20]

In many ways, Kentucky's geographical situation as a border state engendered complicated sectional allegiances among its citizens. Many Kentuckians felt a filial tie with their mother state of Virginia, while others held family and economic connections to "newer" northern states like Illinois, where numerous former residents of the commonwealth settled in the first half of the nineteenth century. The state shared financial ties and trade relations with both the South and the North. Politically speaking, most white Kentuckians shared in Whig ideals. Even in the years after the Whig Party dissolved, they remained committed to the political philosophy of their beloved political icon, Henry Clay. In both their electoral behavior and their political sensibilities, they carried a sense of integrated nationalism that the idea of secession offended. They also tended to see the national government as a potentially constructive force that had, despite decades of effort by citizens and politicians to destroy slavery, managed to protect the institution.[21]

Yet Unionist sentiment in the state was not without weaknesses. As E. F. Drake, a Louisville resident, wrote to Salmon P. Chase in 1861: "If the late vote of Ky is relied on, as an indication of the strength of the Union party it will deceive you. The vote showed a large majority, but when carefully considered it will be found that nearly all old men are unionists at heart and in action while their sons, living in their fathers houses are heading rebellion. There is another large class, who sympathize with the rebels, yet from policy vote and talk Union, and almost *every* Union man considers the *South* aggrieved, and expects an end of the war only by agreeing to any demand by way of guarantee which the South may demand. . . . I am sure Kentucky is only a Union State for fear of the consequences of being the seat of war as a border Confederate State." As Drake suggested, the war did pit fathers against sons, and it was not unusual for families to be divided in loyalties along generational lines. Robert J. Breckinridge committed himself to the Union and two of his sons fought in the Federal army; two others fought for the rebel cause. As George Prentice, the prominent editor of the *Louisville Journal*, preached the Union cause in the pages of his newspaper, two of his sons were off fighting for the Confederacy. The families of Kentucky's great compromisers Henry Clay and John Crittenden were similarly divided. Kentuckian James Speed, who served as Lincoln's attorney general, argued that generational tensions and familial bonds aided the southern cause, writing early in the war, "So many of our giddy young men have gone into the Southern army, that almost every man who goes into our army, knows that he has to fight a neighbor, a relative, a brother, a son or father—I have been astonished to find out how many persons permit family ties to override their allegiance to the government."[22]

One Kentuckian who illustrated how complicated the relationships among slavery, family, and sectional loyalty could be was Brutus Clay, a Bourbon County farmer and politician. Brutus, brother to abolitionist Cassius and related more distantly to Henry Clay, owned a considerable number of slaves, who worked his sizable estate. Brutus also exemplified a number of Kentuckians who played absentee landlord to large cotton plantations in the South. In the late 1840s, Clay and his family began to purchase interest and land in Bolivar County, Mississippi, so that even as a border southerner he shared the business interests and dependency on the peculiar institution of Deep South planters. Yet, throughout the crises of 1860 and 1861, he maintained an unwavering commitment to the Union. This loyalty survived the warnings of his brother-in-law and plantation manager, who wrote him pointedly in 1862: "How any *slave owner* in Kentucky can now sustain this war and administration is a mystery to me."[23]

Brutus Clay's devotion to national unity transcended whatever fears he may have harbored regarding the fate of slavery or his own livelihood, but the same could not be said for several of his children, whose varying personal, political, and economic allegiances caused the Clay household to splinter over the course of the war. In April 1861, Brutus's son Christopher described himself as a "Union man" but pronounced that Lincoln's declaration of war had "forced me to share my fate with the South, my present home & salvation." By May, he was firmly in the secessionist camp. Another of Brutus's sons, Zeke, snuck out of the house one night the following September to join Confederate forces. Clay's daughter, Martha, also became a secessionist, while another of his sons, Green, fought briefly for the Union.[24]

Despite their rampant uncertainty about Lincoln's intentions regarding the peculiar institution, white Kentuckians like Clay generally believed that the Union provided a safer bet for protecting their political and economic interests, *including* slavery. Other proponents of Unionism invoked this point in their efforts to secure Kentuckians loyalty to the Union as well. In late 1861, Robert J. Breckinridge wrote: "The profitable continuance of negro slavery anywhere on this continent, and its continuance at all in the Border Slave States, depends absolutely upon the existence of a common national government embracing both the Free States and the Slave States." "Our political system," he asserted, "affords not only the highest, but the only effectual protection for interests that are local and exceptional—and at the same time out of sympathy with the general judgment of mankind. And of all possible interests, that of the owners of slaves, in a free country stands most in need of the protection of such a system." He predicted that secession would "do nothing more surely than drain the slaves, owned by secessionists in the Border States, farther south—and leave the slave interest in the restored Union, a far weaker political element than when they sought to strengthen it by revolution."[25]

Unionist politician Joseph Holt also employed arguments about slavery in the interest of capturing public sentiment for his cause. Holt, who served as secretary of war under James Buchanan and whose political wrangling was largely responsible for a Unionist victory in the state legislature in 1861, asserted that the federally supported Fugitive Slave Law, "effective in its power of recapture, but infinitely more potent in its moral agency in preventing the escape of slaves," alone "save[d] the institution in the Border States from utter extinction." Noting that the privilege would be unavailable to them if they joined the Confederacy, Holt appealed to white Kentuckians' fear of losing their property. Kentucky, he argued, "will virtually have Canada brought to her doors in the form of Free States, whose populations, relieved of all moral and constitutional obligations to deliver up fugitive slaves, will stand with open arms inviting and welcoming them, and defending them, if need be, at the point of the bayonet. Under such influences, slavery will perish rapidly away in Kentucky, as a ball of snow melts in the summer's sun." Unionist Kentucky politicians urged their constituents not to secede for the sake of, not in spite of, their property rights and the retention of the status quo.[26]

Ultimately, after choosing their sides, between 66,000 and 76,000 white Kentuckians fought for the Union, and an estimated 25,000 to 40,000 enlisted in the Confederate ranks. Many, it seemed, believed, as Cassius Clay argued, that "the only safety *is* in the government of our fathers." Interestingly, Kentucky's participation in the Federal military and in the Confederate military was nearly even when it came to the leadership ranks. The Confederacy boasted thirty-eight Kentucky-born generals; the Union had forty-one. What is most telling about Kentucky's participation in the Civil War is the number of men who *did not* fight. Of Kentucky's eligible white males, 71 percent chose not to fight at all. Lincoln attempted to draft white Kentuckians twice during the war. In the first effort, the Federal government called for a little over 9,000 troops. Only 421 offered personal service, while nearly 4,000 provided proxies or monetary commutation. In 1864, the vast majority of eligible men dodged the draft completely. Unionist sentiment was not enough to compel people to fight. In July, Lincoln tried again, this time calling for over 16,000 troops. Fewer than 1,500 responded for personal service, with almost 2,000 finding substitutes of some sort. In sum, fewer than 25 percent of those targeted responded to the draft in any form. The state incurred a quota deficit of 15,472 men. By contrast, 24,000, or 40 percent, of Kentucky's able African American males served the Union. Of the southern states, only Louisiana boasted more black recruits. White Kentuckians' reluctance to fight reflected their irresolution about the war, the Federal government, and a president for whom they did not vote.[27]

From the outset of the struggle, Kentuckians endured an environment of fear, suspicion, and violence. The instability and distrust that emerged among the state's civilians as sectional and political partisanship, racial fears, and economic deprivation increased fostered violent and unlawful behavior that often took the form of irregular or guerrilla warfare. Armed and mounted bands of men roamed primarily the rural areas of the state, robbing, stealing, and destroying property. Although their goals varied, these marauders were most often Confederate partisans who resorted to destructive tactics to disrupt Union supply and communication lines, procure supplies for the southern war effort, punish Unionist sympathizers, and, later in the war, torture and stymie African Americans who attempted to enlist in the Federal army. Whatever the motivation behind it, this "citizen's warfare" plagued all areas of Kentucky throughout the war. In August 1862, Hopkinsville resident Ellen Wallace assessed: "Treason is plotting at every corner of the street. The Union men of this place feel unsafe in person and property without an armed force to resist the Gurillars." In eastern Kentucky the following spring, Booneville resident Hiram Hogg wrote his son who was serving in the Union army that "for the last three or four weeks there has been more horse stealing and robbing than anywhere I know at this time. Our country is in a deplorable situation at this time." In Allen County along the Tennessee border, J. R. Thornton reported that "guerillas has bin in our Country lately and taken a good chance of money and killed two men. . . . Our Town is nearly burnt up. . . . We don't know when we lie down at night what we will be killed by Guerillas before the sun rises next morning."[28]

Less distrust existed, however, within the divided populace than between civilians of all stripes and the military government, which had occupied the state since September 1861. In a state that was teeming with southern sympathizers, Federal army officials had no way of knowing who was loyal and who might betray their cause. By 1862, Kentucky had evolved into what amounted to a police state under the command of General Jeremiah Boyle. People suspected of southern sympathies could not hold elected office or serve as teachers, ministers, or jurors. Federal authorities suspended the freedom of the press, and several editors shared the fate of Louisville minister Stuart Robinson, who found his newspaper, *The True Presbyterian*, seized and himself arrested. Union forces pulled former governor Charles Morehead from his Louisville home in the middle of the night and led him handcuffed through the streets, before imprisoning him at Fort Lafayette in New York City.[29]

As the war continued, the military government cast its punitive nets wider and wider, and civil liberties virtually disappeared. Fearing that women could not be trusted any more than men, Boyle created a prison in Newport for females whom he deemed disloyal and put those incarcerated to work sewing for the Union army. In October 1862, General Don Carlos Buell ordered the arrest and exile of anyone who had aided the recent Confederate invasion. In 1863, General Ambrose Burnside declared martial law statewide. In western Kentucky, one military authority tried "rebels" at random and often upon flimsy evidence, in some cases executing them. Citizens could be arrested for aiding the Confederacy and even for simply sympathizing with it. While the Federal government did not mandate such activity, it turned a blind eye toward it. Such heavy-handed treatment of southern-sympathizing citizens often turned Union partisans against their own war effort. Such was the case with George Smith, a small farmer from Henderson County, who wrote bitterly in his diary after seeing his friend "murdered by a band of armed men who styled themselves Union soldiers." Designed merely to squelch rebellious activity, Federal attempts to suppress guerrilla activity often had the unintended consequence of inspiring anger among once-loyal citizens.[30]

The vast majority of white Kentuckians, regardless of their sectional loyalty, were outraged by the actions of the Federal military, and time and again prominent Kentucky unionists pleaded with Lincoln and Secretary of War Edwin Stanton to intervene, often with mixed results. From the outset, Lincoln treated Kentucky's citizens gingerly in a resolute effort to maintain their loyalty. "I think to lose Kentucky," he famously said, "is nearly the same as to lose the whole game. Kentucky gone, we cannot hold Missouri, nor I think Maryland. These all against us, and the job on our hands is too large for us. We would as well consent to separation at once, including the surrender of this capitol."[31]

But lenient treatment of the state became increasingly difficult as the war stretched on and white Kentuckians appeared more and more set against the Union cause. Relations between white Kentuckians and the Federal government disintegrated into an untenable quagmire. The government and its local authorities could, with good reason, never count on a loyal populace. As such, the white citizens of Kentucky, though they remained within the Union, were never treated as a part of the Union but often as part of the rebellion. This, in turn, only compounded the antipathy and hostility many Kentuckians felt toward the Federal government. By 1862, many white Kentuckians felt as Green Clay did when he wrote that the state "would have to pay for her loyalty. . . . As soon as all hope of winning us to the cause of the rebellion should disappear, it was natural to expect that we should then become the object of their bitterest hate! A border state, we would suffer from their injuries, their barbarities, and their vindictiveness." Still, he decided, "it was probably wiser for Ky. to adhere to the old Union even at this sacrifice & retain the benefits in other respects to a good & beneficent government." By 1863, Garrett Davis, one of Lincoln's closest Kentucky advisers, estimated that one-third of all Kentuckians were "disloyal."[32]

Perhaps no individual did more to turn the loyalties of white Kentuckians against the Federal government than General Stephen Gano Burbridge, whom Lincoln appointed military commander of Kentucky in August 1864. Burbridge took his post just a month after Lincoln had suspended the writ of habeus corpus and exercised with zeal his free rein to quell the rampant extralegal warfare infesting the state. Under his Order 59, Confederate sympathizers proximate to guerrilla attacks might have their property seized to compensate for destroyed Union property and could even be deported from the state. The most sinister stipulation of the order was Burbridge's mandate that for every unarmed loyal citizen killed, four guerrillas were to be taken from prison and publicly shot. An estimated fifty executions followed. Many Kentucky Unionists may have been uncomfortable with the grisly manner in which their Confederate sympathizing neighbors were treated, but many more were outraged by Burbridge's efforts to ban books, interfere in local elections, and even fix the prices received by the state's pig farmers in the scandal known as the Great Hog Swindle. By the time the Lincoln administration removed him from command, in February 1865, Burbridge was widely regarded as "the most hated man in Kentucky" and had severely damaged Union loyalty in the state.[33]

Nothing, however, shifted the sentiments of white Kentuckians away from the Union cause more than Lincoln's evolving policies regarding slavery. From the outset of the war, Kentuckians were wary of his intentions regarding the peculiar institution. As Garrett Davis wrote to Salmon P. Chase in September 1861, "There is a very general, almost universal feeling, in the state against this war being or becoming a war against slavery." The president had taken pains at its outset to obstruct any proemancipation legislation that might cause Kentucky to join the Confederacy. Most white Kentuckians, it seems, banked on an agreement, presented in a resolution by the state legislature and carried tacitly in the minds of many, that they would be rewarded for their loyalty to the Union with Federal protection of their slave property. Thousands of Kentucky's African Americans, however, nullified this agreement with their own feet by escaping their masters and flocking to military camps as soon as Federal forces entered the state. While Jeremiah Boyle prohibited army personnel from admitting slaves into the camps, the need for their labor often outweighed his demands, or those of masters seeking the return of their property.[34]

In July 1862, the president proposed to give slave owners up to $300 for each slave they freed. For years, most white Kentuckians had been opposed to the idea of compensated emancipation, and they certainly were not going to alter their views now at the behest of a Federal government that they had once held responsible for upholding their property rights. They resented the suggestion that they, as loyal southerners, would be expected to relinquish their property privileges, when the other South, the rebellious South, remained unaffected. On a more practical level, many Kentuckians doubted that Congress would approve the compensation funds. A committee appointed by the state legislature responded to the proposition unequivocally, pledging to combat the plan "by all peaceable means." Should that course of action fail, the committee promised, "Kentucky [would] rise up as one man and sacrifice the property, and, if need be, the lives of her children in defense of the Constitution under which alone we can ever hope to enjoy natural liberty."[35]

When, only a few months later, Lincoln issued the preliminary Emancipation Proclamation, most white Kentuckians understood its implications. Although the document applied only to the rebellious states, they recognized that it sounded the death knell of slavery everywhere. The Proclamation convinced white Kentuckians that their faith in the Federal government was badly misplaced. For many, the sense of betrayal was excruciating. Unionist Benjamin Buckner, a young attorney who left his Clark County law practice to enter the 20th Kentucky Volunteer Army as a major, exemplified this sense of deception. At the outset of the war, Buckner had had little respect for secessionist sentiments, which he felt made "men forget all the restraints of law and morals." Though he was politically conservative and certainly not antislavery, Buckner, like many Kentuckians, saw the Union and the Constitution as the bedrock upon which American principles rested. "Just remembering always," he wrote to his fiancée in June 1862, "that I am fighting for a great government and not for any particular administration and that Lincoln has as yet not permitted any anti slavery steps to be taken by his Generals, and that until we are convinced that there is positively no hope, I think it is better to fight for that side, which has heretofore given us peace prosperity and happiness, than for that which only promises us lawless violence and commercial ruin."[36]

Yet within a few months, as Lincoln's intentions regarding slavery became clear, Buckner did an about-face. In response to the preliminary

Emancipation Proclamation, he wrote, "It is an abominable infamous document, and falsifies all his pledges both public and private. The Union Kentuckians are most shamefully treated, and by reward of the presidents want of good faith, which is only equaled by his lack of sense, we find ourselves in arms to maintain doctrines, which if announced 12 months ago, would have driven us all, not withstanding our loyalty to the Constitution & the Union, into the ranks of the Southern Army." He added, "No Kentuckians can have any heart for this contest. We joined the people of the North (a people whom we did not love) to fight the South (a people with whom we were connected by ties of relationship, interest, the identity of our hearts and intuition) verily upon principle and to preserve that Constitutional form of government which was the wonder and admiration of the world." By the end of the year, Buckner had decided to tender his resignation in the Union army and predicted that other officers in his regiment would as well.[37]

Buckner was certainly not alone in his evolving sentiments. To Andrew Pirtle, a Federal soldier from Louisville, news of emancipation came as a shocking disappointment. "To us that are fighting the battles of the Union," he wrote his father from the frontlines, "it seems as if we had been deceived and that we are fighting the battles of a party and not of a great people." In January 1863, John Harrington, of the 22nd Kentucky Volunteer Regiment, wrote to his sister in dejected tones: "I enlisted to fight for the Union and the Constitution, but Lincoln puts a different construction on things and now has us Union Men fighting for his Abolition Platform and thus making us a hord of Subjugators, houseburners, Negro thieves, and devastators of private property." Yet, despite the overwhelming disdain many Kentucky Federal soldiers felt for Lincoln's policies, there were others who put larger war aims above their feelings about slavery. Robert Earnest, a member of the 26th Kentucky Volunteer Regiment, wrote to his brother in April 1863 that, although he opposed emancipation "upon the ground that it has had the affect to give strength to the Rebellion & prolong the war," he believed that Lincoln was "to a very great extent warranted by the enormity of the crime against whom he [was] contending."[38]

Thus, the reactions of most Union service men to emancipation highlighted their sense of betrayal at being asked to fight for a cause in which they did not believe, and the sentiments of Kentucky civilians revealed their belief that the government failed to protect their constitutional property rights and also their personal safety. Ellen Wallace, who lived near Hopkinsville, voiced these key concerns. Though her husband owned around thirty slaves at the outset of the war, Wallace began the war as a staunch Unionist who projected in April 1861 that any decision by Kentucky to secede would lead to the state's "ruin." But over the course of the next two years, Wallace came to believe that ruin came to Kentucky anyway in the form of Lincoln, a "vile wretch" of a president, and his "infamous proclamation."[39]

Some of Wallace's outrage stemmed from the difficulties she experienced in dealing with her increasingly "unmanageable" and "insolent" slaves and what she knew would be the eventual and complete loss of her slave property. At the same time, she also repeatedly confided to her diary in vividly racist terms her fears of physical harm and sexual threat that emancipation would bring to the women of Kentucky. Wallace charged Lincoln with placing "innocent women and helpless infants at the mercy of black monsters who would walk in human shape." "Servile insurrection will be the consequence [of emancipation] unless the strong arm of the nation prevents it," she wrote on another occasion, "and the blood of helpless women and children will flow in torrents if [Lincoln's] wicked and fanatical policy is not over ruled." It could be, Wallace feared, "St. Domingo all over again."[40]

Perhaps the greatest indignity for white Kentuckians came in March 1864, when, in an effort to offset the deficit of white draftees, the Union army began recruiting African Americans. This was not the first time that black Kentuckians saw service. From the outset of the war, the armies of both the Confederacy and the Union impressed African Americans as they moved in and out of the state. The Federal army initially limited impressments to the slaves of those white citizens deemed disloyal, but as labor needs intensified, it began to conscript slaves of Unionists, a move that provoked public outcry. By the summer of 1864, the Federal army began to enlist all slaves, a move that essentially guaranteed freedom to able-bodied black men who were willing to walk away from their homes and families. Slaves arrived at recruiting centers from all corners of the state. At Camp Nelson alone, over 5,000 black Kentuckians joined the Union army. Thousands of women and children also fled their masters, seeking refuge behind Union lines. According to one account, by March 1865 an estimated seventy to one hundred were enlisting in the army daily, freeing an average of five women and children per enlisted man. Historian Victor Howard described the atmosphere: "The spirit of freedom was contagious, and insubordination became the order of the day as many slaves refused to be whipped or determined to take to the road because they had been beaten."[41]

Decades later, John Fields would remember fleeing servitude with his brother and trying to join the Union army in Owensboro. Army officials accepted his brother, but they turned John away because he was too young. Undeterred, he escaped to Indiana and tried again, first at Evansville and then at Terre Haute and Indianapolis, but without success. Slave owners, however, did not give up their property easily and combed the banks of the Ohio River with baying bloodhounds, tracking down those who were attempting to escape to Ohio to join the Federal ranks. Provost marshals from around the state reported that black Kentuckians faced imprisonment, beatings, and death as they attempted to enlist. As Marion Lucas writes, Kentucky's African Americans "contributed more than their fair share of the physical labor and much of the military power that ran the Federal war machine in Kentucky. Out of their effort came victory and, eventually, freedom of a sort."[42]

For many Kentucky whites, who had traded their loyalty to the Union in return for protection of slave property, black enlistment was the ultimate blow, the final realization that the Union cause had evolved and was no longer their own. They articulated their dissent many times over. In his 1863 inaugural address, Governor Thomas Bramlette claimed that arming African Americans "humiliates the just pride of loyal men." Perhaps anticipating postwar rapprochement between Unionist and Confederate whites, he added that black soldiers could "never remain and live amongst those against whom they have been set in battle array." The provost marshal from Kentucky's Fourth Military District described white Kentuckians as being "ripe for mutiny" over the issue. One of Kentucky's most esteemed men in blue, cavalry commander Frank Wolford, exclaimed in 1864 that people of Kentucky would refuse to "keep step to 'the music of the Union' alongside of negro soldiers." Throughout the spring and summer of that year, Wolford made a series of long-winded speeches—one purportedly lasting for four hours—in which he denounced Abraham Lincoln as a "fool" and a "tyrant" and his policy of enlisting African Americans as illegal and "disgraceful to the people" of Kentucky. He encouraged Kentuckians to resist any efforts to enroll them in the Union army. Wolford's series of extended protests led to his arrest and dishonorable discharge from the Union army and elevation to the status of folk hero among many in his home state. One Bluegrass resident noted, "Whilst the policy of his course is doubted, even censured by some, the gallant Wolford is now the most popular man in our part of the State & the President universally condemned for his tyrannical course in dishonorably dismissing [him]."

Rank-and-file Union soldiers concurred with Wolford's feelings. While on picket duty in 1864, Elphas Hylton, a volunteer from Lawrence County, reported in his diary seeing "three thousand negro soldiers on a grand review, a black cloud to see." "Here," he wrote, "I became dissatisfied as a soldier on account of the negro, negro, negro." Benjamin Buckner went even further, declaring that with enlistment of African Americans, "all men of decency ought to quit the [Union] army."[43]

African American enlistment offended Kentucky whites on several fronts. In addition to the fact that the draft hastened the loss of their slave property, many felt that the very dignity of the Union war effort was compromised by having black troops join the fight "side by side and shoulder to shoulder" with whites. As Ellen Wallace put it, "The master and his former slave must keep time to the same musick, share the same rations." But of more immediate concern to many whites was the shift in power relations between white and black Kentuckians that came as a result of emancipation through enlistment. Not only did enslaved African Americans gain and use this new access to freedom, but they did so with the strength of the Federal government at their backs and guns in their hands. In November 1863, Wallace described with dismay hearing about a group of Hopkinsville slaves caught riding off toward Federal lines on horses they had taken from their masters. She wrote only a month later that Lincoln had "made the negro master of the white man as far as his power goes putting arms in their hands. Stationing negro pickets at the toll gates and bridges where they defy their former masters to pass on peril of their lives. The white man has to turn his horses head and obey Lincoln's negro troops with clenched teeth." As Ellen Wallace's writings reveal, the change in racial order stung all the more because in Kentucky the Federal army often employed black troops locally, rather than sending them to fight on some distant battlefield. This led to contentious confrontations between masters, mistresses, and former slaves. Ever worried about her personal safety, she declared: "I think if affairs go on as they have been doing the white women in town will find it necessary to carry daggers and revolvers in their girdles instead of pin cushions and scissors."[44]

As white Kentuckians struggled to make sense of what the war for the Union had become, it led politicians like Brutus Clay to articulate and defend the unique position of Kentucky Unionist slaveholders in the wake of emancipation and black enlistment. In 1863, voters of the Seventh Congressional District elected Clay to fill the seat left vacant by the death of John C. Crittenden to represent them as a Union Democrat. On the floor of Congress, Clay consistently defended the property rights of border state residents. When congressional representatives discussed drafting African Americans into the army, he warned that it would alienate loyal Kentuckians: "It will create a civil war among us" and "crush out the Union sentiment" in the state. Clay consistently maintained that the Union was selfishly stealing and enlisting the property of loyal slave owners for the sole purpose of lowering white draft numbers. As impressments of slaves into the Union army escalated, Brutus wrote to his wife, Ann, in March 1864, to "tell the negroes to run off and get away if [Federal forces] attempt to take any. Tell the negroes what their object is, to put them in the war & have them all killed off under the pretense of giving them their freedom. They will win no liberty but all [will] be killed off with hard work & exposure & in battle in place of the *cowardly scoundrels* from the North." Whatever the true roots of Clay's opposition to African American enlistment, the Federal policies hit his pockets and his household hard. Between May 1864 and January 1865, seventeen enslaved men belonging to Brutus Clay joined the Union army. At the same time that Clay was arguing in Congress that the exchange of military service for freedom was not in their best interest, his former bondsmen were enjoying their first taste of freedom. The formerly enslaved David Hill wrote home to his mother, over whom Clay still claimed ownership, from his encampment in Russellville: "I eat when I get hungry & drink when I get dry. I joined the Union Army to live until I die."[45]

Not surprisingly, Confederate Kentuckians viewed the change in public and military sentiment brought by emancipation and the enlistment of black troops with more optimism. Edward Guerrant, who served under John Hunt Morgan, noted in June 1864 that Union recruiting in Kentucky had "about 'played out'" and that he had seen fewer than a dozen Union recruits since coming into the state that summer. "The young men," he declared with delighted contempt, "are a shameless, spiritless, downheaded, subjugated, elegantly dressed, and starched set of unconscious slaves to Lincoln and his negro soldiers." The addition of African American soldiers to the ranks of the Federal troops would forever shape the subsequent memory of Unionist military efforts.[46]

By late 1864, several factors—the Union army's treatment of civilians and, above all, the Lincoln administration's inclusion of black freedom as a war aim and its willingness to arm African Americans in order that they might achieve it—caused many formerly loyal Kentuckians to turn their sympathies against the Federal government. As early as October 1863 visitors to the state, like Andrew Phillips, issued assessments claiming that "since the emancipation proclamation the people of Kentucky are all secesh except at Louisville and along the river at Covington." In December 1864, the once-Unionist Ellen Wallace celebrated as 2,000 Confederate troops took over Hopkinsville after several months of occupation by a multiracial Federal contingent. "Oh how our hearts leaped for joy at the sight, after being subjected to Negro troops and black republican outrages. I could not refrain from weeping as I saw the brave heroes, half clad and half frozen pass, with a song of defiance on their lips, to their northern foes, who well fed and well clad had fled on their approach with their black hords," she waxed in romantic tones. Confederate Micah Saufley aptly summed up the altered state of public opinion in Kentucky by the war's end, writing: "The African question has worked a marked change in the sentiments of the people. Strange they could not see the foley [folly] four years ago when every thick headed Contraband had no doubts!"[47]

The end of the war held varying meanings for Maria Hawes, for Mammy, and for all Kentuckians. Confederate sympathizer Belle Simrall was circumspect about southern defeat: "We must now acknowledge it to have been a grand rebellion rather than a Revolution," she wrote of Lee's surrender. She comforted herself with the dignity afforded to returning Confederates: "Everyday, the Southerners are coming to Ky. yielding themselves to the authorities. Surely they have no need to be ashamed of their tested valor, even though they are not victorious." For fellow Confederate Micah Saufley, however, defeat was a more bitter experience, and reunion with former foes would be a long time coming. "If I am never to be a Christian until I love my enemies," he wrote his wife after the war, "I am doomed to practical infidelity."[48]

In a state where families had split in their allegiances, the end of the war meant not only coming to terms with defeat or victory, but with friends and family as well. Susan Bullitt Dixon, a Union sympathizer from Henderson, had two brothers who served the Confederacy. She wrote to her beloved brother Tom, an inmate of a Union prison in Delaware, that peaceful reunion was her deepest desire. "I hope the nation is recovering from its madness and its passion, and that the white wings of peace will again shed over our land a radiance of the sunshine of prosperity, to which our eyes have been strangers for many long and weary months," she commented poetically. Although dedicated to her cause, she hoped that when "talking politics . . . I may convince them that we 'good Union' people were always right, and that the *mediums*[,] those between both extremes, were the *only* ones in the right all the while—Oh, peace, blessed peace—how happy it would make this entire nation!"[49]

Kentuckians like Micah Saufley, Maria Hawes, Susan Bullitt Dixon, and Brutus Clay may have been divided in wartime politics and loyalties, but they found much to unite them in the postwar era. The same whites who had disagreed over the question of secession in 1860 found new common ground in the aftermath of Federal intervention and the end of slavery. In a congressional debate over the Thirteenth Amendment, Brutus Clay summed up what was at stake in terms of the connections among property rights, emancipation, and the loyalty of Kentuckians. "If you take away from a man that which he considers to be justly his own," he warned, "you make him desperate, and he will retaliate upon you. You can never by oppression make a man obey willingly the laws of his country. Act justly toward him; let him see that he has a Government which will project [protect] him, and he will love that Government. But oppress and rob him, and he will despise and hate you." Years earlier, in March 1862, Clay's secessionist daughter Martha had written him an angst-ridden letter in which she pleaded: "Would to Heaven the eyes of the Union people of the Border States could be opened to the real object of this war." Now it appeared those eyes did open. With many white citizens of the commonwealth stripped of their property and illusions and all left to question what a new postwar racial and economic order would bring, many soon found that after four years of bloody war their memory of the experience would quickly unite them in peace.[50]

The Rebel Spirit in Kentucky

THE POLITICS OF READJUSTMENT, 1865–1877

"The Psalmist and I are alike in one respect at least," wrote Lizzie Hardin of Harrodsburg, Kentucky, in her diary in July 1865. "We both have seen the wicked flourish like a green bay tree and the vilest men exalted. I wish I had the power to describe the state of this country. The Constitution so much wasted power, the civil law a dead letter, slavery in such a condition that neither masters nor Negroes know whether it exists or not, lawlessness of every shade, from the lawlessness of the government at Washington to that of the Negro who steals his master's chickens, and in the midst of it all, between the Southerners and Union people a hatred, bitter, unrelenting, and that promises to be eternal." When Hardin penned these words, she had been back in Kentucky for less than a month. Two years earlier, in July 1863, Hardin and some of her family members had joined a crowd in the streets of Harrodsburg to cheer the arrival of famous Kentucky Confederate cavalryman John Hunt Morgan and his men. As prominently disloyal citizens, the Hardin family quickly drew the attention of federal authorities, who arrested them as part of an effort to quell rebellious activity in Kentucky. Banished from the state, the Hardins spent much of the remainder of the war in Madison, Georgia.[1]

Although Hardin's somewhat extraordinary experience of arrest and dislocation, as well as her grief for the doomed Confederacy, may have caused her particular rancor about the condition in which she found her home state, her feelings of bitterness and confusion were far from unusual. The concerns she raised—the failure of constitutional rights to protect slavery, the abrogation of racial order, and sectional tensions—plagued Kentuckians long after the great struggle ended. But as white Kentuckians argued among themselves about the significance of the Civil

War in the coming years, they would find surprisingly quickly that, contrary to Hardin's prediction, the hatred among them was not as bitter or unrelenting as might have been expected.

ONLY A MONTH after writing her dispirited sentiments, Lizzie Hardin gained some vindication from the results of the August statewide elections. Colonel William E. Riley, the provost marshal who had arrested Lizzie and her family three years earlier, ran for a seat on the state Court of Appeals. In a state where people had grown tired of the federal government's heavy-handed treatment of civilians, the Hardins actually became rhetorical weapons in the campaign against Riley when one of his opponents publicly charged that he had "arbitrarily caused the arrest of several ladies of high social position, without warrant and without authority for so doing." An acquaintance of Riley wrote a letter to a Louisville newspaper defending his actions. "The state was then full of rebel spies and guerrillas," he charged, "and these ladies were notorious and babbling rebels, and in full sympathy with Jeff Davis." But such appeals based on sectional bitterness had lost much of their resonance with white Kentuckians, even those who had been staunch Unionists, in the face of their current concerns. As Hardin wrote with satisfaction in her diary, "The Colonel's friend could not save him."[2]

In the coming years, many Unionist politicians would share Riley's fate as Conservatives would seek and receive vindication in ballot boxes across the state by consistently voting conservative Democrats into office. Never disenfranchised, white males in Kentucky used the polls in their attempt to shape the state's postwar society. For some, voting Democrat was retaliation for the tight reign of martial law during the war, for the perceived injustice of Reconstruction further south, and, most of all, for the violation of racial order in their own state. As a Lexington paper stated in 1866, "Whether they have been Federal or Confederate soldiers, or neither; whether they served in Camp Chase or were exiles in Canada, or unmolested during the war; were Union or anti-Union in the past," the people would endorse the Democratic Party "with an almost unanimous majority."[3]

Indeed, politics became one of the first meeting grounds for former foes as they soon realized that their wartime sympathies were less important than their postwar problems. Even if the phenomenal level of Unionist Democratic voting was, as some historians have argued, a bitter reaction to past grievances, it was for many whites not simply an attempt to redress the past but rather to seize control of the present. Together they

faced personal loss, physical and economic devastation, the legacy of rup-
tured families and communities, and, most of all, a world in which African Americans lived outside of bondage. With this issue in mind, many
former Confederates and former Unionists would come together at the
polls, making the politics of race become common ground for white Kentuckians following the Civil War and leaving the state dominated by what
would be termed the "rebel Democracy."

Although C. Vann Woodward wrote that, "despite Kentucky's failure
to secede and join the Confederacy, no state below the Ohio River presented a more solidly Confederate-Democratic front in the decade after
Appomattox," not all Kentuckians "seceded" after the war. A significant
number of African Americans and white Republicans imbued their politics with a different vision of Kentucky's wartime experience, one recalling the state's loyalty to the Union. For these whites, the end of slavery
had been a long time coming and held open the possibility that Kentucky
might finally become fertile ground for industry and white labor. Black
Kentuckians, meanwhile, pointed out their service and sacrifice for the
Union in their efforts to seize their freedom, negotiate new labor arrangements with whites, and extend their claims of citizenship to the court-
room and the ballot box.[4]

Regardless, it was Democratic politics enveloped in a Lost Cause narrative that came to define Kentucky in the years following the war. The voting tendencies of white Kentuckians quickly gained national attention,
and in northern eyes, especially those of Republican newspaper editors,
the ballot box became the first grounds on which Kentucky rebelled ex
post facto. As one disgruntled Kentucky Republican lamented, it soon became clear that "a majority of her voters believe[d] the war for the Union
was wrong and that their hearts as well as their voices, [were] in sympathy
with the 'lost cause.'"[5]

AT THE WAR'S END, Kentucky was a place where slavery was neither
dead nor alive. Although nearly 70 percent of Kentucky slaves ended their
bondage by serving in the U.S. army or marrying someone who did, an estimated 70,000 of them existed within a weakened form of slavery through
the spring and summer of 1865. This meant, ironically, that a place
where slavery once existed in its most tenuous form became one of the
institution's last outposts. Indeed, with the exception of Delaware, Kentucky clung to the dying institution longer than any other southern state.
Kentuckians did so partially out of a desperate attempt to control African
Americans and partly in the hope that they might still receive some sort

of compensation for their property. Moreover, slavery was still legal in the commonwealth. On his postwar journey through the South in 1865 and 1866, Whitelaw Reid noted that Louisville was the only place on the trip where slaves waited on him. "They were the last any of us were ever to see on American soil," he noted. Not coincidentally, Reid found the city to be a "rebel community," whose residents displayed about as much loyalty to the federal government as those of Charleston, and even less than those in Nashville.[6]

To those who owned slaves and those who did not, the uncertain status of slavery and its incumbent ever-shifting racial relations proved to be the biggest source of anxiety in the aftermath of the war. While African Americans began to fully test the boundaries of their new freedom, whites wondered how long they might count on their labor and subservience. Even as whites clung tenaciously to slavery, they anticipated its demise. "We would not however be surprised to see the whole flock take flight someday," Lizzie Hardin said of her family's servants in July 1865, knowing it was only a matter of time before they would "blossom into freedom."[7]

Indeed, the very next week, Hardin reported that "liberty fever" had "broken out" among the family's servants. One of them, whom the family referred to as Uncle Charles, left his work at the Hardin household and walked to the nearest army encampment to obtain his "Palmer pass," the eponymous document the Federal military commander of Kentucky, John Palmer, began granting to African Americans in the spring of 1865, enabling them to travel freely in and out of the state. Emboldened and determined to take advantage of this freedom, Uncle Charles told Hardin's grandfather that his pass "allowed him to hire himself to whom he pleased." Hardin denounced it as "only a permission to go to Cincinnati, or in other words, to run off." Her grandfather, trying in vain like many Kentucky slaveholders to wield any coercive power he had left, threatened to sue anyone who would hire the black man. For Uncle Charles, however, the documentation was assurance that he could act upon this liberty if he wished, and for a time Hardin noted that he seemed "perfectly satisfied with the consciousness of having the pass in his pocket, and came back and went to hauling wood without any mention of his freedom."[8]

Doubtless, hundreds of such encounters between "slaves" and "masters" took place in the summer and fall of 1865. Across the state there existed a three-way struggle between the occupying Union forces who tried to extend and protect the rights of black freedom, freedpeople who were seizing those rights, and whites who attempted to limit them. As thousands of African Americans moved away from rural areas and congregated in urban centers around the state, white fears about their concentrated numbers escalated. In October 1865, Lexington mayor Josiah Wingate, in denial that slavery was dead, demanded that slave owners retrieve the African Americans and "take care of them" or face legal charges. Federal commander Palmer countered, threatening use of military force should any people calling themselves "owners and claimants" endeavor to seize them. Furthermore, he asserted, "all the people of the state are presumed to be *free and protected as free until orders are received to the contrary.*" In November 1865, one Kentucky judge, seeking economic remuneration while he could, tried to sell the child of one of his slaves. In an attempt to save her child, the mother feigned marriage to a Federal soldier, and the judge narrowly escaped the embarrassment of being arrested by a group of black soldiers. Everywhere, there were reminders that the prewar order was irrevocably gone. During the August 1865 elections, armed black troops stood at Mercer County polls to deny access to expatriated Confederates. When a white sheriff seized two black men accused of a crime, a group of black soldiers on a train passing through Bowling Green seized the prisoners and threatened the sheriff and anyone who attempted to interfere.[9]

As African Americans seemed to challenge the racial order in myriad ways, Kentucky whites voiced a multitude of fears in newspapers and other public forums. They worried about lack of control over where bitter and possibly retaliatory former slaves lived and traveled. Landowners and those who rented slaves for seasonal labor worried about the labor supply and whether African Americans could be compelled to work without the coercive power of slavery. One former Kentucky slaveholder described the feelings of many Kentucky whites when he stated candidly: "The negroes have been among us for centuries. They are among us now. The mere fact of the negroes being a part of our society, is not offensive. It is only when the negroes are free that it is assumed they will be a bad element of the population." To the problem of control and the matter of "reconstruct[ing] a system of efficient labor out of the ruins of slavery," he proposed the passage of the same sort of stringent vagrancy laws as existed in other southern states and provisions for every county with a large number of freedmen to manage a farm "under a competent overseer" upon which vagrants would be forced to work for the county. Trading one vision of coercion for another, he argued that "wise, judicious, and humane laws can be readily devised, enacted, and enforced as the new exigencies of the new system may require."[10]

Other Kentuckians shared with their fellow southerners the fear that freedom would lead to sexual equality and miscegenation. "The great staple argument of the Kentucky Conservatives who oppose the [Thirteenth] amendment," scoffed the *Cincinnati Gazette*, "is that if slavery is abolished, negro equality will result, and their daughters will walk with and marry colored men," to which the paper added, "they have a very poor opinion of their daughters." Other slaveholders simply mourned their loss of authority. As one man told a reporter regarding slavery, "It wasn't the pecuniary loss that hurt me. The truth is, I had all my life, been accustomed to having someone call me master, and I can't get along without it now." Hardin County resident D. C. Phillips wrote his friend in 1865 that "Negro's are getting verry saucy in Ky. They go to speaking, hear their Apostles advacating the doctrine of their freedom: the darkest cloud that has ever gathered around our political institutions is now over us." These worries often took on an apocalyptic tenor, as when the *Lexington Observer and Reporter* stated: "The African at home is the lowest of savages, and although enlightenment of two centuries of contact with whites has wonderfully improved this savage of four thousand years, his domination means ruin and decay."[11]

Though they shared many of the fears of their fellow southerners, Kentuckians soon faced them without either federal aid or federal interference. In October 1865, President Andrew Johnson finally heeded Kentucky's request to end martial law. "Loyal" border state status exempted Kentucky from federal Reconstruction, leaving whites free of its implications and African Americans without its protective measures. As a result, white Kentuckians charted a political path unique among the border states. While Maryland, Delaware, and Missouri each had strong proslavery, antifederal factions, they all, for various reasons, came under Republican control by the end of the war. Even when the Democratic Party later revitalized in these states, Republicans had strong enough footholds to be an effective minority party.[12]

In Kentucky, where the political landscape had been a mass of shifting alliances described by ever-changing monikers since the demise of the Whig Party in the 1850s, the story was quite different. Despite voting for Constitutional Union Party candidate John Bell in 1860, the majority of Kentucky voters considered themselves Democrats at the war's outbreak. After the war, white Kentuckians began carving out new political identities for themselves based on their wartime experiences, the outcome of the war, and their vision of the future. Voters formed political coalitions around their economic interests, their level of support or disapproval for presidential and congressional Reconstruction, and the role that they felt African Americans should play in postwar life.

This resulted in a political environment that scrambled the lines of wartime loyalties. As Kentucky voters searched for the party that shared their best interests, some Unionists pledged allegiance to the Republican Party, which also went by the titles Unconditional Union Party and Union Party. Self-styled to be more moderate than the congressional radical Republicans, the state party nevertheless wished to see Kentuckians embrace, or at least accept, a new economic and racial order. Between 1865 and 1867, another party faded in and out of influence. The Conservative Union (also known as the Union Democrats) steered a middle course between the "radical" Republicans and the "reactionary" Democrats. It became the party of choice for those Unionists dismayed by the federal government's altered war aims but unwilling to ally themselves with former secessionists. Most Unionists, however, feeling betrayed by the Lincoln government and fearful of its successors, called themselves Conservatives or Democrats.[13]

In August 1865, in the first postwar elections in the state, eligible Unionist voters—ex-Confederates still could not vote under the terms of expatriation—filled five of the state's nine congressional seats and the majority of the state legislature with Conservatives and Democrats. Anti-Republican sentiment accounted for some of the vote, but it was also an expression of the racial conservatism of white Kentuckians. As a Cincinnati paper observed, the Democratic Party had "one single rallying point and that is the negro. On that narrow neck of ground they find common ground. Every other principle which has governed these different factions in days that are past is laid aside, and the negro is made the one grand cornerstone of their building."[14]

In November, the Conservative-dominated legislature proved this point when members rejected the Thirteenth Amendment as well as the federal/Republican initiative to admit black testimony in state courts. When, despite its best efforts, Congress ratified the amendment the following month, the state General Assembly repealed the Act of Expatriation to mark its protest, thereby restoring full constitutional rights to ex-Confederates. The reward for such insubordination came when General Oliver O. Howard established the Freedmen's Bureau in Kentucky in December 1865. For the next four years, blacks would look to the bureau for help and protection, while whites would add the bureau's presence, which they considered a "naked usurpation," to their list of grievances. In February 1866, the state General Assembly adopted resolutions requesting the removal of the troops from the state, condemning the Freedmen's Bureau, requesting restoration of the writ of habeas corpus, and yet again rejecting the constitutional amendment.[15]

Some Kentuckians looked on with anger, frustration, and embarrassment at the Conservative intransigence. Louisville native James Speed, who had served as Lincoln's attorney general, was particularly pained by the attitude of his home state. "Kentucky seems to know less than a blind puppy that has not the sense to find the mother's teat and not to wound it," he wrote to his mother from Washington in December 1865. In striking at the agenda of the federal government, he continued, the state was "making ugly sores upon her own body, and future history will not let the scar disappear. I blush for her record in history. . . . Kentucky is more unbelieving than Thomas. She has had her hand in the death wound of the monster slavery, the last desperate struggles of the hideous creature have been upon her soil, and yet she is unbelieving. Poor Kentucky!"[16]

The loudest voices of protest appeared in northern newspapers whose reporters watched the intransigence of Kentuckians with keen eyes and critical pens. Although the ever-proximate Cincinnati dailies—the *Gazette* and the *Commercial*—had reported wavering white loyalty in the state throughout the war, they responded to the state's postwar actions with invigorated resentment and rhetorically linked Democratic voting to Confederate sentiments and what they called "the rebel spirit." The *New York Times*, the *New York Tribune*, and the *Pittsburgh Gazette* soon joined them on a regular basis. "He is hardly a responsible being," said the *Cincinnati Gazette* of the Kentucky slaveholder in 1865; "he sees his idol, his beloved, his adored about to be torn from him, and he is too much distressed, too overborne by his unruly passions. . . . We pity him. . . . [The] poor, silly creatures are standing with their short-handled brooms attempting to sweep back the ocean tide of this mighty revolution." "Oh, wise Democracy of Kentucky," the paper later chastised, "hugging the relic of slavery to your bosoms, bowing before this your idol, and worshipping—calling everybody fanatical that opposes your foolishness, holding on to slavery because it used to pay, forgetting that the times have changed. . . . The people of this country are not going to take a single step backward on this slavery question."[17]

In 1866, with their voting rights restored, Confederates quickly reentered political life in the state. They soon joined ranks with Conservative Unionists, and, despite the fact that much of the Conservative/Democratic constituency consisted of former Unionists, the Confederates quickly began to lead and define the party. In 1866, Alvin Duvall, a southern sympathizer, ran for clerk of the Court of Appeals against a Unionist, Edward Hobson. Though the contested office was a relatively minor one, the sectional credentials of the candidates and their racial politics resulted in an election played out in terms of wartime loyalties. Democrat Alvin Duvall gained his rebellious reputation when military district commander Stephen Burbridge forced him to leave the state in 1864 because of his well-known Confederate proclivities. Meanwhile, Hobson, whom both the Conservative Union and the Republican Party backed, forged his valiant reputation by capturing the hard-riding, elusive John Hunt Morgan on one of his Kentucky raids. Furthermore, he was a racial moderate who supported the passage of the Thirteenth and Fourteenth Amendments.

In the public debate surrounding the contest, commentators wrapped the contemporaneous politics of race completely in the sectional rhetoric of war. J. Stoddard Johnston, the ex-Confederate editor of the *Daily Kentucky Yeoman*, admonished the people of Kentucky to "remember that they have been robbed of more than one hundred millions of slave property" by Hobson's party. On the other side, George Prentice, editor of the *Louisville Daily Journal*, attacked both Duvall and his party for their wartime connections, charging that "every man in Kentucky" knew the Democrats to be "pro-rebel and rebel-sympathizing." He later cautioned, "If you vote for Duvall to-day Kentuckians, you vote BLACK AND BLOODY SECESSION." Criticism of Duvall and those planning to vote for him rained down from across the Ohio River. "Democracy in Kentucky means secession is right, the rebellion was a patriotic duty, the rebels patriots and heroes, and all Union men murderers and tyrants. . . . If a man is a Union man he is not a Democrat. If he is a Democrat now, he is not a Union Man." On another occasion, the *Cincinnati Gazette* wrote of Conservative Democrats: "These men hate the Union, hate the flag, hate its defenders."[18]

Despite the preoccupation with wartime loyalties, the election also turned on practical concerns for white Kentuckians. Along with sectional rhetoric, state newspaper editors used economic issues to make their case. By voting for southern sympathizer Duvall, Walter Haldeman reminded *Louisville Courier* readers, they could curry favor with the southern states and help secure trade for Kentucky merchants. Meanwhile, George Prentice's *Louisville Daily Journal* argued that Kentuckians should vote for Hobson if they wanted any congressional compensation for their lost slave property. One Louisville merchant and former slaveholder inquired of this dilemma,

Now how ought a Kentucky Unionist to vote? If I vote for Hobson, I throw away my chances for a snug share of the Southern trade; for the reconstructed rebels of Georgia and Mississippi understand the question at issue in this State and they are all for Duvall. If they find out that a Louisville merchant votes for such a Radical Johnson man as Hobson, won't they at once pass me by, and hereafter make their purchases in Cincinnati? On the other hand, I am an ex-slaveholder and I want pay for the two slaves of mine who went into the Union army, and who, for eighteen months, fought in the Union cause. If Duvall is elected, this snug little cake of mine is at once changed into dough, and my six hundred dollars must be charged up to "profit and loss." So you see, I don't know exactly "which chute to take."[19]

Tensions came to a head on election day as violence broke out and at least twenty people were killed in conflicts around the state. White Kentuckians, it seemed, really were refighting the war at the polls. Some Republican observers had optimistically estimated that Hobson would win by 20,000 votes, but when the ballots were counted Duvall emerged victorious, winning by a margin of 37,000. Recognizing that Duvall's success had as much to do with racial fears as his Confederate status, the *Tri-weekly Commonwealth* in Frankfort reported that the Unionists had been "outnumbered, or out-generaled, the great engine used against them having been, as usual, the negro."[20]

For northern onlookers, Duvall's election appeared to be "a straight out rebel victory." Once and for all, Kentucky had exchanged war loyalties. "It is a sad record for Kentucky, claimed to be the most thorough Union state in the Union. That she is rebel and thoroughly rebel is proven beyond doubt by the election," wrote the *Cincinnati Gazette*. The *Gazette* continued: "The rebel gray has whipped the Union blue at the polls and as humiliating as it may be, it is nevertheless true. The same rebel spirit that rules in Memphis and New Orleans against all who sustained the Union there, voted . . . in Kentucky against all that respected the Union here." Furthermore, recognizing that Kentucky's loyalty to the Union had been based in part on the preservation of slavery and had been lost with the institution's demise, the *Gazette* asserted that the state had "been rebel" since the fall of 1862, when Lincoln issued the preliminary Emancipation Proclamation. In the end, the Court of Appeals race in 1866 exhibited not only the extent of Conservative sentiment in Kentucky but also the power and pervasiveness of sectional rhetoric in postwar politics. In an atmosphere where whites feared the loss of their place in the racial hierarchy above all else, having been a Union hero not only carried little weight but when coupled with the rhetoric of race could be spun into a liability.[21]

The contentious political atmosphere continued in 1867. The *Triweekly Commonwealth* heralded the new political year with a warning about "the designs of the conspirators in our midst, who are plotting and scheming to place this State under the rule of those who favored the rebellion." "In every portion of the State," they warned, "the Rebel Democracy are organizing to obtain complete control in the State." Sending up a political battle cry, they declared that this Confederate insurgency "should be met and counteracted by the united efforts of all Kentuckians who earnestly desired the suppression of the rebellion, and who now rejoice that the Union was not destroyed by the traitorous efforts made to that end."[22]

Despite the Republican call to arms, however, 1867 proved to be another successful year for the Democrats. They defeated the proposed Fourteenth Amendment in the state legislature, 62 to 26 and 24 to 7, in January, and, in a special congressional election held in May, Democrats swept all nine seats, prompting one angry Republican to claim, "Kentucky is today as effectually in the hands of rebels as if they had every town and city garrisoned by their troops. With a rebel Governor, rebel Congressmen, rebel Statehouse and Senate, rebel Judges, rebel Mayors, rebel municipal officers, rebel policemen and constables, what is to become of the poor blacks and loyal white men God only knows." The election results so angered Republicans in Congress that they initially refused to seat four of the newly elected congressmen.[23]

The most important victory of the year for the Democrats came when John L. Helm won the governor's seat. The race featured three parties: the Republicans, the Democrats, and the Conservative Union, which was led by several prominent Unionists who could not tolerate the Confederate-dominated ticket. Significantly, the Conservative Union garnered just 13,167 votes, with the Republicans netting 33,939 and the Democrats 90,225. The lopsided Democratic victory caused the Republican editor of the *Kentucky Statesman* to lament, "What Bragg failed to do in 1862, with his army and banners, the people of Kentucky, five years later have done; they have given the State over into the hands of those who have been enemies of the Union."[24]

Newspapers in Chicago, Cincinnati, and Washington, D.C., responded to the election results by calling for the state to be federally reconstructed. Republican congressional candidate Sam McKee did the same after his defeat in the election. "Kentucky needs reconstruction, and must have it," he proclaimed. "She is to-day the most disloyal of all the states. To-day she is more hostile to the national authority than any other State. . . . Today we witness in Kentucky a State avoiding and defying the acts of the nation's Congress. Here the theory of State rights, as contended for by Davis and his collaborators, is a success. . . . Why should congress treat Kentucky different from any rebel State," he asked, concluding that "the mistake of the administration was treating her thus during the war. . . . Now that [Kentuckians] have been conciliated to such an extent as to join the rebel ranks and vote the rebel ticket . . . there is no excuse for Federal government not to intervene."[25]

In the aftermath of the election, the *New York Times* printed a list of all of the newly elected "rebel" state officers. The list included Helm, whom federal authorities arrested twice during the war for disloyalty, and lieutenant governor John Stevenson, a "Calhoun school politician," who was once arrested while trying to raise a regiment of Confederate fighters. The list also contained scores of rebellious lower officers, including the state's attorney general, auditor, treasurer, and superintendent of public instruction. Last, there was James Dawson, the register of the State Land Office, who had during the war climbed to the rank of lieutenant in the Union army but had since "expressed regret that he ever wore the blue." Dawson, the paper claimed, "would have preferred seeing the South succeed, to witnessing the incidental overthrow of slavery, in the triumph of the Nation." When John Helm died after only five days in office, his lieutenant governor, John Stevenson, succeeded him. Stevenson won the seat in his own right in an 1868 special election, becoming second in a line of six men to serve as governor between 1867 and 1894 who had been Confederates or Confederate sympathizers.[26]

Indeed, though the rank-and-file of the Democratic Party had been Unionist during the war, former Confederates quickly assumed leadership of the party. As ex-Confederate William Preston put it diplomatically, "Without a doubt after the close of the war, the Southern element was the most energetic power in reviving the exanimate Democracy of the State." Confederate credentials soon became almost a precondition for election. One southern veteran stated that a majority of the Democrats in his area refused to vote for anyone who had not "seen service in the Confederate army." According to historian Lowell Harrison, "If you wanted to be elected, it was by far best to be an ex-Confederate. If you had lost one or two limbs, for public display, you were almost a shoo-in." Unionists, in many cases, could only get ahead in the party by denouncing their wartime cause. A "rebel" county committee purportedly gave a former Unionist the position of county sheriff after he remarked that he had become ashamed of the Union uniform after "the negro had worn it."[27]

NORTHERN OBSERVERS VIEWED the quick assumption of power by returning Confederates with dismay. "As a loyal organization in that region," wrote the *New York Times*, the Democratic Party had "ceased to exist." The *Chicago Tribune* noted that "service in the rebel army" was a necessary criterion "for any office of honor, profit, or trust in Kentucky." Unionist Democrats wondered whether this was healthy for the party. Former governor Thomas Bramlette expressed concern that a candidate's Confederate war record was becoming more important than actual qualification for office. "Being put forward as a 'soldier boy'—as a 'wounded Confederate soldier,'" he noted, "makes a distinctive issue whether we, as Democrats of Kentucky, will claim it as a super-eminent merit to have been wounded in the Confederate service, or whether we will repudiate the proscriptive spirit which seeks to force upon us the war issues, and forces the old Union element now to surrender to the defeated."[28]

The lopsided prominence of Confederates in postwar politics obscured another important phenomenon that was perhaps more important to Kentucky's apparent exercise in postwar rebellion: the conversion of many of the state's staunchest Unionists to conservative politics. Numerous high-profile examples of staunch Unionists who turned against federal government policies after the war abound. For example, Garrett Davis, who had been so influential in convincing Kentucky slaveholders to remain with the Union, served as a U.S. senator from 1861 to 1865 as a member of the Union Party. Davis changed his loyalties after emancipation, however, and when Kentuckians reelected him in 1867, it was as a Democrat. Similarly, Kentuckians elected successful Union general Lovell Rousseau, who had commanded the 5th Kentucky Volunteers, to the U.S. House of Representatives as an Unconditional Unionist in 1864. Mirroring his constituency, however, Rousseau strongly opposed federal Reconstruction policies, and these views came to a head in 1866 when he debated radical Iowa congressman Josiah Grinnell over extending the power of the Freedmen's Bureau. The discussion turned ugly as Rousseau opposed the bureau and its purposes, and Grinnell insulted Rousseau and insulted the entire state of Kentucky for its racial conservatism. In a subsequent confrontation reminiscent of the Preston Brooks–Charles Sumner incident almost ten years prior, Rousseau struck Grinnell with a rattan cane until it broke. Because of the incident, Rousseau resigned from Congress in July 1866 but promptly returned to fill his old seat several months later, this time elected as a Democrat. As ex-Confederate J. Stoddard Johnston would later write, "In fact the State was as ready for revolt under the leadership of those once most loyal as it had ever been under the State rights domination."[29]

A common rejection of emancipation and radical federal Reconstruction policies lay at the epicenter of the common political ground on which prominent Confederate and Union politicians met after the war. Dismissed Union colonel Frank Wolford underscored this fact when he addressed a group of men of formerly divided sympathies at a Democratic political meeting in 1867. "If history shall show, in the end," he intoned, "that the war was for the overrunning and subjugation of the Southern States, for the purpose of elevating the negro to political power at the expense of white men, born freemen, descendents of our revolutionary sires, then I shall turn from that sword with sorrow, if not with shame." Kentuckians later elected Wolford to the U.S. Congress twice as a Democrat. Thus, although the political ascendancy of former Confederates became the most obvious symbol of Kentucky's postwar conservative turn, the behavior of former prominent Unionists was perhaps the more telling indicator of the political climate in the Bluegrass State.[30]

Meanwhile, whites who chose to align their politics with the "old Union element" found themselves held political hostage by Conservatives. The Republican men who were on the winning side of the war became pariahs, persecuted by those whom they had defeated on the battlefield. They faced social ostracism, lawsuits, threats to their property, and violent mobs. One radical lamented: "Combinations formed to ruin you in business, to exclude you from society, to turn you out of your houses of worship, to compel you to send your children to school to [be taught by] rebels." In Mason County, a landowner informed one of his tenants that if he voted the radical ticket he would have to leave the farm. The man followed through on his political convictions and left. Other tales emerged of former Confederates refusing to buy goods at stores whose owners did not vote Conservative. The *Cincinnati Gazette* claimed that after the 1866 political contests many men who had voted Republican were "discharged from work" and replaced by Conservatives. One veteran feared for those Union veterans who were unable to "earn a living, owing to the wounds received battling for this Government. Place the Government in the hands of rebels, and God help all such."[31]

Republican candidates often ran for public office at the risk of their lives. When Sidney Barnes, a former Union colonel in the 8th Kentucky

Regiment and Unconditional Unionist from Somerset, ran for governor as a Republican in 1867, the Ku Klux Klan hounded him throughout the unsuccessful campaign. The Klan labeled the former slaveholder a "Black Republican" and forced him to sleep atop his revolver at all times. Barnes ran and lost a campaign for a congressional seat in 1868, and several years later, at the age of fifty and "disgusted with Kentucky politics and thoroughly tired of the whole situation," he decided to leave his home state and move to Arkansas.[32]

Perhaps the most dire assessment of the political fallout of this period came from Jesse Kinchloe, who wrote to fellow Kentuckian Army Adjutant General Joseph Holt: "A consistently loyal man in Kentucky, is of all men most miserable,—persecuted, trodden under foot, hooted at by rampant rebels—And disowned & Cast off—by the government, he hazarded all to Support—he finds no security, no ray of hope Any where—It is a political mystery if not iniquity, that a triumphant government, should exalt its enemies—and abase its friends—This is a Strange Conclusion to a Triumphant war." The view of one Confederate summarized the thinking of most Kentuckians on the subject of radicals: "They helped old Lincoln ruin us, that they might get reputation, power, and spoil; but thank God, the people of Kentucky know them, and they will always occupy back seats in this State."[33]

The fact that Kentucky African Americans so willingly engaged in the political life of the state from the earliest days of their freedom was both helped and hindered by white Republicans. Despite the mighty effort whites put forth to limit the scope of black citizenship, black Kentuckians wasted little time after emancipation organizing political action. As they gathered at Emancipation Day and Fourth of July celebrations and at church assemblies and conventions around the state, they not only celebrated their freedom but demanded full rights of American citizenship.

In January 1866, 4,000 black Kentuckians gathered in Louisville, where military commander John Palmer told them to seek the aid of the Freedmen's Bureau and declared that legally they were on "equal footing" with whites. In March of that year, at a convention in Lexington, African Americans in Kentucky launched their fight for suffrage. Thousands pursued both the right to vote and the right to testify in state courts in the following years within groups such as the Colored State Central Committee and the Fayette County Justice Association and worked within fraternal societies such as the Union of Benevolent Societies and the United Brothers of Friendship to gain civil rights. One Cincinnati correspondent asserted, "Any one who supposes that the negroes are indifferent spectators of what is going on in Kentucky is greatly mistaken. They observe closely all that transpires and reason with a logical clearness which is perfectly surprising. White men tell them that they shall never have the right to vote in Kentucky, but the negroes laugh and say, 'It's a comin', massa.'"[34]

White Republicans in Kentucky did recognize that their party's meager numbers could potentially swell if African Americans could vote, helping them gain a share of political power, and they counseled potential voters accordingly. With the promise of black suffrage hanging in the air, white Republicans quickly realized that black memorial celebrations provided excellent opportunities to capture votes. Prominent Kentucky Unionists and Republicans made themselves a fixture of black public celebrations soon after the war. James Speed addressed Louisville celebrants in 1867, offering them "some very good advice" and, as the *Cincinnati Commercial* reported, urging them to "continue in their exertions for promoting their race." At another political gathering, General John Palmer underscored the difference between white Confederates and Unionist blacks and the potential of black citizenship: "All of those intelligent white men were *rebels*—therefore *foolish*; and all of these senseless, ignorant niggers were loyal—therefore wise; and I am in favor of giving the right of suffrage to wise men."[35]

White Republicans also tied black political rights to their role in defeating the Confederacy. At an 1867 convention sponsored by the Benevolent Society of Winchester, J. S. Brisbin sent the following advice: "You black people have a great mission to perform in Kentucky—no less, indeed, than regenerating your native State, disenthralling it from rebel rule and making it what it ought to be, a loyal member of the Union. . . . You helped to cut the head off the rebel rattle snake down South, and now with ballots you must trample the life of the tail in Kentucky." In 1868, one white Republican spoke at a picnic in Winchester where he offered twenty commandments, which, if followed, would lead to African American prosperity. The first was to read the Bible and trust God; the second was never to vote for a rebel or a Democrat for office.[36]

African Americans understood that the Union victory and their role in that triumph formed the basis of the rights they sought. When the Negro Republican Party held its first convention in Lexington in November 1867, Louisvillian William Butler proclaimed, "First we ha[d] the cartridge box, now we want the ballot box, and soon we will get the jury box." Tying black armed service in the Union army to the rights of citizenship, he declared, "We went out and fought the battles of our country, and gained our liberties, but we were left without means of protecting ourselves in the employment of that liberty. We need and must have the ballot box for that purpose." Butler also stated what African Americans knew well, namely that Confederates stood against their freedom after the war, just as they had during it. But if armed with the vote, they could fight back. "I stand here for universal suffrage for rebels as well as black men," he claimed. "I'm not afraid of rebels voting if you give us the same weapon of dissent." But such assertiveness made the latent African American electorate a curse as well as a blessing for white Republicans. The more African Americans staked their claims of citizenship on the scaffolding of Union victory, the more dissonance Conservative Unionists, with their fear of "Negro Domination," saw between their own interests and the rhetoric of Union victory.[37]

Hemmed in politically, white Republicans had to fight their battles on more symbolic fronts. After the 1867 Conservative victories, Republicans and Union veterans in several towns and cities across the state resolved to take back their regimental battle flags and banners that they had deposited at the state capitol for safekeeping after the war. In Warren County, Union soldiers met and resolved that they would not allow the "custody of those cherished emblems of our country's glory . . . pass into the hands of the accredited representatives of a party whose every sympathy has been with rebels and traitors, and whose highest recommendation to office was their devotion to treason and rebellion, both during and since the war." In Lexington, a similar group met and, in accord with the Warren County men, declared that the recently elected state officials, "some of whom fought us under another flag, and the most of whom would have been glad to have seen ours trailed in the dust," were "plainly not the proper people to have custody of these glorious emblems." In Barren County, Union soldiers acted similarly, resolving not to let their American flags "pass from loyal to disloyal keeping, especially to the keeping of those who tried for four long years of war, to humble and conquer them." Although they might well have to turn over their state government to former foes, they resisted doing the same with the relics of military victory.[38]

In late August, soldiers and officers from every Union regiment in the state met in Louisville to discuss the matter further and resolved as a group that the members of the new administration were "unfit custodians" of the banners, entering their protest in the name of the fallen comrades, widows, orphans, and Union prisoners of war, as well as "all the loyal soldiers of Kentucky and of the nation." They then sent this declaration to the governor, the secretary of the senate, the secretary of war, and the adjutant general of the army. While some considered using force to remove the banners, rumors swirled that no fewer than fifty Confederates had volunteered to defend the Union flags should ex-Federals try to rescue them from the capitol. In the end, written and verbal protest was the only weapon they wielded, making it clear that the Union man's symbols were in retreat along with his politics.[39]

One sign of the political times in Kentucky appeared when Ohio Copperhead Petroleum V. Nasby relocated to the state following the war. The literary creation of Republican *Toledo Blade* editor David Ross Locke, Nasby had been one of the most popular characters of American political satire since 1862. When the coarse, semiliterate scoundrel decides he needs a more hospitable political climate after the war, he moves to the Bluegrass town of "Confedrit X Roads" in Locke's 1868 book *Ekkoes from Kentucky.*[40]

Soon after moving to town, Nasby obtains the position of postmaster of Confedrit X Roads by petitioning Andrew Johnson in person. "I am the only Democrat in ten miles who kin write," he informs the president, "and [you] dare not deprive Kentucky, wich never seceded, uv mail facilities." Locke's Confedrit X Roads represents the "typical village in the unreconstructed South," stocked with a few admirable but mostly unlikable characters who are illiterate and racist former slave owners. As eager to talk politics as they are to imbibe local firewater, Nasby and his friends frequently discuss their fears of "nigger equality" and miscegenation. They applaud the burning of a Freedmen's Bureau school and the occasion upon which Louisville lit up "in a blaze uv glory," in celebration of Johnson's policy of "yooniversal amnesty" for Confederates.[41]

If the nation's readers missed Kentucky's political misdeeds in the newspapers, they could find them in exaggerated form in Locke's satire. Under Locke's pen, Nasby and his indolent associates, Kernal Hugh McPelter, Squire Gavitt, and Elkanah Pogram, became the vehicles of disparaging critique of the postwar political circumstances in Kentucky. The only thing they seemed to work hard at was maintaining the town's prewar social, racial, and political order. One of their more ambitious endeavors to this end comes when they decide to tackle the problem of sectional bias in education. Rather than send their children to colleges in "Ablishn" states, they found "The Southern Classikle, Theologikle, and Military Institoot," where "Southern yooth" can be educated without being "tainted with heresy." Professors are, of course, ex-Confederates, and Nasby and friends even propose to help the down-and-out Jefferson Davis by offering him a teaching position. Nasby and his compatriots thrived in this unreconstructed environment as "the waves uv Ablishinism rolled

Kentucky racism and recalcitrance in David Ross Locke's "Confedrit X Roads."
Courtesy of Special Collections, University of Kentucky Libraries.

over all the other States, but aginst Kentucky they struck harmless." For Nasby, "Kentucky [was] a brite oasis in the desert" where Democratic supremacy means white supremacy: "Here we kin flog our niggers,—here we shall hev the Instatooshen [of slavery] in sperit, ef not in name," claims Nasby; "here Dimocrisy kin flourish, ef nowhere else." "So long ez we're left to ourselves," he states with satisfaction, "so long will Kentucky be troo to Dimocrisy."[42]

Kentuckians continued to be true to the Democratic Party and its racial policies in 1868. Before that year's presidential election, a correspondent to the *New York Times* wrote from Cincinnati, "If the people over there mean anything at all by their talk, they mean fight and, in the event of a Democratic victory, will inaugurate it at once. They seem desperate over the loss of slavery and political power in the nation, and they now feel like doing what they did not in 1861, going into the fight as a State as well as individuals." Horatio Seymour captured 75 percent of the Kentucky vote. In the wake of the election, the *New York Tribune* wrote that the spirit of slavery and rebellion pervaded the state, and that it had "carried the state by a 90,000 majority. The state has not a tithe of the loyalty which is to be found in South Carolina."[43]

Petroleum V. Nasby might have come to represent the prototypical Kentucky Democrat in the national mind had Henry Watterson not arrived in the state in 1868 to take over the editorship of the *Louisville Journal* from the aging George Prentice. As the editor of the *Louisville Courier-Journal* for over fifty years, Watterson played an immeasurable role in defining Kentucky's reputation in the eyes of the world. The son of a Tennessee congressman, Watterson split his childhood between the Volunteer State and Washington, D.C. He enlisted in the Confederate army during the war and in the midst of military exploits edited two secessionist newspapers. After the war, he performed editorial stints at the *Montgomery Mail* and the *Cincinnati Evening Times*, before moving to Kentucky. Within a year of his arrival, he convinced *Louisville Courier* editor Walter Haldeman to merge their two papers with the *Louisville Democrat* to form the *Louisville Courier-Journal*.

During his long tenure as editor, Watterson would link Kentucky to the Confederate states in a new way by casting the state as a pillar of the New South. In the process, he channeled the Democratic politics of the state away from the unreconstructed platform of white supremacy and agricultural economy, to the racially moderate, proindustrial politics of modernization. Watterson preached the gospel of sectional reconciliation and southern development, becoming one of the harbingers of what Paul Gaston called "the New South Creed." He sought to modernize the South following a northern model, while prying the region from the political clutches of the North. To this end, like his fellow New South spokesmen Walter Hines Page, Richard Edmonds, Daniel Tompkins, and Henry Grady, Watterson promoted economic development and industrialization. Watterson wanted to "out Yankee the Yankee" when it came to thrift and resourcefulness. He encouraged the proliferation of railroads and cotton mills and the diversification of southern agriculture, all to be accomplished with the aid of northern investment.[44]

Watterson not only entertained ambitions to make the *Louisville Courier-Journal* the most widely read newspaper in the city and state, but he also envisioned it as a voice for the vanquished South. Held tight in the vise of federal Reconstruction, reasoned Watterson, the South could not articulate the terrible situation in which it found itself. Kentucky alone was free from the "despotic power running roughshod over the liberties and . . . private lives of the [southern] people." From his first days at the *Courier-Journal*, Watterson carved out a unique position for both Kentucky and the newspaper as a political advocate and economic partner to the South as it endured federal Reconstruction. At the outset, Watterson anchored this role by claiming a past for Kentucky that was sympathetic to the South. Only weeks after assuming editorship of the newspaper,

Watterson explained that although the state's head had gone with the Union, its heart had always gone with the South, the result of "the nature of generous and manly people to sympathize with the weak in its struggles with the strong." He defended Kentucky's Democratic voting record against those who libeled its citizens as guilty of rebellion and who sought to inflict "despotism" over them by reconstructing the state. Kentuckians, Watterson wrote, enjoyed the rights of "free citizens of a free republic" to vote their conscience.[45]

Within the state, however, he worked to reform the Democratic Party. Since the war's end, the Bourbon element of the party had dominated it, its conservative and tenacious attachment to the prewar agrarian social and economic order appealing to both former Confederates and Unionists. As Watterson later wrote in his memoirs: "There was an element who wanted to fight when it was too late; old Union Democrats and Union Whigs who clung to the hull of slavery when the kernel was gone, and proposed to win in politics what had been lost in battle." In an even less flattering assessment, he reported, "The party in power called itself Democratic, but was in fact a body of reactionary nondescripts claiming to be Unionists and clinging, or pretending to cling, to the hard-and-fast prejudices of other days." The leaders of this "belated element" regarded Watterson, in his own words, "as an impudent upstart . . . little better than a carpet bagger," doing their best to "put me down and drive me out." Luckily for the editor, a cadre of prominent business-minded Unionists and a number of high profile ex-Confederates, including Walter Haldeman, Basil Duke, Bennett Young, and *Lexington Observer and Reporter* editor W. C. P. Breckinridge, helped form the "New Departure" wing of the party.[46]

As their name implied, New Departure Democrats rejected the idea of a primarily agricultural economy, seeking instead a more modern industrial base for the state. The new Kentucky they envisioned featured exploited natural resources, northern investment, and full-fledged industrialization of Kentucky along northern lines. New Departurists supported railroads, business interests, and state-funded education. In the interest of furthering these measures, they advocated relinquishing any sectional animosities and racial conservatism that might hinder business and counseled acceptance of the Reconstruction amendments. Within a framework of implied white supremacy, they believed in "racial moderation," particularly as it served the interest of southern redemption.[47]

As Watterson would later describe, white Kentuckians "refused to admit that the head of the South was in the lion's mouth and that the first essential was to get it out. The *Courier-Journal* proposed to stroke the mane, not twist the tail of the lion. Thus it stood between two fires. . . . Touching its policy of sectional conciliation[,] it picked its way perilously through the cross currents of public opinion." In the interest of "stroking the mane," Watterson espoused a policy of racial moderation that starkly contrasted with the blatantly racist policies of most of the state's other newspapers. He counseled the passage and acceptance of the constitutional amendments, an act that would serve as a "Treaty of Peace between the sections," and promoted the right of African American court testimony at a time when few other Kentucky papers did.[48]

The *Courier-Journal* rapidly grew into the southern voice that Watterson had envisioned. Between 1869 and 1894, the circulation of the daily edition of the *Courier-Journal* rose from 10,000 to 30,000. By 1875, the paper claimed to have the "largest and most widely diffused circulation throughout the West and South" of any newspaper, and that more boards of trade, chambers of commerce, hotels, Young Men's Christian Organizations, and libraries subscribed to it than to any other paper outside of New York. A weekly edition introduced in 1870 reached even more readers, and by 1883, the *Courier-Journal* had a circulation of 38,000, nearly twice that of the main Baltimore and New Orleans papers and three times the number of Henry Grady's *Atlanta Constitution*. By 1894, the weekly edition had 144,000 readers. Watterson quickly came to wield great influence within Kentucky, but even greater influence over the way outsiders perceived the state and its citizens. Although the views of the *Courier-Journal* were generally more moderate than those of most white Kentuckians, Watterson's readers outside of the state accepted his views as indicative of state opinion. Watterson's editorials gained even more exposure when the Associated Press began distributing them for reprint nationally and internationally.[49]

Even as he painted a progressive face on Kentucky Democratic politics, Watterson embodied the very image of the "Old South" he sought to overturn. Unlike many New South spokesmen, Watterson seldom embellished the charms of the Old South in an effort to build a new one. The Old South, he claimed, was the "unsubstantial pageant of a dream," while slavery had been "the clumsiest and costliest system of labor on earth." He truly believed the South was better without the institution, as he once famously and indelicately said: "We had our niggers and we had our debts. Under the old system we paid our debts and walloped our niggers. Under the new we pay our niggers and wallop our debts."[50]

His appearance, however, seemed a throwback to everything he rejected. Despite his progressive tendencies, Watterson's mustachioed face—a mustachio that later grew white with age—and twinkling eyes obscured by "beetling brows" would make him, according to one acquaintance, "the cartoonist's prototype for the southern colonel." By the mid-1880s, he had become caricatured in popular imagination as a brilliant, if unrestrained, Kentucky colonel with a glass of bourbon in one hand and a deck of cards in his pocket. Admirers gave him the racially loaded title "Marse Henry," imparting Watterson with an image of a southern gentleman that was antithetical to his message of modern industry.[51]

Watterson was largely responsible for giving a kinder face to what the *Cincinnati Gazette* described as "the Kentucky experiment of organizing a living party upon a dead rebellion." His reconciliationist outlook took the edge off Kentucky's perceived rebelliousness, and his New Departure politics diluted the rhetoric of racism. Democratic politicians and editors in the state also toned down their rabidly racist rhetoric, when after 1870 they realized that, despite gaining the right to vote, the state's modest African American population could not stand up to the large number of Conservatives. Though many Kentucky whites would continue to wield the politics of racism—Watterson could still lament in the 1870s that "the chap who talks the loudest and with the least common sense about the probability of 'our daughters marrying niggers' always comes in about four lengths ahead"—other issues in the ensuing decades would occasionally outweigh fears of black domination.[52]

Moreover, in the presidential election of 1872, Watterson's own efforts led most Kentucky voters to break with Democrats and cast their votes for Liberal Republican Horace Greeley, proving that Kentucky's bond with the party was not indissoluble. This meant that at the same time that whites in states further south began to redeem themselves, disenfranchise African Americans, and become solidly Democratic, Kentuckians became more politically fractured. In 1895, they elected the state's first Republican governor when the Populist movement split the Democratic vote. The fact remained, however, that in the years following the war "the 'Lost Cause' [had been] found again in Kentucky," as "the hands that feared to assault the armed Republic, [were] swift . . . to become accessories after the fact."[53]

Wicked and Lawless Men

VIOLENCE AND CONFEDERATE
IDENTITY, 1865–1885

In January 1865, as surveyor Alfred Harrison traveled through Lewis County, a band of armed men attacked the house in which he was staying. The men took his money, his horse and tack, and everything else in his possession. "Few persons," he remarked bitterly, "save those who have had some experience among the rebels can fully understand and appreciate the ravages and unmitigated crimes perpetrated by a set of monsters in the shape of men, banded together for the purpose of robbing, stealing, and carrying out the dark designs of that miserable thing called the Southern Confederacy. . . . Such are some of the doings of southern chivalry. Such are the acts of a set of scoundrels, with whom many of the men living in the Loyal States, and pretending to be good citizens, sympathize. But these are nothing more or less than fair specimens of the great masses of the people who are seeking to overthrow this Government." Harrison's vitriolic statements echoed what many people of Unionist sympathy were thinking about the conditions of affairs in Kentucky at the time: that the state's turncoat rebelliousness was manifesting itself in utter lawlessness that victimized loyal citizens.[1]

ONLY A FEW MONTHS LATER, Confederate sympathizer Lizzie Hardin wrote in her diary about "lawlessness of every shade" that existed in 1865, "from the lawlessness of the government at Washington to that of the Negro who steals his master's chickens." It is doubtful that Hardin, or anyone in Kentucky, had the ability to foresee the extent to which lawlessness would engulf the Bluegrass State in the decades that followed. Although many Kentuckians yearned for the return of peace after the war, they hoped in vain. Instead, as one historian remarked, Kentuckians "degenerated into a sort of private warfare," producing a "saturnalia of crime" that swept across the state in the decades following the war.[2]

This lawlessness, however, could not be laid at the feet of the federal government or of liberated African Americans, as Hardin maintained. Rather, the fault rested with native whites whose loosely organized campaigns of intimidation, shooting, burning, ransacking, and lynching blanketed the commonwealth in an atmosphere of terror and disorder for decades. Like the dominance of conservative Democratic politics, the incidents of bloodshed, which surfaced across the state like angry boils, were largely the product of white Kentuckians' efforts to restore as much of the prewar social and racial order as possible. Often deployed in the interest of suppressing African Americans, Union veterans, and white Republicans, the violence proved to many that the same forces of conservative white supremacy were at work in Kentucky as had been in the former Confederate states during the Reconstruction era.

Between 1865 and 1885, Kentucky emerged as one of the most lawless states in America. The commonwealth exhibited many of the same forces of conservative white supremacy that were wreaking havoc in the former Confederate states and in other border states, especially Missouri. The fact that many Kentuckians adhered to antebellum codes of chivalry only compounded the ruthless postwar behavior. Kentuckians, more than ever, became associated with brutal behavior as they engaged in and suffered from vigilantism, mob violence, and lynching on an unprecedented scale, reminding the rest of the nation that, wartime sympathies aside, Kentucky shared the violent tendencies of the former Confederacy. At the same time, an increase in personal violence, which was not necessarily connected to Civil War grudges, fed into preexisting notions of southern honor and justice and further cemented Kentucky's association with the Confederate states to the South.[3]

Kentucky's wartime loyalty to the North further compounded the problem by placing the state outside the framework of federal Reconstruction, giving the federal government far less power in Kentucky to curtail the violence than in southern states that seceded. Internally, the lack of a committed or efficient response from the governor and legislature reflected poorly on the entire state, making its government seem sympathetic to, or at least ambivalent about, the extralegal activity. By 1885, Kentucky's dubious distinction as one of the most violent states in the nation's most violent region helped reshape the memory of the state's wartime loyalties.

Importantly, violence in Kentucky was not simply a postwar phenomenon but rather a natural outgrowth of the pervasive and intense guerrilla activity that had plagued the state during the war. Hundreds of Kentuckians who had not joined either army turned to extralegal and deadly means to fight a veritable civil war within a civil war, and violence among civilians increased as the conflict wore on and the general upheaval of war rendered the legal system ineffectual. After 1865, crime became the hallmark of a state full of wandering deserters and a populace fallen on hard times, still reeling from social, political, and racial upheaval and intent on fighting a "war after the war." That year, Union veteran and Wayne County resident John Tuttle wrote of seeing "great numbers of soldiers from both the Federal and Confederate armies lately discharged, deserted, or sent out in loose detachments for various purposes" and noted that they "created considerable disturbance" throughout the region, the "civil law" having "but little effect in curbing their turbulent spirit." These former soldiers committed "a great many depredations . . . on defenseless citizens." Although the military officials in the state dispatched units to suppress the disorder, they proved, according to Tuttle, "not at all efficient for the purpose for which they were sent here." "The public mind here these days is excited, restless, and uneasy," he added.[4]

Henderson resident Susan Bullitt Dixon described another incident in which a group of twenty robbers rode into town "and acted more like devils than humans." In the process of robbing one townsperson of his money and watch, "they beat him over the head and shoulders with pistols, cutting one of his ears in two, and finally shot him through the neck." The men claimed to be from John Hunt Morgan's regiment but were actually deserters from both the Union and the Confederate armies, banded together not only "for plunder and murder" but also for survival. Indeed, joining together to both perpetrate and fight crime became one of the first fronts of reunion among Kentucky's divided populace. In the face of such a threatening situation, Dixon remarked, "I am thankful that I do not come of a coward stock and that I am not easy to scare." Allen County citizen J. R. Thornton described his town as having been "nearly burnt up" by marauders, adding, "We don't know when we lie down at night what we will be killed by Guerillas before the sun rises next morning."[5]

In addition to the general crimes of horse theft and robbery, it was not uncommon for armed groups to derail trains by destroying track and then plundering the passengers. John Tuttle considered his corner of southern Kentucky to be "in a most deplorable condition," with lawless bands

"continually prowling through this region of the country stealing, robbing, plundering, burning, and committing all manner of depredations,
cruelties, and atrocities upon helpless and unoffending citizens." At their
most benign, the mobs would journey to the county seat of Monticello,
drink, and "insult and abuse citizens, swagger about using the most pro-
fane, vulgar, and obscene language."[6]

Much of the violence, however, was less random. Just as in the states
of the former Confederacy, violence in Kentucky became a hallmark of
the Reconstruction period. During the transition from war to peace, and
from a slave society to a free one, violence, in all of its chaotic cruelty, became a way for many white Kentuckians to assert order over what they
viewed as a destabilized world. As they dealt with the anxieties regarding the place newly freed African Americans would occupy in postwar
life, "lawless" activity became a means of instilling order where its perpetrators perceived civil authority to be ineffective or absent. Regulators
were "self-constituted guardians of law and order" who "hanged and shot
people for crimes which state authorities were not given time to punish."
The "crime" was usually some breach of the racial or political hierarchy.
In postwar Kentucky, violent acts became the tools of people interested
in maintaining the prewar racial and political status quo. In the wake of
the radical upheavals brought by the Civil War, extralegal activity became
a way to assert conservative values, Democratic politics, and, most of all,
white supremacy. To this end, the targets of violence were overwhelmingly
African Americans and Union or Republican whites. African Americans in
particular suffered the effects of postwar violence. In their efforts to shape
a world where former slaves remained in a subservient status, thousands
of Kentucky whites used intimidation to prevent African Americans from
violating racial boundaries, or punished them when they did so.[7]

One of the most remarkable ways that Kentucky resembled the former Confederacy during Reconstruction was the widespread presence of
regulator groups and the Ku Klux Klan in the state. As Alan Trelease has
observed, "Kentucky was the only state outside the former Confederacy
where the Klan found any significant lodgment." He has also noted that
although they lacked any real central organization, local Klan and regulator groups "were active sporadically in various parts of the state well into
the 1870's, longer than in any other state." The Bluegrass region which
included Kentucky's major cities of Lexington and Louisville and its capital, Frankfort proved to be the epicenter of the worst violence, with the
heaviest casualties in the southern and western portions of the area. No
corner of the state, however, went unscathed. By 1874, the *New York Times*

declared of Kentucky, "From no State in the South to-day come such frequent and continuous reports of brutal murders and whippings by Ku Klux and other secret organizations."[8]

White efforts to control black labor frequently resulted in racial violence. Whites often acted as slave masters, continuing to beat and flog their black laborers as they had under slavery. More menacing, however, was the threat from groups of armed and mounted men who terrorized African Americans and sometimes their white employers. Whether they referred to themselves as "regulators" or as Klansmen, these groups sought not only to punish blacks for their new freedom but to persuade employers not to hire them, especially those blacks who had served in the Union army. Cycles of violence were often tied to cycles of labor, and conflict intensified during the slack winter hiring season. In 1866, regulators in Daviess, Marion, Henry, and Oldham Counties burned housing farmers had built for laborers. That year, in Lebanon, a gang of around forty mounted outlaws known as Skagg's Men descended upon an enclave of twenty homes inhabited by African Americans. They screamed insults and plundered, tearing apart furniture, roofs, and chimneys, before finally driving the freedpeople from the area. In the Bluegrass region, nightriders, whom some believed to be white tenants displaced by African Americans willing to pay higher rent, whipped and killed freedmen in Franklin and Fayette Counties.[9]

Near Owensboro, in western Kentucky, one group threatened to burn the property of white farmers who rented land to African Americans and warned the black tenants to leave by the next day. Violent competition between white and black workers was not limited to agricultural work or to certain geographic areas. In Estill County, in eastern Kentucky, the Red River Iron Works company replaced white miners with black skilled workers, who would work for lower wages. In 1871, twelve of the white miners raided the boardinghouse in which several of the black workers were staying. The conflict escalated when the local Klan repeatedly conducted raids and effectively shut down mines. The mining company, fearing both the Klan and the interruption in business, failed to challenge the ruffians and allowed the 400 blacks who were working there at the time to be driven from the area.[10]

In the face of this danger, many African Americans emigrated from rural areas to towns, which offered at least a small measure of protection, leading to massive displacement from rural to urban areas, and thousands of African Americans left the state altogether. Statistics reveal the extent of this trend. Between 1860 and 1870, for instance, the white population increased in Kentucky by 14 percent, while the state's black population decreased by 7 percent. The number of African Americans in the state's largest towns and cities, however, actually increased, by an astounding 133 percent. Violence, and the changes it created in rural demographics, intensified an already-severe labor shortage in the state, making strange bedfellows of white landowners and black tenants, both of whom appealed to the state (without much success) for better protection in rural areas.[11]

The widespread practice of lynching became another link between Kentucky and the former Confederate states. In his exhaustive study of the subject, George Wright found that 353 people were lynched in the state following the Civil War. Despite the arguments of historians that southern lynching reached its peak in the 1880s and 1890s, Wright's findings show that 117 lynchings, a full third of the state's total, occurred between 1865 and 1874. Furthermore, more incidents occurred between 1865 and 1880 than during any other fifteen-year period, including the time frame generally considered the peak of southern lynching.[12]

In the context of white Kentuckians' desperate efforts to reestablish prewar order to their life, it is not entirely surprising that these lynchings occurred when they did. The practice in Kentucky, as elsewhere, often occurred outside of civil law, aborting the judicial process and imposing the popular will of a few. In 1866, a black man was shot simply for being intoxicated and for "making fight" at an agricultural fair in Paris. Authorities arrested and jailed him, and later that night he was taken from the jail before he could be tried in a court of law and shot to death by "Lynch law." In the Reconstruction era, both legal and extralegal executions became didactic opportunities for whites to remind African Americans that their place was on the bottom rung of society. At the execution of one black youth found guilty of rape in Monticello, a local clergyman took the opportunity to deliver "a lengthy lecture to the negroes upon their duties in their situation towards whites, one another, their God, and their country."[13]

The alleged rape of white women or girls was, as elsewhere in the South, often cited as the cause of racial violence in Kentucky. Wright's findings suggest that rape was the leading cause of lynching of blacks in the commonwealth and accounted for a full third of all lynchings of African Americans in the state between 1865 and 1940. Although white southerners' extreme fear of black male sexual aggression did not reach its peak until the 1880s and 1890s, accusations of African Americans raping white females were cited as the cause of numerous extralegal executions across

Kentucky as early as 1866 and 1867 and regularly throughout the 1860s and 1870s.[14]

During these years, just as in the 1880s and 1890s, whites equated crossing racial sexual boundaries with breaching political and social hierarchies. In Henry County in 1877, a band of 200 "rough-riders" forced an entire "colored colony" to leave the state because of alleged sexual improprieties between a mulatto man and the wife of a "wealthy and respectable" white man. Writing in response to the *Louisville Courier-Journal*'s denunciation of their actions, several white residents of the county claimed that the man in question was also purported to have had "criminal intimacy" with several other "respectable" white single and married women. "What man with a family," they asked, "would not turn out to rid the county of such a wretch as he. It would seem a white woman could not speak to him but he would turn around and traduce her character."[15]

Instead of a subversion of law and order, many Kentucky whites saw this form of violent activity and intimidation as a means of upholding it. Although much violence was motivated by efforts to suppress African Americans, whites often blamed its presence on the end of slavery and black freedom. The *Lexington Gazette* reported: "In the time of slavery every farmer took cognizance of his dependents and had the power of inflicting punishment." Because law enforcement did not act as a surrogate slave master, however, blacks were free to "harry all over the country without let or hindrance, and render the lives of our farmers and their families one of perpetual anxiety and apprehension."[16]

The prevalence of violence against African Americans in Kentucky motivated Congress to establish the Freedmen's Bureau in the state in late 1865. Indeed, one bureau special investigator who toured the state sent a report to Washington describing the prolific horrors he found. Among them were twenty-three cases of the "most severe and inhuman" whippings, numerous shootings, two women tied up and "whipped until insensible," three women "assaulted and ravaged, [and] the destruction of property and burning of homes." He noted that Union veterans and their wives were well represented among the victims.[17]

From its earliest days in the state, the Freedmen's Bureau faced stiff resistance from conservative whites, who viewed its arrival as more evidence that their wartime loyalty was betrayed by the radical national government. The bureau tried to provide a legal voice for the freedmen by negotiating labor contracts between African Americans and their employers and attempting to quell racial violence, but it had little success. Even with the presence of the Freedmen's Bureau, one man claimed in late 1868 that in Kentucky "almost every breeze comes laden with the wail of freedmen. Almost every night is lit up with the blaze of burning churches and schoolhouses." He added that in one county alone during the period of a month arsonists torched two churches and two schoolhouses.[18]

Bureau agents in Kentucky, unlike in other southern and border states, were not under the protection of Federal troops or a sympathetic state government. Indeed, one historian has written that of the four border states Kentucky suffered "the dubious distinction of being in the forefront of its violent opposition to the activities of the Freedmen's Bureau." Bureau representatives also often became victims of Klan intimidation and violence. In the bureau's two years of operation, regulators and Klansmen blew up one school and burned ten others, and in 1868, a white teacher was threatened and one of her black pupils was murdered.[19]

Internal resentment meant that state authorities gave the bureau little support, and Kentucky's loyal wartime status meant that national authorities rarely backed the local agency. General F. D. Sewall, a bureau inspector sent to appraise operations in Kentucky in 1866, reported that he had found more antagonism toward the agency in Kentucky than in any other state except Mississippi. He blamed this on the "presence of the bureau in a state that had not seceded" and added that in no other state did the freedmen need the bureau's protection more than in Kentucky. Noticing the Freedmen's Bureau's fate, most other freedmen's aid societies avoided Kentucky altogether.[20]

Some contemporary observers felt that the agency's presence made life worse for African Americans by inciting white violence. When a Frankfort mob lynched a sixteen-year-old African American for allegedly attempting to rape a six-year-old girl in 1866, a correspondent for the *Louisville Daily Courier* defended the action not only as justice for the particular alleged offense but as retaliation for the indignities of the new postwar racial and political order. The paper described the incident as a "quiet uprising of the citizens who are determined to put a stop to such outrages" as the Freedmen's Bureau and the Civil Rights Bill of 1866. The execution, claimed the paper, had been conducted "decently and in order," with "no mob" or "confusion and noise."[21]

Not surprisingly, black political activity also inspired white violence. African Americans could not vote in Kentucky until 1871, and prior to that, whites aimed their brutality primarily at what they considered African American social and economic violations of racial order. Nevertheless, conservative Kentucky whites often targeted African Americans for anything resembling political activity. In Lexington, the Klan threatened black clergy and teachers working for suffrage. Elsewhere, they targeted physical structures such as schools and churches that were used for black political assemblies. After the passage of the Fifteenth Amendment, violence only intensified. In Woodford County, whites formed a militia to oppose the formation of black political clubs. On the eve of the August 1870 elections, the Democratic-backed militia shot two prominent black Republican leaders. Local officials refused to apprehend or prosecute the perpetrators, and white Republican leaders fled the county in fear.[22]

Black voter organization surrounding the August 1871 election sparked a riot in Frankfort. Two African Americans, reportedly provoked by gunfire from police, opened fire and killed two white men. White authorities arrested prominent black political leader Henry Washington, who had been wounded in the riot, for inciting the incident. Later that evening, a mob numbering more than 250 men descended upon the jail, removed Washington and another black man held on rape charges, and hanged them on the edge of town. In 1872, the Ku Klux Klan lynched Samuel Hawkins, a central Kentucky political organizer, and his entire family because of his efforts to register black voters.[23]

Despite the formidable danger and tremendous terror they faced, black Kentuckians resisted. Many took up arms in defense of their homes and lives. In several central Kentucky counties, armed African Americans surrounded local jails to prevent the Klan from removing black inmates. In the Bluegrass town of Stamping Ground, a few black residents successfully halted a Klan attack, killing one of the white raiders. Elijah Marrs, a black Union veteran who settled in Henry County to teach in a freedman's school, started a local chapter of the Loyal League. He drove off the Klan mobs several times by firing on them and claimed to have "slept with a pistol under [his] head, an Enfield rifle at [his] side, and a corn knife at the door." African Americans near Stanford successfully fended off a Klan mob, killing three of the hooded men. Many whites considered black self-defense an affront to white supremacy. As one critic noted of the situation in Kentucky, "The moment 'Mr. Negro' touch[es] a gun and t[akes] sides, 'the war of races' beg[ins]. It makes no difference whose fight may be in progress, or what may be the danger to non-combatants, the instant the colored troops take a hand, that instant the aspect of the melee is changed, and the outraged 'Southron' points to the combat as a result of negro emancipation, and as an argument against granting further rights to the emancipated race."[24]

In addition to physically defending themselves, African Americans appealed to local and state officials for support in ending the crimes committed at their expense. In 1872, six of Kentucky's most prominent black citizens went before the U.S. Congress with a petition on behalf of the African Americans in the Frankfort area. "We respectfully state that life, liberty, and property are unprotected among the colored race of this state," they read. "Organized Bands of desperate and lawless men mainly composed of soldiers of the late Rebel Armies, armed disciplined and bound by Oath and secret obligations, have by force terror and violence subverted all civil society among Colored people." They implicated the Democratic state legislature for allowing the disorder, which was "perpetrated only upon Colored men and white Republicans," asserting that they had become "the special objects of persecution" at the hands of the Democratic Party. They documented sixty-four cases of brutality, which included robbing, ravishing, killing, and forcing black Kentuckians to "bathe" in the frozen Kentucky River.[25]

The African American representatives used their citizenship as grounds for protest, arguing that they were law-abiding, tax-paying citizens deprived of their constitutional rights to vote and testify in court. Although Congress could do little to directly quell violence in the state, Kentucky's black citizens successfully created political pressure for action by bringing these abuses to the attention of the nation. Moreover, by laying the blame at the feet of ex-Confederates, they illustrated to a largely Republican Congress that rebels held an unjustifiable level of power and influence in the Bluegrass State. Thus, even as they asserted their rights won by Union victory, they gave credence to the idea that Kentucky was in the hands of rebels and Confederates.

Racial violence and intimidation shaped everyday life for Kentucky's African Americans and informed their memory of the postwar period for decades to come. In his autobiography, Madison County native Thomas Burton remembered the Klan being "quite thick in [his] vicinity" and recalled the nightly ritual in the African American community: "About nine or ten o'clock . . . the roaring, thundering sounds from the horses' feet, seemingly about two thousand in number," riding by and yelling at "some people's houses whose lamps and candles were burning, they would shout, 'Lights out!' If the occupants of the house did not extinguish those lights at the command immediately, a bullet from without would." He recalled that "it was the usual custom to go to people's houses at night, and see them greet one another in the dark," with the only dim light coming from a fireplace or a grease lamp.[26]

Hannah Davidson, who grew up in Ballard County, remembered of the Klan: "If they heard anybody saying you was free, they would take you out at night and whip you." She also remembered Klan membership being composed of "plantation owners." "I never saw them ride," she added, "but I heard about them and what they did. My master used to tell us he wished he knew who the Ku Kluxers were. But he knew, all right, I used to wait on table and I heard them talking 'Gonna lynch another nigger tonight!'" John Rudd's fear of the Klan was captured in a long-enduring memory of seeing seven former slaves hanging from a single tree "near the top of Grimes-Hill, just after the close of the war." Even more horrific was Mary Wright's recollection of the Klan placing the heads of African Americans they had killed on stakes "alongside de Cadiz road," where "de buzzards would eat them until nuthin' was left but the bones." According to Wright, they posted signs on the stakes which read: "Look out Nigger You are next." This terrifying admonition, she remembered, kept children close to home. "I jes knowed that dis Ku Klux would do dat to us sho if weuns had been catched," she declared.[27]

Like African Americans, white Republicans also became lightning rods for the violent wrath of conservative whites. In western Kentucky, the Klan placed gallows on the property of Union Party men, poisoned their farm animals, and even expelled them from several counties. In the eastern Kentucky counties of Breathitt, Magoffin, Wolfe, and Perry—Republican strongholds by Kentucky standards—nineteen white men, all Union veterans or Republican supporters, were murdered in a six-month period during 1870. In the western Kentucky town of Russellville, which served briefly as the Confederate capital of Kentucky during the war, assailants killed five Union men during a period of a few months in 1868, including the U.S. marshal for Kentucky, who had been a major in the Union army. In Owen County, the Klan tried to drive out not only African Americans but "all Radicals who were in favor" of them.[28]

As with the crimes whites committed against African Americans, white-on-white violence was tied to wartime allegiance and postwar politics. In a well-publicized 1867 incident, a gang of regulators shot U.S. Major James Bridgewater in the back while he played checkers on the porch of a Stanford store. During the war, Bridgewater had earned a reputation as a fierce guerrilla hunter. After the conflict, he continued his service to the federal government, first with the Freedmen's Bureau and then with the Internal Revenue Service, in both capacities using sometimes violent tactics to stanch regulator activity near his Lincoln County home. This same gang purportedly whipped or hanged at least thirty other people. Their victims included an entire African American community in Lebanon and Unionist luminaries General Speed Fry and John Marshall Harlan, both of whom they drove from their homes. Bridgewater's murder became a symbol inside and outside of Kentucky of the virulent hatred of and dangers faced by those who still supported the Union cause after the war. In June of the same year, a band of regulators descended upon a political meeting in an attempt to capture two Union candidates. Although locals thought that the mob included several civil officers, citizens were reluctant to identify members by name, for fear of jeopardizing their property or their lives. One observer reported to the *New York Times* in 1868 that "in some districts ex-Union soldiers are persecuted by their more numerous rebel neighbors until they are forced into a resistance which sometimes ends with the loss of their lives, or they are compelled by self-defense to emigrate." Violence was not solely the province of conservative whites, however. In 1871, the Loyal League was reportedly active in the state, especially in the eastern portion. In the eastern Kentucky county of Harlan, they threatened Democratic voters and reportedly whipped them in Madison County. By and large, however, the targets of lawlessness were Republicans and Unionists, white and African American.[29]

As victims of violence, those who supported the Union after the Civil War became marginalized. They may have been on the winning side of the struggle over disunion, but they were demoralized by the conservative backlash of their neighbors who had been Confederate partisans. Seemingly helpless to defend themselves, on occasion they looked to the federal government for help. In 1870, a group of Scott County Republicans wrote a letter to the *Cincinnati Gazette*, a Republican paper, calling for Federal troops to offer protection, promising to retract their demand only when the "formidable rebel army" in the county was no longer a threat. Meanwhile, political class and racial tensions collided when enraged Booneville Republicans wrote to President Grant demanding that he send a regiment of African American troops who might "subsist off those rich Rebel Ku Klux and hunt down and punish those midnight assassins."[30]

Yet Kentuckians intent on remembering their state's wartime loyalty remained strong in their convictions, even as "rebel" elements intimidated and tortured them. One Kentucky man reminded readers of the *New York Times* that despite the behavior of many citizens there were "no firmer friends of the National Union than those Southern men, who have always been such," and that even "amid the circle of ex-gray-coated warriors, their adherence to a united nation is as firm as ever." He also begged them to remember that their devotion was all the greater for the risks they incurred to defend it. "It costs them nothing to express their sentiments," he wrote of people in the North and the East, while Unionists in Kentucky faced constant threat for their convictions.[31]

Violence, race, and Democratic politics were impossibly intertwined in Kentucky, and old sectional tensions often mixed with politics to create volatile results. In Carlisle County, during the 1876 presidential contest, some of the town's Republicans signaled their political leanings by displaying a large number of Union flags. Soon after, a group of "rebels," who were reportedly "stimulated by bad Whiskey and a prospective hope of victory in November," congregated around a flag belonging to the widow of a Federal officer and "raised a fierce howl of derision," threatening to burn down her house if she did not take it down. Later that evening, the crowd began yelling and cheering for the rebel flag and the Confederacy. When James Blair, a "gallant young fellow" from a Unionist family and brother of a Republican candidate for the legislature, rushed into the crowd, he was shot and killed.[32]

The *New York Times*, which covered the story under the headline "The Rebel Spirit in Kentucky," called him "a victim to the intolerant rebel spirit which pervades the Kentucky Democracy—a brave, fearless man, murdered by the unreconstructed rebels who compose the Democratic Party of the State." The *Times* correspondent went on to complain mockingly that the incident was not even reported by the "loyal, patriotic, Union-saving Tilden mouthpiece, the *Courier-Journal*." He warned that a Democratic victory would "for Republicans in Kentucky and the South" mean "brutal ostracism," "violence and outrage." It would signify, he asserted, "what the rebels have repeatedly said, when they are victorious, 'You must leave the State,—you, white and black.'"[33]

With African Americans and white Republicans the prime targets of violence, Republican newspapers offered the most vociferous protests of conditions in the state. The Cincinnati papers, situated only a stone's throw from Kentucky borders, were as exasperated by the lawless conditions in the state as they were by its political leanings. The *New York Times* assiduously covered the situation in shocked and angry tones, attacking crime in the state both for its sheer brutality and as part and parcel of their larger criticism of Democratic dominance of the South. They saw outlawry in Kentucky as an apparatus of the Democratic Party and its conservative politics and often referred to state politics as "the Ku Klux Kentucky Democracy." In 1868, a *New York Times* correspondent described the entwined nature of race, politics, sectionalism, and violence in Kentucky when he wrote, "The opposition to [African Americans] and their higher interests has been and is assuming organized shape in many parts of the State, and the bands of wicked and lawless men, under the saphonious name of the Ku Klux Klan, bearing until quite recently the banner of [Democratic candidates], and practices in the 'rebel yell' are almost daily committing outrages and depredations which disgrace the name of Kentucky, but which are passed over in silence by civil authorities."[34]

As the columnist suggested, perhaps the most outrageous aspect of the violence in Kentucky was how little the state government did to curtail it. Although Kentucky governors periodically issued proclamations denouncing the lawlessness and encouraging punitive measures, they had little effect in curbing the reign of terror that engulfed the state. In 1867, when Thomas Bramlette asked the General Assembly to appropriate reward money for the capture of regulator bands, the legislature allocated only $500. Later that year, his successor, John Stevenson, ordered that all renegade groups disband and dispatched the state militia to Mercer County to quell mob violence. In 1869, he again sent armed units to Boyle, Garrard, and Lincoln Counties in the central part of the state and pledged to do whatever was necessary to "arrest and [bring] to justice all of those who combine together, no matter under what pretense, to trample the law under their feet by acts of personal violence." In 1871, the General Assembly did pass a law banning concealed weapons.[35]

Generally, however, such proclamations and legislation proved only mildly effective. When the General Assembly brought anti-Klan legislation up for debate during its 1871–72 session, both Henry Watterson and J. Stoddard Johnston, the distinctly more conservative editor of the *Daily Kentucky Yeoman*, enthusiastically supported it. On the assembly floor, however, sectional overtones dominated the debate. Many conservative politicians argued that if the Klan were to be singled out for prosecution the Loyal League ought to be as well. Mired in animosity, the bill went down in defeat. Outraged, Watterson railed: "The legislature has done nothing. It has sacrificed us. It has violated all its obligations to the state, to the people, and to the Democratic party." To add insult to injury, at the very moment the legislature was debating the ill-fated bill on the assembly floor, thirty Klan members were rescuing a man being held for murdering an African American from a jail "not a hundred rods" from the capitol.[36]

The following year, the new governor, Preston Leslie, proved more successful in quelling crime in the state. He appealed to the General Assembly in 1872 to strengthen the state's response to those supplanting the rule of law with vigilantism. "When men organize themselves into vigilance committees, clans, or leagues, . . . with the vowed purpose of taking the law into their own hands, to inflict punishment upon any member of the community who may be obnoxious to them," he asserted, "they become themselves the most dangerous class of lawbreakers." In response, the General Assembly passed several laws that struck at both the Klan and the Loyal League, banning writing or posting threatening notices, conspiring to harm, and being "armed and disguised." The legislation made these crimes punishable by fines and imprisonment and also threatened local officials with fines, prison terms, and removal from office.[37]

The Democratic General Assembly largely failed, however, to give teeth to such legislation. Although the Democratic Party never officially sanctioned lawless activity and regularly denounced it, partisans often viewed those who carried out violent acts as "political allies . . . not sought but accepted." Furthermore, local authorities often failed to enforce the law, sometimes because they were in sympathy with perpetrators but more often because they were too frightened or outnumbered to do so. The rapid proliferation of Kentucky counties in the nineteenth century meant that the state was composed of "little kingdoms" whose tax bases proved insufficient to support effective law enforcement. Even after Governor Leslie's proclamation, for instance, white outlaws commandeered power from local authorities in fifteen central Kentucky counties. Indeed, it seemed that state laws and those charged with enforcing them were incapable of countering the lawlessness. The state, it appeared, could not even protect the well-being of its citizens, leading a Carroll County judge to lament in 1877: "The blood of the slain cries for justice everywhere. Human life in Kentucky is not worth the snappings of a man's finger. The finger ends of many men who go unpunished are dripping with the gore of their victims. Acres of grass grow on the graves of murdered men in my district."[38]

As Kentucky became further mired in disorder, Henry Watterson continually accused the legislature of "extraordinary inaction." During a particularly intense spate of Klan outbreaks in Owen and Henry Counties in 1873, Watterson decried the "utter lack of respect for state authority" that existed in Kentucky. "The state government," he lamented, "is virtually bearded in its stronghold. The proclamations of the governor are laughed at as were the fulminations of the ancient monarch against the waves of an angry sea, the civil authorities are stricken with the palsy of fear, courts of justice are mere mockery, and their . . . hooded villainy almost invades the grounds of the capital." He claimed things had nearly come to the point where he expected the representatives of the state government to be driven from the capital. Meanwhile, the *New York Times* echoed Watterson's point, declaring that the state was being "ruined" by the lack of law administration.[39]

By March 1871, white officials' unwillingness and inability to deal with the lawlessness made Kentucky's problem the focal point of a U.S. Senate debate over southern violence. On the Senate floor, Ohio senator John Sherman and Kentucky senator (and former governor) John Stevenson launched a shouting match in which Sherman blamed the Democratic state legislature for doing too little to repress the outrages and Stevenson countered by denying that Kentucky was any more lawless than the city of Cincinnati. In October 1871, President Grant himself responded to mounting problems by sending the U.S. attorney general to Kentucky to investigate Klan activities and to do whatever he could to destroy the organization in the state.[40]

It is difficult to overestimate the extent to which lawlessness in Kentucky shaped the state's reputation among outsiders. From the end of the Civil War through the 1880s, much of what journalists, authors, and travelers wrote about the state centered on violence, and the comments of widely read newspapers like the *Louisville Courier-Journal* and the *New York Times* helped define the way many Americans viewed Kentucky. As early as 1866, outsiders such as John Hawes made note of disorder and "barbarism" among Lexington residents. In a letter to a Kentucky friend, he stated his dismay at the "degree of non-chalance with which they handle edge tools and fire arms and stand neither in awe of the laws of man nor God." Casting this behavior as Civil War rebellion, he continued: "The opinion I would express if called upon, would be that the war ended at least two years too soon[—]that while we were whipping this class of people we did not make our blows sufficiently heave to create the impression that we were in earnest." Hawes's opinions were, no doubt, influenced by newspaper accounts. Throughout the 1870s publications like the *New York Times* printed tales of lawlessness regularly, portraying the state as the home of "American Banditti" and "midnight assassins," a place where violence reigned and the law was ill respected.[41]

Kentuckians, for their part, were keenly aware of their reputation in the eyes of the outside world. They were especially cognizant of the views of northerners, and state newspapers often reprinted what other newspapers said about their state. This was especially true of Henry Watterson's *Courier-Journal*, which launched an all-out public relations battle against both the violence itself and the perception the state's lawlessness. As a racial and political moderate, Watterson lamented the cause of the violence, and as an elite white business prophet, he disdained the disorder. But most of all, as a New South visionary, he feared the threat lawlessness posed to the economic development of Kentucky. In 1873, he wrote that the deleterious effects of the violence, in particular the Klan variety, had driven away "good citizens," deterred immigration into the state, depreciated property values, and "made [the] Commonwealth a byword and a reproach among our people." If the lawlessness was not quelled, he warned, it would "plunge us into bankruptcy and ruin."[42]

He had good reason to worry, as those themes recurred frequently in the outside press. The *Pittsburgh Commercial* warned that if the perpetrators were allowed to continue "wreaking their rebel hatred upon peaceable and law-abiding citizens" and achieve the "sober order and tranquility which lie at the base of all order and progress," Kentucky would never be able to capitalize on her ample natural resources. The *New York Times* similarly reported that "troops of immigrants" avoided the state, "repelled by the sorry tales which they have read of the turmoil and disorder in the interior." In 1878, the paper opined, "Kentucky may not care for her reputation morally, but her material interests demand that she should use all her powers to compel respect for law and order within her bounds. . . . Kentucky is, as everybody knows, a fine state, which needs development; but she never will get it, nor will she ever stand fair in the eyes of the world, until she suppresses effectively the spirit and practice of butchery with which her tarnished name is associated."[43]

Watterson and his newspaper found themselves in a thorny position. At the same time he robustly denounced lawlessness, calling for military force to "rid us of violence of every hue and shade" and demanding legislative reform, he fended off attacks of Republican newspapers that blamed the bloodshed on Kentucky's Democratic politics. Watterson condemned the attacks of the Republican *Louisville Commercial* and asserted: "Former Confederate soldiers, Democratic property holders, have suffered equally with the negroes at the hands of those villains." The perennially embattled editor also endured accusations that his Democratic paper did not do enough to denounce the violence. In defense of himself and his paper, Watterson issued statements such as: "The *Courier-Journal* has consistently denounced the Ku Klux of Kentucky with every outrage ever committed in the state in text, and in the strongest and most uncompromising terms at its command. Recently it has been at great expense in its endeavor to finally suppress them, and will never cease its efforts until the last one of the wretches has been properly punished or driven beyond the State."[44]

Despite his best efforts to curtail the lawlessness and to minimize its impact on the reputation of the Bluegrass State, Watterson himself ultimately contributed to Kentucky's violent image. In 1876, Watterson was in Washington serving out the unexpired congressional term of E. Y. Parson when he became embroiled in a public relations scandal. That year, Watterson campaigned relentlessly for presidential candidate Samuel Tilden and became intimately involved in the political wrangling of the disputed election. On January 8, 1877, Watterson delivered a speech at a Jackson Day meeting in Washington, D.C., in which he condemned the Grant administration's bungling of the election and suggested that on February 14, the day the electoral votes were to be counted, 100,000 unarmed citizens come to the nation's capital to exercise their right of petition, to ensure that the majority would prevail. Joseph Pulitzer, then an unknown political figure, spoke after Watterson and suggested that the 100,000 come armed and prepared to fight. All of this might have seemed innocuous enough if Watterson had not, in a *Courier-Journal* editorial published the same day, encouraged the attendance of "at least ten thousand unarmed Kentuckians in this city the coming 14th of February." "Less than this," he claimed, "will be of no avail. So much, supplemented as it will be by other States, will secure through civil agencies the peaceful settlement of the most dangerous issue that ever menaced the existence of free government."[45]

The Republican press purposely commingled the wording of Pulitzer's remarks with the content of Watterson's speech and editorial. In the hands of the national press, it appeared that Watterson had called for a mob of 10,000 armed Kentuckians to march on Washington, D.C., and threaten peaceful transfer of the power of the presidency. In response, President Grant threatened to put down "any demonstration or warlike concentration of men threatening the peace of the city." As a contemporary of Watterson's later wrote, the incident seared into the national imagination "visions of a hundred thousand Kentucky colonels, their white mustaches quivering with anger, advancing upon the national capital with horse-pistols and mint juleps."[46]

Watterson quickly became a symbol of volatile irresponsibility—as one biographer said, a "resurgent rebel, yelling for war." Cementing this into the national imagination was Thomas Nast's cartoon appearing in *Harper's Weekly* on February 3, 1877. It featured a wild-eyed Watterson, looking like an agitated Kentucky colonel, with a mustache and goatee and a crazed look that recalled Edmund Ruffin on the eve of secession. Playing cards spilled out of Watterson's suit sleeves, a ticket in his pocket said

"Red Hot for Tilden," and steam gushed from his mouth as a dignified Murat Halstead, editor of the *Cincinnati Commercial*, poured a pitcher of ice water over his head. Next to him lay two broadsides, one reiterating his call for citizens to assemble at the capitol and another that advertised, "Henry Fire-Watter-son (of the Louisville-Courier-Journal) will let off steam To Night." In the aftermath of the scandal, Watterson wrote his friend Whitelaw Reid, "You know me not to be an extremist. And yet; if I were a mad dog I could not have come in for greater disparagement." This image raised Watterson's profile on the national radar and undermined his credibility both as a critic of violence and, especially in the context of the election, as a spokesman for sectional reconciliation. The most outspoken critic of violence in the state came to embody the very stereotype of the incendiary Kentuckian.[47]

In 1880, journalist H. V. Redfield profiled Kentucky in his book *Homicide: North and South*, widely considered the first work to compare violence along sectional lines. Along with the former Confederate states of South Carolina, Tennessee, and Texas, Redfield awarded Kentucky an entire chapter unto itself. "The condition of society in Kentucky,—with respect to taking human life," he asserted, was "so deplorable that often in sixty days there are more murders and manslaughter than in all of the six New England States in one year, with four millions of population." Moreover, he noted, there were more homicides reported in Kentucky in six days than happened in a span of seven years in Vermont. "Both in character and in frequency," he wrote, "these personal difficulties and street fights [in Kentucky] . . . bear a close resemblance to one another in all the Southern States." In 1882, the editor of the *Nation*, E. L. Godkin, continued the negative comparisons of Kentucky with other states when he claimed that the Bluegrass State had suffered more homicides in 1878 than eight other states, including Maine, New Hampshire, Vermont, Massachusetts, Rhode Island, Connecticut, Pennsylvania, and Minnesota, which among them had "an aggregate population of ten millions."[48]

Violence in the commonwealth mimicked postwar lawlessness in the former Confederacy, in both its methods and its victims, and it also shared something else: a common context of honor and chivalry. Kentucky had a reputation as a violent place long before the Civil War. Pioneer lore celebrated the exploits of early settlers of the "dark and bloody ground" who, like Daniel Boone, lived and died by their long rifles. By the early nineteenth century, Kentucky had also become famous for the Cavalier culture of its Bluegrass region. As the fame of the white Bluegrass gentry (close kin to the venerable stock of its mother state, Virginia) and their palatial

Henry Watterson portrayed by Thomas Nast as a hot-headed Kentucky colonel in *Harper's Weekly*, February 3, 1877. Courtesy of Special Collections, University of Kentucky Libraries.

estates increased, Kentucky easily inherited the mantle of chivalry and honor.

The system of honor, Bertram Wyatt-Brown has shown, dictated that southern society conform to a patriarchal hierarchy that valued female deference, kinship, and, above all else, a man's reputation in the eyes of his peers. By the early nineteenth century, elite white Kentuckians were famously entrenched in this system, which, as Daniel Singal has noted, "lent frontier gunplay a respectability it had never enjoyed before." Bloodshed, so long associated with Kentucky, from the days of Indian warfare, was given a patina of gentility. "Whether in dancing, horse racing, or any other competition," Stephen Aron has argued, "Bluegrass planters were quick to answer all insults to their dignity as gentlemen" and to defend their southern honor, often through dueling. So marked were their Cavalier pretenses that one observer in the antebellum era remarked that "a Kentuckian [was] an Englishman with a little more pride."[49]

The southern code of honor played out within the legal system as well as in folkways, including the prevalence of concealed weapons, dueling, and lynch law. Though illegal, Kentuckians engaged in dozens of duels prior to the Civil War. Henry Clay, consummate politician, who came to typify the Kentucky gentleman in the first half of the nineteenth century, notoriously participated in two duels, including one with Virginian John Randolph in 1826. Many of the state's most prominent citizens viewed violence as a viable method of resolving disputes and defending honor.[50]

People generally looked benignly and even romantically upon this type of justice in the antebellum and Victorian eras. Within the strict social and racial hierarchy of the southern code of honor, the Cavalier's "natural impulses were held in check," William Taylor has written authoritatively. Thus, "the gentleman planter was not simply a Southerner, he was the principal civilizing agent in a society where everything tended toward anarchy and disorder. . . . Only the Cavalier possessed the heroic force of character which was required to hold back the restless flood of savagery that threatened to overflow the country." Daniel Singal has reiterated that, with his perfect self-control, the southern gentleman had a "heroic ability to bring order and culture to all he surveyed" and could "convince themselves and others that the South enjoyed the most stable and civilized society in America." This genteel self-restraint often meant that personal justice shared as much authority as the letter of the law.[51]

This emphasis on personally sanctioned justice continued in Kentucky and in the rest of the South after the Civil War, but middle-class northern views regarding the southern code of honor began to change. Intensely preoccupied with the status of human evolution and society's trajectory toward human progress, people in the Victorian era tended to divide human behavior into two categories, the "civilized" and the "savage." Civilized status, furthermore, could only be achieved by mastering savage impulses. During the nineteenth century, as Gail Bederman has argued, middle-class ideology put a premium on the "ability to control powerful masculine passions through strong character and a powerful will as a primary source of men's strength and authority over both women and the lower classes. By gaining the manly strength to control himself, a man gained strength, as well as the duty to protect those weaker than himself: his wife, his children, or his employees."[52]

An increased insistence on legalism also changed the way northerners viewed the relationship between honor and violence. As historian James Klotter has shrewdly observed, in postwar Kentucky there existed "two competing ideals of honor—the one seeking violent actions, the other seeing such violence as a threat to social order." Victorian sensibilities regarding manly self-control and civilization meant that the integrity of the letter of the law, especially after the Civil War, was increasingly at odds with the flexible community-based southern vision of justice. Along with broad precepts of legal and social behavior, the northern public demanded that Kentucky comply with the federal constitutional amendments and their implications for racial equality and that violence not be allowed to undermine the war imperatives. Many white Kentuckians, however, tended to base their legal behavior "on community standards and beliefs about what constituted a correct response," rather than Victorian legalism. "The honorable man followed the law, but reserved a higher law unto himself," states Klotter, and this "higher law" was increasingly at odds with those Americans outside the South.[53]

The actual violence, it seemed, had also become less romantic since the days of the Cavalier. "In place of the relatively civilized duel," C. Vann Woodward has written, "there arose the barbarous custom of shooting on sight." Kentucky, it seemed to both residents and outsiders, lay in the grip of the savage element of the state. In 1878, the *New York Times* remarked that the conditions in the Bluegrass State "would not have been strange sixty or seventy years ago, for many of the early inhabitants were so rude and uneducated as to be half-civilized," but that Kentuckians had seemingly failed to evolve, the violence being as "barbarous and disgraceful to humanity to-day" as ever before. "The Kentuckian," the *Times* continued, "assassinates his man or men, braves public opinion, or would were it not, so far as his neighborhood goes, wholly on his side, and, backed by his friends, arms himself against the officers of justice, killing them with as much savage alacrity as though they had the murderers of his kin. Such bloody lawlessness could not and would not be but for a certain sympathy with, or indifference to, it on the part of the State, which is really responsible for it." Finally, the newspaper counseled, "she should remember that this is not 1769, when DANIEL BOONE settled there, but 1878, when law and humanity have rights which neither individuals nor Commonwealths can violate with impunity."[54]

Editorials about the violence time and again invoked the language of savagery and civilization and often drew on the contrast between the mythical reputation of Bluegrass gentry and the unsavory ruffianism overtaking the state. "We have been invited to consider the great Commonwealth as a land which produces more beautiful women, unrivaled horses, fine whisky, and Bluegrass than any other section in the universe," claimed one *New York Times* article, "but have heard that some classes of its inhabitants are hostile to innovation . . . and think it no harm to kill a man or two yearly to keep their sense of honor keen and their weapons bright." The language that commentators used to describe the situation in the state often featured almost apocalyptic qualities. Kentuckians had, as the *Times* put it, "arrived at an epoch when they required one-half of the citizens to be ready to march at a moment's notice, to preserve order among the other half. . . . Civil Society within the limits of the Commonwealth which boasts some of the noblest society, and which has produced many of its ablest citizens, seem[s] toppling from its foundations."[55]

As the press both inside and outside of the state addressed the violence, it often drew on the concept of honor—a trait that Kentuckians were at risk of losing, or had already relinquished. The *Princeton (Ky.) Banner* remarked that the violence was an affront "to the boasted chivalry and civilization of the nineteenth century," and one Indiana paper described the lawlessness as a "burning shame to Kentucky, that much vaunted home of chivalry." The *New York Times* turned the language of honor on its head when it described the African American population of Henry County being forced into exile by "chivalrous roughriders." In another story, entitled "A Civil Rights Idyll," the paper recounted the story of a "gallant Kentuckian" who offended his own sense of honor when he unwittingly escorted a veiled black woman through the streets of an Alabama city. Embarrassed that he had inadvertently endorsed social equality of the races, he hurriedly left the state. "Some chivalric men of honor, might, under the circumstances have blown out their wretched brains," the paper remarked sardonically. An Episcopal bishop in Kentucky wrote in 1879 that "every portion of [Kentucky] soil and every year of her history have been tarnished by these acts of mistaken chivalry but real brutality."[56]

Even the geography of violence violated the perceived wisdom regarding civilization. At a time when urban areas were believed to be repositories of human progress, newspaper accounts were agog at the amount of violence that occurred in the more "settled" portions of Kentucky. The notorious Simmons Band operated within thirty miles of Frankfort, the state capital. Although the city was the picture of enterprise, "surrounded on all sides by rich plantations and thriving villages, . . . a band of desperados [was] allowed to operate with impunity. . . . We have been accustomed to regard such a state of things as possible in the mountain districts of Italy," remarked the *New York Times*, "but were hardly prepared to believe that it could have existed in the Commonwealth of Kentucky." Henry Watterson similarly intoned, "If the outlaws infested remote mountain recesses—if they lived in caves and retreated from the pursuit of law officers—there would be at least some apology from the apathy and criminal indifference which have been betrayed by those whose duty it is to drag this cowled band into the light and inflict upon them the penalties of their crimes; but no such plea can be made. The most thickly settled portion of the State—a point within sight of the State capital—has been selected as their headquarters, from whence they make their nocturnal raids."[57]

Perhaps the most vivid symbol of Kentuckians' extralegal proclivities was the prevalence of firearms. One estimate held that "seven men in every ten" in the state carried concealed weapons and that "the average Kentuckian is ready at all times to settle differences in the usual style." The *New York Times* attributed three-fourths of the murders that occurred in the state to the depraved character of the white male Kentuckian, who carried a pistol on his hip as a "universal practice." Watterson faced personal risk by openly criticizing the outlaws, but, tellingly, he sometimes invoked violence himself, writing in his autobiography: "I might not be able to hit a barn door at ten paces, but could shoot with any man in Kentucky across a pocket handkerchief, holding myself at all times answerable and accessible."[58]

Another common theme in the press coverage of Kentucky violence held that brutality was often carried out in defiance not only of human decency but of the nationally defined aims of the late war. One writer attributed Kentucky's violent tendencies to its perceived turncoat insurgency. Kentuckians' "expeditious method of regulating society by the will and physical force of armed, midnight mobs," claimed the author, "grew out of the rebellion as fruit from the parent tree." Writer Henry Field traced the roots of violence even further, to Kentucky's antebellum slave system. "This quick resentment and this habit of violence, showing itself in fights and feuds, Corsican Vendetta and all, is the heir-loom of Slavery—one of the natural products of irresponsible power." "Whoever has given into his hand absolute mastery over other human beings," he counseled, "must have extraordinary self-control not to become a tyrant on a small scale, as the case may be. He who from a boy has been approached with servility by inferiors, does not bear contradiction with composure even from equals." Compounding this effect, Field wrote, was the "temptation of an idle life" under slavery, "when a [white] man had nothing to keep him busy but maintaining his reputation." He optimistically predicted an end to the violence: "As slavery was the brood-mother of many forms of cruelty, now that the old witch-hag that gave them birth is dead, it is fit that her ill-shapen offspring should die and be buried in the same dishonored grave."[59]

AS VIOLENCE STRIPPED the commonwealth of its chivalrous past and derailed its trajectory to modernity, Kentucky appeared to be a place that was antimodern and antithetical to progress. "This is a very singular position for a State of the American Union to find itself in during the latter half of the nineteenth century," stated the *New York Times* in 1874; "one might say, with much show of truth, that the peaceable people of Kentucky are to-day in more danger from outlaws and murderers of their own race than they were at the dawn of the century from hostile Indians." Watterson, too, remarked that the state of affairs was "a disgrace to the times in which we live."[60]

In the two decades following the war, Kentucky's violent behavior cemented the commonwealth's reputation as the prototype of the South and the former Confederacy. Reports about lawlessness in the Bluegrass State were often published alongside those of other southern states, under headlines such as "Phases of Southern Life," or included in assessments of "The Southern Situation." White Kentuckians' recalcitrance in the face of federal measures led observers to speak of it in terms applied to federal Reconstruction of the former Confederacy, as a failed experiment in "Home Rule." This kind of rhetoric applied to Kentucky linked the state to those of the former Confederacy, reaffirming the state's link with the southern customs of honor and chivalry, while describing these traditions as outmoded, even deleterious, relics of the past.[61]

Thus, many white Kentuckians used mob activity and personal justice to restore the pre–Civil War racial, political, and social status quo as much as possible, and Kentucky had by the 1880s gained a reputation for crime that placed it firmly within the context of southern and Confederate violence. By the 1880s, outsiders saw the Bluegrass State as a place where the code of honor was turned upside down and where cities, the supposed repositories of civilization, were overrun by barbarity. The behavior of its citizens was antimodern, and state laws and institutions proved unable to contain their base impulses. In northern eyes, Kentucky was outdoing its fellow southern states in dishonor, prompting one correspondent to write from Louisville to suggest that "the northern face of Mason and Dixon's line be inscribed with the legend, 'All hope abandon, ye who enter here.'"[62]

What Shall Be the Moral to Young Kentuckians?

CIVIL WAR MEMORIAL ACTIVITY
IN THE COMMONWEALTH, 1865–1895

For the divided populace of Kentucky, the Fourth of July 1865 was a day that reflected the fractures of the previous four years. Confederate sympathizer Lizzie Hardin noted that in Harrodsburg "the 'glorious fourth' passed . . . in a very inglorious manner, the citizens refusing to make any demonstration whatever. . . . I suppose the men thought there was no use in making a fuss over the day on which our forefathers gained their liberty." She remarked contemptuously, however, that it was a different story only twelve miles away, at Camp Nelson, a Federal army base, where "the Negroes had a grand jubilee." As the first Independence Day that had ever applied to them, July 4, 1865, was a day of particular rejoicing for black Kentuckians. Thousands attended a similar celebration at Camp Dick Robinson, near Lancaster. Though he was only eleven at the time, decades later Samuel Sutton remembered the "big time" African Americans had speaking and celebrating that day. Never again, he claimed, would he see so much rejoicing on Independence Day.[1]

In other areas of the state, among other citizens, the Fourth seemed to go unnoticed. One loyal Kentuckian wondered, "Where are our liberty poles, where are our fireworks, the ringing bells, and the loud resounding report of cannon?" Things were, instead, "as hushed and quiet as the midnight hour." In Clark County, Confederates planned their own alternative celebration for July 5, in honor of the day on which, two years before, John Hunt Morgan and his men had ridden into Lebanon, raiding Unionist-owned businesses and destroying $100,000 worth of property. Alarmed at the prospect of such a symbolic affront to a national holiday, Federal troops garrisoned the town to quell any Confederate activity.[2]

The various ways Kentuckians observed or ignored the Fourth of July 1865 and the significance they accorded it were early indications of divisions within public postwar memory in the state. Whether white or black, Confederate or Unionist, Kentuckians grappled with what to remember and what to forget and with what kind of meaning they should assign to the tumultuous half-decade that lay behind them. In their comportment, memorial activities were quite unlike the electoral politics and violence that painted Kentucky as a Confederate state. Carefully choreographed and decorously executed, memorial activities were full of symbolic meaning and rarely invoked the public controversy that Kentuckians' electoral politics or extralegal violence did. Yet the cultural expressions Kentuckians used to either appropriate or reject various memories of the war were loaded with political meaning and became as much a potent means to shape the present as they were a vehicle to remember the past.

In this way, July 4, 1865, was an early occasion of remembrance that was indicative of the varied courses historical memory would take in the next thirty years. Holidays marking Confederate achievements or losses became more compelling reasons to celebrate for ex-Confederates than national holidays. As new heirs to American citizenship, African Americans would successfully lay claim to national memorial days and create new holidays out of Emancipation Day and the anniversaries of constitutional amendments. Meanwhile, left out of the Confederate Lost Cause and repelled by African American claims on Union heritage, Kentucky's white Unionists found themselves with little to celebrate. They, too, would mourn their dead and remember their sacrifice, but in very muted ways.

AT WAR'S END, Kentuckians of all wartime sympathies mourned the nearly 30,000 of their citizens who had given their lives in the great struggle. They took part in the national effort to collectively grieve and honor their fallen men, adorning their graves with flowers and flags on specified Decoration Days. Southern partisans assembled in late April at cemeteries across the state to lay flowers and wreaths on the graves of Confederate soldiers, while Union sympathizers did the same on congressionally designated Memorial Day in May. The rituals of burial and reburial were also important ways Kentuckians remembered their dead, and they worked tirelessly in the years following the war to reinter the dead in Kentucky. While the federal government assumed responsibility for the reburial of Union soldiers, Confederates had to fund and arrange the reinterment of their dead independently. By the early 1870s, Kentucky had a chapter of the Confederate Burial Memorial Association, the Nashville-based organization, headed by E. Kirby Smith, dedicated to burying the remains of Confederate soldiers and erecting monuments "worthy of their memory" in battlefields and northern prisons. The organization also purchased land on which to build monuments and gravestones. Smith appointed several prominent Kentucky Confederates to the state association, including William Preston, Simon Bolivar Buckner, and Basil Duke. In the years following the war, Kentuckians retrieved and reburied the remains of hundreds of Kentucky soldiers who had lost their lives in other states. Some Confederate dead received humble ceremonies, like the one held by Confederate Cynthiana residents in 1870 for forty-seven local soldiers. Other services elicited massive outpourings of public grief and adulation. Such was the case when John Hunt Morgan's body arrived by train from Richmond's Hollywood Cemetery to lie in rest at the Lexington Cemetery.[3]

Although Union and Confederate sympathizers took equal solace in mourning their dead, Confederates quickly became the public face of memorial culture in Kentucky. People of the vanquished South seemed to need the public's sympathy far more than did the victorious North, and although white Kentuckians may have abandoned them in 1861, they certainly did not in 1865. In Lexington and other cities, groups like the Southern Relief Association organized concerts to benefit the "Southern poor," "the orphans of the South," and the "Suffering people of Northern Alabama." In a plea that appeared in the *Tri-weekly Yeoman*, one man appealed to the "generous chivalric sentiment of their natures as men," in an effort to raise money for the destitute former first family of the Confederacy. He proposed that every Confederate officer in the state donate money toward a homestead for Jefferson Davis and his family and offer them "a home in this, his native and ever-fondly loved State." Pro-Confederate relief efforts and memorial activity became part of the larger phenomenon in which the Bluegrass State appeared to embrace the southern Civil War cause. As J. Stoddard Johnston later wrote: "Instead of coming home to be disciplined the Southern soldier was received with open arms as a hero by those from whom he least expected such welcome, as the parable of the prodigal son was exemplified. The fatted calf was killed and the veal was made its portion."[4]

Though the commonwealth had not officially been a part of the Confederate defeat, white Kentuckians appeared to take up the Lost Cause as their own. As an ideology, the Lost Cause combined ideas about an idyllic agrarian past and the Confederacy's righteousness and valor in defending it. Most scholars who have identified this phenomenon interpret it as an emotional and historical antidote to Confederate defeat. Surrounded by the crumbled vestiges of their former civilization, southerners could revel in its former glory, replete with faithful slaves, gracious and submissive women, and beneficent and chivalrous patriarchs. The Lost Cause version of Civil War history contended that southerners waged a war to preserve their way of life and to protect states' rights, and though that valiant and heroic effort failed, it was their duty to vindicate heroes of the conflict, both dead and alive. This impulse grew into a fifty-year movement, which, as Gaines Foster has written, "helped ensure that the Confederate dead became powerful cultural symbols within the New South." Infused with an assortment of conservative racial, gender, and class values, the Lost Cause worked in Kentucky, and in the former Confederacy, not only as vindication for the past, but as a blueprint for shaping the future.[5]

The most visible and enduring evidence of the Lost Cause in the commonwealth appeared with the stone structures that sprung up in cemeteries and on courthouse lawns and town squares across the state. Confederate monument-building campaigns began soon after the war, with one of the earliest efforts taking place in Cynthiana. When, after a two-year effort, residents completed and dedicated the twenty-five-foot Italian marble shaft in 1869, they considered the finished product to be not only a tribute to the dead but to the righteousness of the living. Town resident A. J. Beale recalled decades later that local Confederates could not afford to have the monument inscribed at the time it was built. "We were all too poor to do much in that line at that early date. The wolf and the Yankee were both after us. . . . We were deterred by the persecutions of our friends in the farther South and the continued waving of bloody shirts by [Unionists]." In the 1870s, Kentuckians erected Confederate monuments in Morganfield, Campbellsville, Crab Orchard, Bowling Green, and Versailles, and by 1890, they stood in Woodsonville, Mt. Sterling, Hopkinsville, Georgetown, Maysville, and Paris.[6]

In Kentucky, as throughout the rest of the South, women performed much of the work of Confederate commemoration. Lexington Confederate women began meeting in 1869 to plan and raise funds for monuments. By 1874, they had formed the Ladies Memorial and Monument Association of Lexington and had commissioned a sculpture that *Frank Leslie's Illustrated Newspaper* dubbed "probably the most perfect thing of its kind in the South." Situated among the Confederate graves in the Lexington Cemetery, the monument was sculpted to look like a wooden cross, perched upon a mound of carved rocks, surrounded by an empty scroll and a broken sword. "The conquered banner," whose "stricken folds, caught by the arms of the cross, but with the stars and bars still showing, droop[ed] as lifeless as the martial forms which are moldering around." "This monument exhibits in its design one of the highest qualities of true art," praised the magazine, "for it tells its own story—the tragic story of the Lost Cause—without the use of a single word."[7]

Because most commemorative endeavors in Lexington and the rest of Kentucky involved women, females quickly gained enormous power over the way people would come to interpret the state's Civil War experience. Southerners saw white women as especially suited for memorial work and considered mourning and memorializing as an extension of their maternal and domestic functions. They became "keepers of the past," curators of public memory. Furthermore, in many areas of the Reconstruction-era South, women's memorial activities provided an important political function, allowing southerners to express political and historical views that would have been seen as treasonous coming from men. With the Lost Cause in their hands, white women gained broad cultural authority over the southern past. Moreover, for white women, disenfranchised and unable to shape society directly through legal, legislative, or electoral means, Lost Cause activities became a way to imprint the contemporary world with their conservative values. W. Fitzhugh Brundage has pointed out that white women, "by both explaining and mystifying the historical roots of white supremacy and elite power in the South, performed a conspicuous civic function at a time of heightened concern about the perpetuation of social and political hierarchies." In their veneration of the dead Confederacy, white southern women took on an additional task: "rehabilitating" southern men to the positions of power they had held before they were defeated morally, economically, and militarily by the Union.[8]

Although the commonwealth was exempt from Federal military occupation and white men had little trouble exercising political agency no matter their wartime sympathies, memorial activity conducted by Kentucky women still proved to be a powerful political medium. As one member of the Robert E. Lee Monument Board of Managers wrote to Kentucky Confederate William Preston in 1878, "Woman is a powerful factor in Southern society and it would be almost a vain thing to attempt a work of love without their aid." One early example of their influence came in 1869, when Lexington women set about "rehabilitating" a very prominent Bluegrass ex-Confederate, John C. Breckinridge. Following the death of Henry Clay in 1852, Breckinridge became Kentucky's most prominent politician, spending two terms in the U.S. House of Representatives defending slavery and state sovereignty. In 1856, at the age of thirty-five, he was elected vice president of the United States under James Buchanan. Four years later, he ran for president as the Southern Democratic candidate, winning the electoral votes of nearly every southern state but losing those of his home state to John Bell and finishing second nationally to Abraham Lincoln. Though their Unionism precluded them from offering him their presidential votes, Kentuckians sent Breckinridge to the Senate, where he served for nine months before joining the Confederacy. After serving under Braxton Bragg and Jubal Early, Breckinridge became the Confederate secretary of war, in February 1865, just as the Confederacy was about to expire. Following Lee's surrender, Breckinridge fled to Cuba, and then to Europe and the Middle East before settling in Canada.[9]

When the federal government granted him amnesty in 1869, Breckinridge returned to his home state, after an eight-year absence. As he reentered Kentucky by train, people met him at every station with "perfect ovation." His fellow Lexingtonians greeted his arrival with bonfires, fireworks, and music; a large crowd waited in pouring rain to hear him speak. The *Lexington Observer and Reporter* claimed that "the old chords of affection" between Kentuckians and their famous statesman had not been broken but were stronger than ever. "There is not a thing he could ask; within their gift, that his fellow-citizens would not confer with alacrity." Though diminished in fortune and health, he lived as a hero until his death in 1875.[10]

Shortly after Breckinridge's death, Lexington whites began plans to erect a monument to him, a project that drew widespread attention and criticism from outside of the state. The *New York Times* pointed out with derision that the Kentucky General Assembly had appropriated $10,000 toward the monument but had voted 23 to 1 against earmarking a similar amount for a monument to a Union veteran. "Thus are we conciliated," the newspaper remarked mockingly. Several years later, the *Cincinnati Gazette* also raised some obvious questions regarding the implications of a monument to John C. Breckinridge. "As an early secession conspirator, and a Confederate soldier, statesman, and man, he is probably as statuable as any Confederate," they conceded, but wondered, "What shall be the moral to young Kentuckians?" The *Lexington Daily Transcript*, situating itself and the people of Lexington within a Lost Cause context, rebutted, "Those who have hated [Breckinridge] in the past because of his locality and the spur which his greatness gave to that resistance of oppression, futile at last, out of which has since grown all manner of distemper in the victorious North, may assume to criticize the pride and tenderness with which he is held by his people; but what right have they to invade the sanctity of a Southern necropolis in which his life is commemorated in stone?" The people of Lexington completed their bronze and granite tribute to Breckinridge in November 1887 and accorded it a prominent position on the west side of the city's courthouse.[11]

Of all the monuments constructed in the state, perhaps none were as distinctive as the "martyrs" monuments. Dedicated specifically to the memory of "victims" of federal war policy in Kentucky, these monuments stood as a testament to the singular position of Kentucky memory regarding the Civil War. In 1864, when guerrilla warfare was decimating Federal troops in the state, General Stephen Burbridge instituted a policy known as Order No. 59, which mandated the execution of four Confederate guerrilla prisoners for every Union soldier killed. Kentuckians of all sympathies came to despise all of Burbridge's policies, but they saw Order No. 59 as the most draconian and eventually built several monuments to his Confederate victims. St. Joseph residents erected the first martyrs monument to two Burbridge victims in 1864; the citizens of Eminence later built a monument to three Confederates executed to avenge the deaths of two African American Union soldiers. The monument inscription noted that the Confederates had died "in pretense of retaliation of two Negras who were killed near Port Royal." "Sleep on ye braves," advised the inscription, "for you have got our last breath. We would not have thee buried on a lot with him who has caused thy death." Referring to the racial identity of the Union dead, the monument's architects implied that the Confederate deaths were even more futile and outrageous because the men for whom they had been killed were African American.[12]

The martyrs monuments were a phenomenon particular to Kentucky's status as a Union state. Most Confederate monuments commemorated the bravery of heroes felled in battle, but these sculptures remembered them as *victims* of federal war *policy*. They also served as reminders of how federal actions embittered Kentuckians and, in their permanence, helped to preserve that memory. Kentuckians built two more Burbridge martyrs monuments, one in Midway in 1890 and another in Jeffersontown in 1904, indicating that the memory of these Union transgressions was long-lived.

Mourning and memorializing the dead were community activities, but relating combat experiences and reconnecting with old comrades was the sole province of those men who had fought. Soon after the war, several Confederates began to pen reminiscences and accounts of Kentuckians in battle. The two most notable were Edwin Porter Thompson's *History of the First Kentucky Brigade* (1868), an account of Kentucky's famous

Orphan Brigade, and Basil Duke's *History of Morgan's Cavalry* (1867). Duke, a Scott County native, married Henrietta Morgan, John Hunt Morgan's sister, in 1861. Four months later, he became second-in-command of his brother-in-law's cavalry company, where his fellow soldiers elected him first lieutenant. Federal forces wounded Duke twice and imprisoned him in 1862. Only a month after Duke's release from prison, Morgan was killed and Duke assumed leadership of the cavalry, rising to the rank of brigadier general. On his last martial assignment, he served on the force that helped Jefferson Davis flee Richmond. Returning to Kentucky in 1868, he set up a law practice in Louisville and soon became an important attorney for the L&N Railroad. Duke's historical testimony of Morgan's command would be only his first foray into honoring the history of the Confederacy, as he and his wife, Henrietta, quickly became leading organizers of Lost Cause activity in Kentucky.[13]

Soldiers' reminiscences became outlets for what David Blight has called their "burdens of memory," and they became a way to vindicate specific interpretations of the war as well. When Edward Guerrant, one of Morgan's men, contemplated writing memoirs of his war experiences under John Hunt Morgan, his friend Humphrey Marshall counseled him on the importance of offering "reasons given to posterity *why we were in army against the government.*" Urging him to "make for all time our justificatory plea" before telling the exploits which led to "*the lamented conclusion,*" Marshall suggested Guerrant act quickly, because "the public greedily swallows up whatever is first presented, and often retains for truth whatever it has accepted."[14]

In addition to recording individual accounts of service, Kentucky Confederates joined a regional movement to collect relics and records of their historical experience. In 1878, Lexington Confederates established a chapter of the Southern Historical Society, an organization devoted to gathering historical materials relating to the Confederacy. First organized in New Orleans in 1869 and relocated to Richmond in 1873, the Southern Historical Society sought to archive war memorabilia and also to vindicate both the war record of the Confederacy and its cause, within the *Southern Historical Society Papers*. Under the leadership of Simon Bolivar Buckner and then of William Preston, the Kentucky chapter aimed to collect "historical material relating to the Confederate war."[15]

In 1880, Louisville Confederates founded their own chapter under former mayor Major William O. Dodd, and, although several Louisvillians became officers in the Lexington branch, the two entities remained separate against the suggestion of the main organization. Interest in the Lexington chapter ultimately faded, and by 1880 the secretary at headquarters wrote to Preston to collect dues owed as well as historical contributions, both of which, it seems, they had been slow to send. The Louisville chapter flourished, however, and by late 1880 the *Southern Historical Society Papers* reported that the branch had been "sustained with a good deal of spirit and interest." Within a few years of its founding, the Louisville branch was one of only two subsidiaries to prosper.[16]

In 1882, attempting to reach a larger audience, the Louisville society began publishing a magazine entitled the *Southern Bivouac*. Printed by the *Courier-Journal* Job Printing Company, the periodical served as a vehicle for soldiers' reminiscences and sketches of the war. Reflecting its border state home, however, the publication presented a distinct effort on the part of Louisville veterans to break away from the focus of the *Southern Historical Society Papers*, which tended to be Virginia-centered and to focus on the experiences of military elites. *Bivouac* editors sought a broader audience and held to a milder political stance than the stridently pro-Confederate, backward-looking leaders of the Virginia coalition. The *Bivouac* glorified the southern cause but did so while pushing a more pragmatic message of sectional reconciliation. The magazine was founded in a time when northerners and southerners were increasingly willing to recognize each other's claims of martial valor. Serving these dual interests, the magazine claimed that its "truthfulness, candor, and fairness, made it as popular with those who wore Blue, as those who wore the Gray" but also insisted that its role as a voice for southern veterans was its most important. "The survivors of the lost cause," its editors believed, "can least afford to be silent. The fairest history a victor may write never does justice to the cause of the conquered." As testimony to its sectional rapprochement, the magazine offered joint subscriptions with a Boston Grand Army of the Republic magazine, *Bivouac*. The *Southern Bivouac* successfully appealed to a cross-sectional audience and by 1883 listed a number of Union veterans among its subscribers.[17]

In 1885, the magazine changed genres and editorial hands when Basil Duke, who was by this time a successful Louisville attorney, and Richard W. Knott, editor of the agricultural magazine *Home and Farm*, took charge. Once Duke and Knott assumed editorship of the *Southern Bivouac*, they transformed it into a literary journal, self-described as a "distinctively Southern Magazine, [which] while appealing to lovers of good literature everywhere, [would] deal chiefly with the aspects of Southern life, thought, action, with Southern history and scenery, with Southern traditions and prejudices, in accordance with the accepted rules of art." In this new incarnation, the magazine continued to publish war papers but extended its contents to literary accounts of southern life as well as regional poetry and fiction.[18]

Under Duke's editorship, the *Southern Bivouac* often printed politicized editorials and literary pieces espousing conservative views regarding African Americans' place in society. In an 1887 editorial, for instance, Duke castigated George Washington Cable's efforts to engender sympathy for black southerners among northern whites. Giving credit to northern whites for realizing that Reconstruction was nothing less than "white southerners engaged in a desperate struggle with influences which threatened to destroy their civilization and reduce their country to barbarism," Duke cast southern whites' reactions to federal policy as "the efforts of the superior race to defend and conserve society." The *Southern Bivouac* also attributed an alternative and less-threatening face to African Americans in the form of sentimental tales about contented "darkies" in the Old South. In these stories, slaves toiled devotedly for their benign and paternalistic masters, presenting southern whites with a pleasant and reassuring alternative to contemporary racial uncertainties.[19]

By 1886, the *Southern Bivouac* had developed a sizable circulation of 7,500. The next year, after the publication of only two volumes, *Century*, the popular New York literary magazine, which had become known for its extensive coverage of Civil War history, offered to buy the magazine. Because the *Southern Bivouac*'s success had not translated into significant profit, the publishers agreed to sell the magazine. In the closing issue, the editors lamented that instead of becoming a "permanent exponent of Southern thought," the journal was "only a mile-stone in the progress of southern literature."[20]

Thus, Kentucky Confederates penned memoirs, built monuments, and founded successful historical organizations and periodicals, but the efforts of Kentucky's white Unionists to honor the Union cause in Kentucky were more limited. The story of the Grand Army of the Republic (GAR), the primary Union veterans' organization, in the state is indicative of this. Founded in Illinois in 1866, the GAR was devoted to both fraternalism and Republican politics. The Department of Kentucky gained provisional status in 1867 and by 1872 claimed eight white and four "colored" posts. From its earliest days in the state, the organization faced stiff, sometimes violent, opposition from outside its own ranks. At the 1871 GAR annual encampment, a national officer reported that a comrade from one Kentucky post had been assassinated and the commander of another post lashed fifty times, "because they dared to declare openly their allegiance to the Order." When a commanding officer from Rhode Island visited Kentucky on a trip through the South in 1872, he found twelve posts "in fair working condition, though working under disadvantages."[21]

Though he did not explain under what specific "disadvantages" the GAR was laboring, the organization's hardships were no doubt related to anti-Republican sentiments in Kentucky and throughout the South. At the same encampment, one GAR official asserted, "There is considerable feeling in the minds of the people of the South against our Order, that can only be dispelled by careful and prudent action on the parts of our comrades there, proving that the prejudices against us are wrong and ill-founded." Membership in the GAR declined nationally in the 1870s because of economic depression, and even more noticeably in Kentucky. By one account, it became "harder for poorer men to keep up with dues," and many posts "fell into arrears." The Covington Post reportedly failed to meet between 1871 and 1874, and by the middle of the decade the state's provisional department did not even keep contact with the national organization, leading the inspector-general to report at that year's annual meeting: "The Order there is apparently not prosperous, nor do the people understand its objects." A newspaper account later remarked of that assessment: "This was not unjust criticism, just the simple truth."[22]

The biggest challenge Kentucky's GAR members faced, however, came from within their own ranks, as they struggled to discern racial boundaries for their organization. Early in the GAR's existence in the state, internal dissent bubbled up within Kentucky's divisions when an officer, H. K. Milward, ordered delegates from African American posts to be seated on an equal basis with white delegates at the annual state encampment. The Joe Holt Post of Newport and the Nelson Post of Covington balked at this demand and appealed to national commander-in-chief General John A. Logan, who ultimately decided that Milward's order must stand. Although Logan's decision quelled the debate, the whole affair, according to one account, "hurt the order in Kentucky for several years." Most white Kentuckians who served the Union army resented fighting alongside African Americans in the war, and many of them felt no more camaraderie with them after the Union victory. White veterans may have shared the fight with African American soldiers, but in Kentucky they did not want to grant them their full share of the victory, or even a part of remembering it. Even those white Kentuckians not deterred by the Republican politics of the organization could not escape the challenges to racial hierarchy implicit in the Union victory.[23]

Kentucky African Americans, on the other hand, proved less divided and more committed in their celebration of Union victory. From the first days following the war, they marked holidays such as the Fourth of July and anniversaries of constitutional amendments and the Emancipation Proclamation. James Smith, a former slave, described the scene in Louisville on July 4, 1865: "For the first time the people celebrated this day as free people. . . . They came from the factories, the work-shops and the fields to enjoy themselves in the pure, fresh air of freedom." An estimated 10,000 African Americans paraded through the city streets while at least as many looked on. Leading the march were 800 troops from the 123rd U.S. Colored Infantry with a band in tow. Sunday school students from local churches followed, as did delegates from several fraternal societies. A "tastefully decorated" horse-drawn carriage carried women representing the Fifth St. Baptist Aid Society. Behind them came other aid societies, and a carriage carrying "working men, plying the saw, plane, hammer and mallet," followed. The parade concluded with 600 members of the 125th U.S. Colored Infantry and another band.[24]

The Louisville parade revealed much about the new way in which Kentucky African Americans viewed themselves and their new freedom. The procession was both a function of their independence and a reminder of an older sense of community and past accomplishments. It symbolized the military valor that had helped African Americans gain that freedom and would empower them to keep it. Moreover, it celebrated the hard work and skills that black men had exercised in the past and would use to their own advantage in the future. For black women, however, there was no reminder of their labor. Instead of walking the streets of Louisville as domestic workers, toiling in the background for their white masters and employers, they rode high as the center of attention. As Kentucky African Americans marched through the streets that day, filling the public space so recently reserved exclusively for whites, they spoke of free life, free labor, free manhood, and free womanhood.[25]

Rather than looking back at the gains they had made, however, black Kentuckians used these occasions to look ahead and to stake further claims of citizenship. At one 1866 Louisville emancipation celebration, between 4,000 and 5,000 African Americans petitioned the Kentucky legislature for full legal equality and the right to testify in state courts. Frankfort African Americans echoed those demands in a local celebration. At another Louisville celebration the following year, black leader William F. Butler asserted, "We claim . . . a position of political equality with whites as a matter of right, as a matter of justice." "We ask no man for pity," he stated. "We only ask you to take your hand off the black man's head and let him grow to manhood." At the 1869 Emancipation Day celebration in Louisville, Henry Young, a black minister, encouraged those in attendance to "use every lawful means to obtain manhood suffrage." At the Paris Fourth of July festivities that year, African Americans again reiterated demands for suffrage. Less than a year later, 6,000 men, women, and children of the town rejoiced again after the passage of the Fifteenth Amendment. In May and June, African Americans in Winchester, Lancaster, and Bardstown also publicly celebrated the passage of the amendment. Despite their jubilation over the right to vote, they continued to push for further privileges, particularly the right to testify in state courts.[26]

African American invocations of war memory did not go unnoticed by Kentucky whites. In September 1867, the Benevolent Society of Winchester invited interested African Americans from neighboring counties to attend a mass convention at the town fairgrounds to discuss how to exercise their impending right to suffrage. A crowd consisting mainly of black men formed a procession and marched through Winchester's main streets to the fairgrounds. As an observer reported: "The procession was under charge of colored marshals on horseback, wearing sashes and carrying sabers. They had all been soldiers in the Union army, and knew something about marching." During a speech, Dr. A. M. Davison reminded the crowd of their valorous service in the U.S. armed forces, "but soon you joined the ranks of the Union army and joined in the chorus, 'We will rally around the flag boys, We will rally once again, Shouting the battle-cry of freedom,'" a call to action that caused the crowd to erupt in cheers and applause. The large attendance at Winchester typified the significant public presence Kentucky African Americans often exhibited in their memorial activities. White observers consistently noted their numbers, their use of the main thoroughfares, even the amount of noise they made.[27]

With African Americans so successfully appropriating the Union war victory to further their political goals, it is not surprising that mainstream conservative whites who sided with the Union during the war found it difficult to honor that past. As long as Union victory was so strongly equated with black emancipation and Republican politics, there remained little cultural and political ground upon which conservative white Unionists could celebrate. Many had defended a Union of white men, not of black and white men, but by the end of the war, there seemed no way to celebrate the national triumph apart from what David Blight has termed an "emancipationist narrative." This fact was evidenced by the relative lack of white Union monuments and public commemorations of the Union victory in Kentucky.[28]

The few Unionist heroes who were honored with monuments were often as widely known for their conservative politics as for their military service. Citizens of Columbia, Kentucky, built a monument to Colonel Frank Wolford, one of Kentucky's most esteemed Union warriors. In March 1864, however, he openly criticized Lincoln's decision to enlist black troops in the Union army at several venues throughout the state and threatened to deploy his troops against army enrollment officers who complied with the president's order. Wolford's insubordination caused Stephen Burbridge to arrest and jail him several times for disloyalty, which increased his popularity and earned Wolford a dishonorable discharge from the president. One of the few other Kentucky Unionists to be honored with a monument was Joseph Holt, the prominent politician who before the war convinced Kentuckians to remain loyal by arguing that the national government was the best protector of slavery. Although Louisville African Americans began and quickly ended an effort to erect a monument to antebellum revolutionary John Brown in 1891, most Kentuckians considered only racially conservative men worthy of a statue.[29]

In the absence of a broad-based white celebration of Union victory, many Kentucky whites actively embraced statewide and, more broadly, sectional reconciliation. Signs of rapprochement between former enemies appeared soon after the war's end. In 1867 and 1868, when former Confederate commander Admiral Raphael Semmes traveled the state on a lecture tour meant to raise funds for the Confederate Monumental Society, he drew audiences of both Unionists and Confederates. When southern-sympathizing former governor Beriah Magoffin hosted a Christmas dinner featuring Semmes as a guest, the turnout included a large number of "prominent ex-Federals and ex-Confederates, 'hobnobbing together, and forgetting their animosities.'" Magoffin toasted the crowd, saying, "The fame of American soldiers and sailors, whether rebel or federal, is the common heritage of our people."[30]

By the 1870s and 1880s, signs of reconciliation were everywhere in Kentucky. When Robert E. Lee died in 1870, white Kentuckians of both wartime affiliations publicly mourned him. In Louisville, Confederates joined with city leaders to organize an extensive funereal demonstration that engaged citizens "irrespective of party" and "represent[ing] every shade of political opinion and all conditions of society." At Mayor John Baxter's request, the city went into mourning for Lee, businesses closed, and church and engine-house bells tolled. City buildings and even steamboats on the Ohio River flew flags at half-mast. Along the city streets, buildings were shrouded in funeral drapery. An estimated 1,000 Confederate veterans planned to march wearing badges of mourning from the courthouse to services at St. Paul's Episcopal Church. "I think that such an expression of respect may very properly be manifested by our whole community without doing violence to any political or party feeling," Baxter declared. "We should simply view the deceased as an upright American citizen, against whose private character there was no reproach." The Republican *Louisville Commercial* also took on a conciliatory tone, noting that such an outpouring of grief for Lee "was to be expected" and commended those organizing the festivities for "studiously endeavor[ing] to divest them, as far as possible, of all sectional and political bias. It would be well for the country if the heart-burnings and dissensions to which the war gave rise could be buried out of sight in the graves of the great leaders who are passing one by one from among us."[31]

The impulse to reconcile with former enemies appeared in various forms. In 1872, Louisville hosted a "Peace Reunion," an industrial exposition "dedicated to the works of peace," where, promoters advertised, "'one hundred thousand' patriots" would "shake hands across the bloody chasm." The *Southern Bivouac* sounded the bell of conciliation, deeming the reunions held by both armies "proper and becoming." The magazine promoted the cross-participation of Union and Confederate armies in symbolic reunions, lauding their ability to "recognize in each other the same spirit animated by the same motives—patriotism impelling all, only pointing them to different roads." "The old veterans are right," the *Southern Bivouac* continued. "They are commemorating noble sentiments, honorable deeds, generous sacrifices on both sides." In one issue, the magazine printed side-by-side notices of the reunion of the Orphan Brigade to be held in Glasgow and the reunion of the 4th Kentucky Cavalry and asserted, "The BIVOUAC will always gladly publish notices of these reunions of either army." Another symbolic union came in 1885, when Owensboro ex-Confederates and ex-Unionists formed an association.[32]

Symbolic reconciliation in Kentucky, however, was often Confederate-hued. On May 1, 1877, white Louisvillians showed broad support for the former Confederacy when an estimated 25,000 of them celebrated the removal of Federal troops from South Carolina and Louisiana and the end of congressional Reconstruction in the South. Louisville officials decorated the city's public spaces, hanging locomotive headlights and candles on City Hall, the courthouse, the jail, and other official buildings. Citizens burned gas lamps on their porches and in their front windows, illuminating the city for blocks. When darkness settled across the city, as the *Courier-Journal* headline read the next day, Louisville appeared to be "A Blaze of Light." The courthouse yard was "jammed with humanity," as people delighted in the public concert given by the Liederkranz Singing Society.[33]

That night, the musical repertoire represented the spirit of sectional reconciliation, as the singers interspersed the "Star Spangled Banner" and "Yankee Doodle" with "Dixie" and "Bonnie Blue Flag." Despite the political party divisions so recently exacerbated by the Hayes-Tilden election, Democrats and Republicans came "into line, making it entirely a nonpartisan affair," as members of both parties "numbered among those who saw fit to remember the Southern people." Yet Louisville's celebration marked more than cooperation between political parties. As the *Courier-Journal* remarked, the citywide public jubilation "proved most clearly how much in sympathy with the sorely distressed southern people Louisville [was]."[34]

White Kentuckians also reunited along class lines. In 1877, Louisville experienced the wave of railroad strikes sweeping the country when a group of predominantly black sewer workers walked off the job, on July 24, and roamed the city convincing other sewer workers to strike for higher wages. When Mayor Charles Jacob called for the formation of a citizen militia to aid the city's police force, ex-Confederates Bennett Young and Basil Duke, as well as prominent ex–Federal army officers Eli Murray and Benjamin Helm Bristow, led over 700 citizens in confronting the rioting laborers throughout the night. Future Supreme Court justice Louis Brandeis joined the operation after coming home from a party to find that the workers had targeted his parents' house.[35]

The legendary detective and labor antagonist Allan Pinkerton later praised what he considered the bipartisan composition of the militia. "Political party fences were thrown down in the crisis," he said, "and the sharp distinction between 'Yankee' and 'Rebel' which the years had been slowly melting away, was obliterated entirely by the shadow of common danger." Old enemies, Pinkerton asserted, "met as friends in a common cause; and down through all the ranks, old soldiers of the 'Blue and Gray' mingled as comrades true." Such a show of solidarity, he projected, would "remain as a perpetual warning to the turbulent and lawless elements of Louisville." Pinkerton thus perceived the class defensiveness of wealthy white Louisvillians, who must have felt all the more threatened because the workers were black, as a positive force for quelling sectional animosities. Class interests inherent in antipathy toward organized labor became yet another way to obliterate sectional lines.[36]

Indeed, Lost Cause sentiment went hand in hand with antilabor rhetoric. Under Basil Duke's corporate-minded leadership, the *Southern Bivouac* regularly carried antilabor messages. In June 1886, just after Chicago's Haymarket Riot, the magazine published a story entitled "The Destruction of Louisville." The piece was a futuristic account of a Knights of Labor riot projected to occur in late 1887, during which workers carrying red flags pillaged the city and murdered prominent citizens. Upon the narrator's return to Louisville in 1889, he found the city's population of 180,000 inhabitants reduced to only 40,000 and its streets reduced to "a barren showing of blackened walls and eyeless windows." He discovered grass growing in the middle of Main Street, where "only two or three feeble factories [endeavored] to sustain the ancient reputation of the city, but apparently in vain." At the story's close, the narrator stood looking at a human skeleton in the street and expressed hope that humanity "may be warned by our fate, and remember that 'eternal vigilance' is not only the 'price of liberty,' but the price of self-preservation also."[37]

Duke wrote an editorial in the same issue in which he attacked the Knights of Labor and their leader, Terrence Powderly. The organization, asserted Duke, was "now being used for mischief." Its members "served no good purpose and were fit only to incite contentions and to foment prejudice." Although Duke claimed to be far more concerned with "the right of a non-union man to work for a small wage," he clearly worried about the "condition of disagreement" he saw the Knights of Labor creating between workers and employers. The *Southern Bivouac* published antilabor articles alongside tributes to the Old South, providing an outlet for contemporary postindustrial fears and venerating an idyllic past.[38]

The ascent of Henry Watterson as a nationally known New South spokesman and proponent of sectional reconciliation also enhanced Kentucky's reputation for promoting reunion within a Confederate framework. Watterson continually disseminated his nationalist message in the pages of the *Courier-Journal*, and in 1877 he began a speaking tour of northern cities. He saw his role as that of a "mercenary," trying to convince northerners that the South was on the road to reform, politically, racially, and, most of all, economically. Lecturing around the country on "The Oddities of Southern Life," Watterson regaled his audience with stories filled with stock characters of Dixie. Once he had the audience laughing, he assured them that the difference between northerners and southerners was "purely exterior."[39]

Furthermore, at a time when many northerners believed that southerners were able to handle the "negro problem" better than they, they saw the advantages of reuniting with southern whites on the basis of common whiteness. "No people in the world are more homogenous" than Americans, Watterson declared, bound together by "the vestal fire of our Anglo-Saxon race" and the principle of self-government, which proved "strong enough to maintain our system of Anglo-Saxon freedom and law to the farthest ends of the earth." Thus, Watterson assured northern crowds that America would reunite by virtue of white superiority. African Americans, by default, argued Watterson, would not play a role in reunion, for "the negro is an African in Congo or in Kentucky, in Jamaica or in Massachusetts."[40]

In 1877, Watterson delivered the Decoration Day address at the National Cemetery in Nashville. The event was an important one for the editor, coming only months after the "10,000 unarmed Kentuckians" debacle had stripped him of some of his credibility as a reconciliationist. He announced before a crowd of thousands, "The day has come when the animosities of war, growing less and less distinct as the years have passed, should disappear altogether from the hearts of brave men and good women. I can truly say that each soldier who laid down his life for his opinions was my comrade, no matter in which army he fought." Newspapers throughout the country reacted favorably to Watterson's speech; the New York Daily Tribune praised him as representing the "best class of public men in the Southern Democracy."[41]

Whenever Watterson addressed an audience, he did so as a Kentuckian and as a Confederate. Representing the state as a southern veteran with a colonel-like bearing, he could not help but enhance its identification with the Confederacy. He compounded this association by rarely making reference to Kentucky's divided Civil War history. Instead, he liberally peppered his speeches with vignettes about the state to illustrate the character of southern life, old and new, further blurring the distinction between Kentucky and states that had seceded. When Louisville hosted the American Bankers Association meeting in 1883, Watterson gave an address entitled "The New South." Speaking to the northern bankers, he claimed, "The South! The South! It is no problem at all. I thank God that at last we can say with truth, it is simply a geographic expression." "I no more believe that that river yonder, dividing Indiana and Kentucky, marks off two distinct species than I believe the great Hudson, flowing through the state of New York marks off a distinct species." Speaking in the context of reconciliation, Watterson reset the borders of the Union and the Confederacy (the very geographical boundaries he was trying to transcend) at the Ohio River, to make no distinction between Kentucky and the rest of the former Confederacy.[42]

Despite the dominance of reconciliationist memory that white Kentuckians cultivated, they were not able to claim sole possession of public memory in the state. In September 1883, a national convention featuring the nation's most prominent African Americans convened in Louisville to assess and call attention to the ways in which the country had come up short on its promises to its black citizens. The meeting came at a time when the national black leadership found itself divided on a number of issues: whether members should, as a group, support a Republican Party that increasingly took them for granted; and whether African Americans, in the aftermath of Reconstruction and its amendments, should even hold conventions separate from those of whites. The main object of the convention, however, was, in Frederick Douglass's words, no less than "the advancement of the condition of the colored race." When asked if the delegates would ask Congress to enact more protective laws or further amendments to the Constitution, he replied, "No, we shall merely growl because those that we have are not enforced."[43]

Conference organizers had originally planned to meet in Washington, D.C., but eventually decided that Louisville, a southern city, where "the problem for solution is to be found," would be a more fitting setting. Not all African Americans supported the new location, and the hostility likely to be encountered at a Kentucky site may have driven some would-be attendees away. Although one Arkansas delegate anticipated the success of the conference, he maintained that the nation's capital would have attracted a larger crowd. Alluding to Kentucky's widespread reputation for racial violence, he predicted that "those Kentucky bullies down in Louisville will be apt to do some killing when the negroes come there."[44]

The Louisville conference was truly a spectacle of black influence and power. Nearly three hundred delegates representing twenty-six states and Washington, D.C., gathered in Louisville, descending upon Liederkranz Hall. In the same city where six years earlier whites had celebrated the end of federal Reconstruction, African Americans stood firm in demanding that the federal government once again stand behind the advances that the Civil War and Reconstruction had promised them. They elected Frederick Douglass as chairman of the convention, and in front of 2,500 people he called attention to the dissonance between the assurances of liberty and citizenship offered to blacks in the federal amendments and the persistent problems they faced in the South. "It is our lot to live among a people whose laws, traditions and prejudices have been against us for centuries, and from these we are not yet free," he declared. "Though we have had war, reconstruction, and abolition as a nation, we still linger in the shadow and blight of an extinct institution. . . . In his downward course he meets with no resistance, but his course upward is resented and resisted at every step of his progress." Douglass then addressed nearly every challenge facing African Americans at the time: violence and lynch law, the stereotype of black indolence, black exclusion from trade unions, debt peonage, and educational and political inequality. Speaking of the "color line," he asserted that the convention itself proved that African Americans believed in white Americans and their capacity for "reason, truth, and justice." "If liberty, with you, is yet but a name," he said to whites in the audience, "our citizenship is a sham, and our suffrage thus far only cruel mockery."[45]

Douglass grounded his demands in the very memories of the past that whites in Kentucky and, by 1883, all over the nation tried to put behind them. "It should be remembered by our severe judges," he intoned, "that freedom came to us not from the sober dictates of wisdom, or from any normal condition of things, nor as a choice on the part of the land-owners of the South, nor from the moral considerations on the part of the North." African American freedom came "not by gentle accord from either section," but had been "born of battle and of blood." It had come "across fields of smoke and fire, strewn with wounded, bleeding, and dying men. Not from the Heaven of Peace amid the morning stars, but from the hell of war—out of the tempest and whirlwind of warlike passions, mingled with deadly hate and a spirit of revenge, it came, not so much as a boon to us as a blast to the enemy." Black rights were an act of war, not of beneficence, he reminded the audience. In this way, Douglass used the Louisville convention to undermine the spirit of white reconciliation by reminding them of both the sectional animosities and the racial consequences of the war.[46]

The *Courier-Journal* hailed the event as "the first national colored convention that ever assembled in the United States" and praised the delegates for forming a "fine-looking body" of "representative men of the race." "There was no disputing the fact that an unusually large number of them were men of intelligence, learning, industry and familiarity with parliamentary laws," continued Watterson. "Certainly there was nothing to make any colored man feel ashamed.... It was a fine body of men—men of spirit and energy who would attract attention anywhere." Observing the concern of local whites, who watched the event with "an unusual degree of interest," he wrote that there seemed to be "in the minds of many a suspicion of this convention. Its aims are not well understood, its purpose seems somewhat vague and indefinite." He claimed, however, that whites should pay attention to the issues under discussion. "The negro is a citizen," he noted paternally, "[and] whatever improves his condition, increases his intelligence, gives additional value to his labor, whatever, in short, makes him a better man and a more independent voter, is an advantage to society."[47]

In an editorial entitled "The Negro and His Leader," Watterson was more measured in his approval, arguing that the grievances Douglass aired were not "any more justly the complaint of the negro than of the white man." Furthermore, he counseled, the answer to the country's racial problems could only come over time. "We look too soon for results," he said; "we forget that the mills of time grind slowly; and because sentence against an evil work is not executed speedily we harden our hearts." "The regeneration of society," Watterson advised Douglass, "can not be accomplished by a manifesto. The walls of Jericho do not now fall down at the sound of the trumpet."[48]

The editors of the *Southern Bivouac*, by contrast, found the "colored convention" more menacing. The magazine lamented the fact that the blacks in attendance glorified Abraham Lincoln and "displayed an aggressiveness upon popular sentiment that is the sign of the times, by demanding perfect equality, social as well as political." After dismissing such an idea, the editors declared their intention to "turn away from the revolting subject with a sigh for the future of the [white] race," warning readers that "from the sentiments of the [convention] speakers, one thing may be assured: that if our literature is to be molded and our national councils are to be dominated by African stock, the name Confederate will be a synonym for all that is infamous and despicable. If we do not see to the making of our own history, our only hope for justice will be in the magnanimity of the North." The editors not only worried about African American political and social equality but also feared their interpretive influence over the past, knowing it would inevitably lead to a version of history directly opposed to their own. Louisville's Confederate magazine spoke in both sectional and racial terms, believing it was a Confederate history and a white history that needed defending.[49]

The 1883 national African American convention added another dimension to Kentucky's discussion of war memory. African Americans continued to invoke the state's Union past in their efforts to both gain new rights and defend existing ones. In 1892, they enlisted Civil War history in their efforts to fight a proposed Jim Crow law that mandated that African Americans ride in separate train coaches. Many of the state's prominent African Americans galvanized quickly to oppose the legislation. Their carefully crafted petitions were meant to appeal to white state officials and public opinion alike, drawing on Kentucky's Civil War history and the roles of black Kentuckians in the conflict.

The delegation of African Americans that took their case to the legislature's Joint Railroad Committee skillfully appropriated memories of black wartime loyalty to whites. J. Allen Ross, secretary of the National Association of Colored Democrats, noted that if African Americans could be "trusted with the keeping of homes of those gallant Kentuckians who rode away to war in 1861" they could be trusted to ride peaceably in the same train cars. Bowling Green minister Robert Mitchell used a similar line of reasoning: "While you were at war fighting for a principle wholly against us," he told the committee, "we were supporting and protecting your homes; on returning you found them as chaste and pure as when you left. Had the colored man been vicious and dangerous great would have been the slaughter of those days."[50]

W. H. Steward took a different tack, reminding the legislature that Kentucky had hesitated to take sides at the outbreak of the war. He asserted that since the state government had not taken the path of other southern states into secession, it should not follow them into legal segregation. "During the war Kentucky remained a neutral State," he declared. "Why not remain neutral now? Why disturb and place a blight upon the increasing prosperity and advancing the intelligence of the blacks?" Perhaps the most impassioned argument using this historical argument came when a group of the state's most prominent African American women appeared before the General Assembly. Frankfort native Lizzie E. Green declared:

> Our mother State Virginia, the grand old Dominion, refused to
> sanction the bill, and also South Carolina, the first State to secede
> from the Union. Can Kentucky, our loyal State, that stood firm and
> unchangeable during the sad and bloody war of rebellion when
> all her border states south had withdrawn their allegiance to the
> Union? Firm and loyal when sympathy for her suffering sister
> States might have led her to espouse their cause. Firm and loyal,

though indignation and hatred be hurled against her by the sister States seceding. Firm and loyal till peace and good feeling had again united our country together. Can Kentucky afford to be less magnanimous than Virginia and South Carolina? May she ever preserve her loyalty, deal justly with her inhabitants and carry unsullied her banner on which is inscribed: United we stand; divided we fall.

Though they were ultimately unsuccessful in halting the law's passage, Kentucky African Americans once again revealed their ability to interpret Civil War history and use it as another weapon in their arsenal for justice.[51]

By 1895, however, the nation's whites seemed stricken with amnesia in regard to Kentucky's divided Civil War experience. This historical forgetfulness was in full evidence when Louisville hosted the 1895 GAR national encampment, an occasion that showed just how much the state's identification had shifted in the thirty years following the war. Recovering from its early difficulties, the Kentucky department of the GAR had reorganized in 1882, and by 1893 it had reached a peak membership of nearly 10,000 members. In 1894, some of Louisville's most prominent citizens, both ex-Union and ex-Confederate, attempted to attract the annual meeting of Union veterans by playing up its role as a border South city. Louisville's general council stated in its invitation that should such a meeting take place, it would "lead to a better understanding and a higher appreciation between the people of various sections of the country."[52]

Echoing that sentiment, the state House of Representatives claimed that a reunion within Kentucky would "drive away forever the fading shadows of the great fraternal strife." At the 1894 GAR meeting in Pittsburgh, where Henry Watterson traveled to advertise Louisville's merits, organization officials debated what sort of reception they might receive south of the Ohio River. One enthusiastic member asserted that a meeting in Louisville could "do more to make this a united Republic than any one act that has been done since the surrender at Appomattox." A reunion in Louisville, as the promoters pitched it, would represent Union veterans coming to formerly hostile territory and would symbolize sectional reconciliation. The implications of the rhetoric surrounding the 1895 reunion are unmistakable. Seemingly forgetful that their city had remained Union territory and had served as a Federal supply base during the Civil War, the citizens of Louisville offered to host the reunion not only as a southern city but also as a Confederate city.[53]

Although another border South city, Baltimore, had hosted the GAR encampment in 1882, members and officials considered the idea of Louisville hosting the event to have special symbolic importance. In anticipation of the reunion, GAR delegations around the country began to tout the sectional ramifications of the gathering. One member of the New Jersey department pronounced that the encampment would be the "entering wedge of harmony which [would] rive asunder all sectional hatred and animosity and leave in its place nothing but peace and good will." The commander of the Rhode Island department anticipated that in Louisville, with the first gathering of Union troops "on Southern soil since the close of the war, . . . the country [would] witness how foemen who have crossed swords in the fierce tumult of battle can now clasp hands in friendly greeting." "Will not the pathos of such a spectacle reunite our countrymen in yet stronger ties of patriotism and loyalty," he asked. One Pittsburgh official declared that "the GAR people should come to a Southern City, south of the Mason and Dixon line, to show that all were Americans, served under one flag, to forget which side they fought for, and be united. . . . Every soldier whether he was East, West, or North stated that he would come to Louisville, shake the rebel by the hand, and show that all were friends."[54]

Optimistic predictions about the goodwill the encampment would foster between North and South abounded. The commander in chief of the national GAR, General Thomas G. Lawler, declared, "I am glad to see that the bitter feeling between the North and South is dying out, and I believe this encampment will do a great deal to unite the two sections of this country." Greatly anticipating the southern hospitality they expected in Louisville, the Ohio delegation estimated that the city would "outdo herself in giving the old soldier a chivalrous welcome." The feeling that the Louisville meeting would further reconcile old enemies was not one-sided. Isaac T. Woodson contributed a column to the *Louisville Commercial* entitled "Plaintalk from an Old Confederate" in which he asserted that "Louisville will consider herself the representative of the rehabilitated South, and will receive with open arms and fraternal greetings."[55]

Despite the harmonious sentiments, the reunion planning process was not without controversy. Friction over several aspects of the event simmered beneath the peaceful public dialogue. One issue arose when local Confederates briefly considered unveiling Louisville's recently completed Confederate monument during the reunion. This prospect elicited an outcry and distrust among GAR members, who, notwithstanding their reconciliationist rhetoric, were not ready to compete with such a symbol of Confederate primacy. Though Louisville GAR members continually denied them, rumors of the purported unveiling had, according to the *Camden (N.J.) Review*, "gained widespread currency in [the] middle and eastern states" in the months prior to the encampment.[56]

Yet another controversy ignited over the appointment of Mary Creel Tyler, wife of Louisville mayor and ex-Confederate Henry Tyler, to head the women's committee for local arrangements. When Nettie Gunlock, the national president of the Ladies of the GAR, an unofficial affiliate of the men's organization, came to Louisville in the spring preceding the reunion, she was outraged at both Tyler's appointment and the proposed Confederate monument unveiling. The *Hopkinsville Kentuckian* wrote mirthfully that Gunlock spent her stay in Louisville "shooting off her mouth in an offensive manner," declaring that unveiling the Confederate monument would constitute "treason" and that even the consideration of such a thing would "keep thousands of veterans from attending." The paper responded sarcastically: "Mrs. Gunlock seems to be un-necessarily alarmed. The 'Confederates' under the monument are dead ones, and no longer dangerous." Another newspaper reported that Gunlock "finally left town convinced that she was in a nest of disloyal Confederates, who were liable to use the national colors as a nose-rag at the slightest provocation." Union planners also made compromises. They cancelled a proposal for Union prisoners of war to march in the parade out of respect for "Southern feeling" and added that "similar reasons might be urged against having a parade of ex-Confederates during the encampment." An "exhibition of the cruelties and tortures they suffered in war times would have a tendency to arouse the old sectional hatred."[57]

A more serious and intractable issue arose over accommodations for African American GAR posts. Many northerners and GAR officials looked upon Louisville's segregated society with great interest and anxiety, wondering how its citizens would accommodate black veterans. The *Louisville Commercial* reported in July that eastern newspapers were circulating rumors that "colored people would not be looked after" by the local arrangements committee and that these stories were doing "a great deal of harm" to the reunion effort.[58]

During the summer preceding the September encampment, the local GAR and local accommodations committee received many letters from northern chapters asking about provisions for African American members. Pennsylvania GAR member Abraham Levering wrote the committee that a "colored comrade" had presented him with a clipping from an Ohio newspaper stating that "the color line would be drawn" during the event. He suggested the committee "make good arrangements for our Colored

Comrades," warning that a failure to do so "might lead to an unpleasant-ness." Another Pennsylvanian inquired about the racial protocol for res-taurants, streetcars, and hotels, asserting that it would "make a great dif-ference in the numbers [from] this mighty post that will visit your city if we are all treated in equality."[59]

The topic of accommodations for African Americans appeared fre-quently in northern newspapers prior to the encampment. The *Cleve-land Gazette* and the *Chicago Record* reported that black troops might not be admitted to quarters or allowed to march in the parade. The *Boston Standard*, however, wrote that there would be "no G.A.R. Color Line" and quoted a Louisville woman who stated that the "colored veterans" would "receive the same attention as the white veterans," the only discrepancy being that "as a rule, the white people of Louisville will not entertain the black veterans in their houses as guests." She reassured the northern pub-lic, however, that the theaters and "all places of amusement, all churches, and all points of interest" would be open to "black and white alike," adding that Louisville's African American community would extend its hospital-ity "and [would] spare no pains to make their stay in the city a thoroughly enjoyable event." The *Boston Standard* observed that one of the sub-chairmen of the local committee was "a colored woman of great ability who is doing good work in bringing matters to a harmonious line on this issue." Not everyone, however, was heartened by the separate-but-equal overtures extended to African Americans. The *Murray (Ky.) Ledger* antici-pated that not drawing the color line more firmly would "keep lots of real white folks away" from the reunion.[60]

The controversies surrounding the Louisville GAR encampment in the months preceding the event underscored the fact that although a genuine willingness existed among white Americans to put past grievances behind them, a number of thorny issues remained embedded within the culture of conciliation that would be hard to surmount. In particular, the matter of black inclusion emphasized that formal racial customs were a tangible, and not yet reconcilable, difference between North and South. Some divi-sions would not be stamped out by the rhetoric of goodwill. Furthermore, in hindsight, the issue underscores the fact that thirty years after the war, race served as a key factor divorcing Kentucky from its Unionist past. When held to northern scrutiny and considered in light of the impending Union celebration, the state's racial customs enhanced its Confederate identity. Try as both sides might to keep matters of race from coloring the tone of the reunion, the issue could not be ignored. Even Commander in Chief Thomas Lawler could not refrain from comment about the racial divide that marked North from South. Although he prefaced his remark by claiming that "the G.A.R. [was] not a political organization," he stated the matter plainly: "The only bugbear of the South is the negro question."[61]

The local Union effort surrounding the encampment defined racial distinctions even more clearly, particularly within women's organizations. The GAR enlisted the aid of two women's groups, the Ladies of the GAR circles and the official arm of the men's organization, the Woman's Relief Corps. The largest of Louisville's four posts, the African American unit of the Woman's Relief Corps remained largely unrecognized by the official encampment women's committee and the press coverage of women's work during the event. Mary Tyler, the controversial head of the women's committee, commended African American women for their "effective work" in arranging hotel rooms and providing lunches for black visitors and assisting the white women in serving white visitors. For all of their efforts, however, the *Courier-Journal* failed to list black committee members individually by name, as it did for the white members. It seemed that white Unionist women were less reluctant to work alongside the great number of Confederate women who figured prominently in the event work than with their African American wartime allies.[62]

In fact, the 1895 encampment took place amid an effort by Kentucky white GAR women to dissociate themselves from black chapters in the state. In 1892, the national vice president of the Woman's Relief Corps, who resided in Covington, Kentucky, declared that "weak departments" like the one to which she belonged could grow only if the organization ceased accepting black members. She urged that all energy be put into increasing membership in the white chapters "and no effort [be] made to push the formation of Colored Corps until that has been done." "My experience has shown," she added, "that, if a Colored Corps is organized in town first, you will get no other." Only two years after the encampment, in 1897, the president of the Kentucky branch of the Woman's Relief Corps petitioned that the twelve white corps in the state be allowed to operate separately from the sixteen African American corps. The request was denied, but when they, along with the Maryland delegation, renewed their plea again at the 1900 annual convention, they succeeded in detaching themselves from the black corps of the state.[63]

Despite the marginalized role whites allotted them at the 1895 event, local African Americans used the GAR encampment as an opportunity to participate in broad-based Union memorial activity. The *Louisville Post* reported that Louisville's "colored people" had "shown no lack of interest in the encampment in this city" and had "spared no means" to "tastefully" decorate the city. African Americans also reportedly made up a significant portion of the 5,000 Kentucky troops who marched in the grand parade. As Nina Silber has noted, African Americans became essential "picturesque" elements that northerners came to expect of any southern setting. Not wanting to disappoint their visitors, white Louisvillians hired them to pour drinks at hospitality bars and assist in other service positions. Will Hays, a nationally known local songwriter, enlisted 300 black singers to perform a musical piece he composed in honor of the encampment. In anticipation of the performance, one paper said of the black entertainment, apparently without any sense of irony, "When the visiting veterans witness that cake walk and hear Col. Hay's colored choir sing—'Dar now, Hanna, aint yo' glad yo' cum?' They will be brought to a full realization of the fact that the bloodiest war of modern times was not fought in vain."[64]

Whites thus objectified African Americans to create in Louisville an atmosphere that evoked trends of popular black entertainment at the time, including the cakewalk and other minstrel performances. As the *Louisville Post* insinuated, the common bond whites, north and south, would feel when enjoying the spectacle of black entertainment would prove a point of reunion. In Louisville, the "smoldering fires of civil strife," which fueled "the passion of hate," would be overcome by "a common ancestry."[65]

As the national press reiterated the theme of reconciliation throughout the encampment, it revealed the extent to which Kentucky had become identified as a Confederate state. The *Grand Rapids (Mich.) Democrat* asserted that Louisville had been "one of the centers of the bitterest opposition to the cause for which the men who marched under the Union flag fought." Another newspaper headline announced the flood of Union veterans as "A Friendly Invasion." Even the Republican *Louisville Commercial* decreed, "Louisville Has Surrendered, The Grand Army of the Republic Owns the City." "Nothing Like It Ever Seen," it proclaimed two days later; "Southern Soil Reverberates to the Tread of a Great Peace Army." The *New York Times* gushed, "Men of Southern birth and sentiment vied with their brethren from the North in their demonstrations of greeting and a white-haired woman who, thirty-odd years ago this week, heard of the approach of the bluecoats with fear and apprehension, petted and pelted them today with flowers." Praising the ubiquitous presence of the American flag, the paper continued, "In all directions from the cabins of the colored folk along the river to the mansions of the wealthy in the suburbs, the small stores in the market place, and the big business blocks, 'Old Glory' in tens of hundreds of thousands is floating for patriotism, peace, and welcome. Never since the war, in a Southern city, has the Stars and Stripes been more in evidence." The newspaper that had always turned a critical eye toward Confederate memorial activity in the state now praised "the abundant display of paintings and pictures of the leading men of the Union" and the fact that "portraits of gallant leaders of the Confederacy have for a week been relegated to the background." "So far as outward signs are concerned," the *Times* surmised, "no greater demonstration of patriotic sentiment could be made, even by a city north of Mason and Dixon's line."[66]

Despite the general goodwill, however, traces of sectional antagonism lingered. An Indianapolis paper reported that some visitors had overheard local people on the street slighting the Union visitors. Complaints also came from Confederate quarters that northerners had disrespected the hospitality of their southern hosts. The *Confederate Veteran* reported happily that "there were a good many noble men among [the visiting veterans], and their surprise at the open hearted greeting from [Louisville citizens] was general." The magazine lamented, however, what it considered the obtrusive manner in which many of the Union veterans were dressed: "To see how thousands of veterans would dress and demean themselves upon coming as guests to their vanquished foes. . . . It would certainly have been in good taste for the Veterans to have worn citizens dress, with simple badges to indicate the state from which they came, and in which they served. But the array of blue tinsel was quite similar to that worn South the third of a century ago. . . . Many evidently did not consider the proprieties on becoming guests, in a large sense, to the South. There were many remarks which aggravated the Southern people."[67]

These sentiments aside, both observers and attendants of the Louisville reunion reached a general consensus that it had fulfilled its promise to create good feelings among people of the North and the South. The *New York Times* lauded the fruition of "the cherished plan of having veterans of the Blue and Gray meet for once in good fellowship on Southern soil, and together eat of the fruits of peace and good will." The *Syracuse Courier* claimed that the reunion was "bringing about a closer union of sentiment in the North and the South." A Birmingham newspaper anticipated that "extremists of both sections will have their sharp angles rubbed off." The *Denver Post* declared the city as a place of "genuine reuniting." The *Minneapolis Journal* proclaimed, "The New South is literally a new South; old things have passed away, all things have become new. The presence of Confederate Veterans in Louisville, welcoming their northern guests, indicates the recognition of that fact."[68]

As white Kentuckians came together to host the biggest Union gathering in the country, they did so on their terms, with their own unique take on their state's Civil War history. The GAR encampment confirmed the reputation Kentucky had garnered over the previous thirty years with its politics, violence, and memorial activities. Importantly, white Kentuckians successfully obscured their Unionist past only with the help of the same northern entities who, once enraged by their state's rebelliousness, now took comfort in the reconciliationist implications of such an identity. Despite its divided Civil War experience, by 1895 Kentucky was a former Confederate state in the eyes of the nation.

Two Kentuckys

CIVIL WAR IDENTITY IN APPALACHIAN
KENTUCKY, 1865–1915

In 1896, James Lane Allen penned an article in *Harper's* magazine in which he claimed that there were "two Kentuckys." "It can never be too clearly understood," he explained, "for those who are wont to speak of 'the Kentuckians,' that this state has within its borders two entirely distinct elements of population—elements distinct in England before they came hither, distinct during more than a century of residence here, and distinct now in all that goes to constitute a separate community—occupations, manners, and customs, dress, views of life, civilization." The two "populations" of which Allen spoke were the one that inhabited the Bluegrass plateau in the central and western parts of the state and the one that populated "that great mountain wall which lies along the southeastern edge of the State." They formed two discrete "human elements," the Kentucky highlander and the Kentucky lowlander, "long distinct in blood, physique, history, and ideas of life."[1]

Allen's writing fell amid a growing stream of travel and local-color literature about southern Appalachia that had, by the 1880s, introduced the American reading public to the idea that the area composed a distinctive civilization populated by a unique people. Within this context of Appalachian exceptionalism emerged the idea that Kentucky had endured two divergent Civil War experiences. One featured the landed, slave-owning Bluegrass aristocrats who sided with the South out of custom, kinship, and a proslavery position. In the other, the Kentucky mountaineer, who, according to contemporary literature, had little or no contact with the peculiar institution, had, by virtue of his century-long isolation and undiluted devotion to democratic institutions and nationalism, sided with the Union. At the same time as the memory of the state's Civil War experience was increasingly shaped by Confederate influences and interpretations, the idea of a Unionist eastern Kentucky came to the forefront and provided a powerful alternative narrative. Yet, ultimately, because Appalachian Kentucky was almost always cast in opposition to the rest of the state and was considered to be the nonnormative area of the commonwealth, the supposed blanket Unionism of Appalachian Kentucky ultimately served only to reinforce the state's general Confederate identity.[2]

THE IDEA OF eastern Kentucky as distinct from the rest of the state was not new in 1865. Significant geographic and demographic differences had existed between highland and lowland portions of the state for a nearly a century before the Civil War. By the late nineteenth century, however, the broader notion that southern Appalachia was unlike the rest of the nation seemed to heighten publicly perceived differences between eastern Kentucky and the rest of the state. In the 1870s and 1880s, local-color writers, geographers, and ethnographers began their "discovery" of a distinctive region called Appalachia. They had a receptive American audience that, in the face of the increasingly homogenized national culture, enjoyed reading about what Henry Shapiro calls "the peculiarity of life in the 'little corners' of America." These local-color accounts found their way into millions of homes within magazines such as *Century*, *Scribner's*, *Cosmopolitan*, and *Harper's New Monthly Magazine*, marketed to a growing middle-class readership.[3]

From the pages of these publications materialized "a strange land and a peculiar people" known as Appalachia. In countless stories and sketches, writers cataloged almost every aspect of mountain life: the mountaineers' strange physical characteristics; their ignorant simplicity; their log cabin homes; and their melancholy music—all elements seen as anachronistic to mainstream modern American life. Eastern Kentucky became one of the most frequently profiled parts of the region, with some of the most notable accounts coming from Kentuckians themselves. Lexington native James Lane Allen was among the most influential local colorists, and after he explicitly defined the notion of "two Kentuckys" in two articles for *Harper's*, the state would rarely be referred to as a single entity. Instead, writers divided the state into two or three discrete sections. In his 1889 "Comments on Kentucky," Charles Dudley Warner wrote that, "like Gaul," the state was "divided into three parts"—the eastern mountains, the central Bluegrass, and the western portion. Furthermore, Warner claimed that these divisions, "which may not be sustained by the geologists or the geographers, perhaps not even by the ethnologists, is, in my mind, one of character."[4]

Often, however, writers ascribed to Kentucky only two discrete sections: the Bluegrass and the mountain. Many times they used these two regions as points of contrast. Warner considered the Bluegrass to be "an open garden-spot," an outpost of civilized society, marked by prominent politicians, large estates, and thoroughbreds. The mountains, by contrast, were isolated and their people were "primitive and to a considerable extent, illiterate" and ignorant of the outside world. Significantly, however, the idealized visions of the Bluegrass region that dripped from the pens of fiction and local-color writers presented another exception to the modern world. As C. Vann Woodward has noted, a certain aura of "lingering grace and simplicity of life" persisted in only a few places in the postwar South as "anachronism[s] from the Old Order," and the Bluegrass region was one of them. Set in opposition to the "otherness" of the mountains, the Bluegrass came to represent the typical, if still distinctive, Kentucky. When compared to the strangeness of Appalachian Kentucky, the Bluegrass region represented the norm.[5]

At a time when white Americans were becoming increasingly concerned with defining their own group identities in opposition to others, Appalachia provided a unique racial and social counterpoint. Moreover, in a period when white Americans were growing ever more concerned about the effects of foreign immigration, Appalachia appeared to be the nation's last untouched bastion of Anglo-Saxon heritage. Perhaps the scholar who best defined this idea was Louisville native and University of Leipzig–trained geographer Ellen Churchill Semple. Semple was a pioneer of a method known as "anthropogeography," the theory that environmental factors directly determine human characteristics. In a 1901 article entitled "The Anglo-Saxons of the Kentucky Mountains: A Study in Anthropogeography," Semple argued that the isolated mountain communities of her home state were the site of "the purest Anglo-Saxon stock in all the United States." As descendants of the English and Scotch-Irish settlers of Virginia and North Carolina, "with scarcely a trace of admixture," they had "about them in their speech and ideas the marks of their ancestry as plainly as if they had disembarked from their eighteenth-century vessel yesterday," she claimed.[6]

Yet the fact that they were "the exponents of a retarded civilization, and show[ed] the degenerate symptoms of an arrested development, [meant that] their stock [was] as good as any in the country," she reassured. As a people, "kept free from the tide of foreign immigrants," argued Semple, the Kentucky mountaineers were sturdy threads in the national fabric. As proof that only their rough and isolated environment stood between the mountaineer and modern enlightenment, Semple related the story of ten Combs brothers, who after the Revolution moved west from Virginia across the Appalachians. Nine of the brothers settled in the mountains of Perry County, but one of them made his way into "the smiling regions of the Bluegrass," where he became "the progenitor of a family which represents the blue blood of the state, with all the aristocratic instincts of the old South." Meanwhile, their mountain cousins went "barefoot, herd[ed] in one-room cabins, and [were] ignorant of many of the fundamental decencies of life."[7]

With its newly bifurcated geography, Kentucky gained another distinctive Civil War narrative. Politicians, writers, and journalists emphasized Kentucky's postwar Confederate proclivities, while chroniclers of Appalachia regularly discussed the region's supposedly steadfast Unionism during the war. Semple claimed, "Such was their zeal for the Union, that some of the mountain counties of Kentucky contributed a larger quota of troops, in proportion to their population, for the Federal army than any other counties in the Union."[8]

James Lane Allen suggested that these internal geographical and sectional divisions within the state determined nothing less than the ultimate outcome of the war:

But for the presence of this wall [of mountains], the history of the state—indeed the history of these United States—would have been profoundly different. Long ago, in virtue of its position, Kentucky would have knit together, instead of holding apart, the North and the South. The campaigns and the result of the Civil War would have been changed; the Civil War might never have taken place. But standing as it has stood, it has left Kentucky, near the close of the first century of its existence as a State, with a reputation somewhat like the shape of her territory—unsymmetric, mutilated, and with certain parts missing.

But for the existence of Appalachia, and therefore of "two Kentuckys," the state would have been free of division, Allen asserted.[9]

The idea of a Unionist Appalachia became a common theme not only in local-color sketches but in historical fiction as well. William E. Barton's *A Hero in Homespun: A Tale of the Loyal South*, which focuses on the forgotten loyalties of the mountain South, typified this movement. During the

Civil War, Barton argued, the southern mountaineer "emerged from his obscurity and turned the tide of battle," only to later return to "his mountain fastness" and to be subsequently forgotten. Though the book was based mainly on the fictional experiences of loyal Unionist soldiers from east Tennessee, Barton took care to map out Kentucky's allegiances. In his story, two men from east Tennessee must travel through the Kentucky mountains to enroll in the Union army in the central part of the state. One character explains the geography of sectional loyalty in the state: "Wall, the Bluegrass thar is secesh, same as West Tennessy is. But the mountings is fur the Union, same's here. An' they'r goin' to raise troops, an'let the Gov'nor go to grass."[10]

This Unionism, held many scholars and chroniclers of the region, was rooted in the supposed absence of slavery in Appalachia. Kentucky's status as a slave state figured prominently in the Confederate memory, but the postwar narrative of Appalachian Kentucky was notable for the absence of slavery. As Ellen Semple declared, the mountains had "kept out foreign elements," but "still more effectually . . . excluded the negroes." "There is no place for the negro in the mountain economy," she wrote in 1901, "and never has been." The impracticality of large-scale agriculture in the mountains, Semple argued, "made the whole Appalachian region a non-slave-holding section." When the Civil War began, "this mountain region declared for the Union, and thus raised a barrier for disaffection through the center of the Southern States." By the early twentieth century, this history supposedly manifested itself in relative racial egalitarianism and loyalty to the Republican Party.[11]

Like Kentucky's Confederate past, the notion of Unionist mountain Kentucky was grounded in both truth and exaggeration. In actuality, residents of Kentucky's eastern, mountainous counties distinguished themselves from their lowland counterparts during the Civil War and Reconstruction era in several ways. Although slave ownership was not uncommon in the Kentucky mountains, it was certainly less widespread than in the rest of the state. Landholdings were often much smaller and staple crop farming even less tenable in the mountainous terrain. Though its prevalence varied widely from county to county, slavery certainly existed in eastern Kentucky. In Jackson County in 1860, African Americans made up less than 1 percent of the population, while in Clay County, enslaved and free blacks composed just over 5 percent and 4 percent of the population, respectively, for a total of nearly 10 percent. Mountain residents were well aware of the buying and selling of slaves, as the mountain passes and rivers provided the southward and westward routes of the interstate slave trade. Mountain towns like London, Pikeville, and Manchester also held regular slave auctions.[12]

Nevertheless, prior to the war, much of the state's antislavery activity took place in eastern Kentucky, with the foothills of Madison County providing the base of operation for both John Fee and Cassius Clay. Moreover, some historians maintain that many residents of the eastern counties were more likely to hold antislavery sentiments. As John Alexander Williams points out, however, with the exception of Fee and his followers, that did not translate into a lack of racism or concern for the well-being of African Americans. By the time fighting broke out in 1860, he has pointed out, "the mountaineers' resentment of slaveowners and their war was coupled with an even stronger dislike of the slaves themselves and of black people generally."[13]

With the failure of Kentucky's neutrality policy, most mountain residents, like their lowland counterparts, remained loyal to the Union. They enlisted in the Union army over the Confederate by a ratio of about four to one. In the Big Sandy Valley counties of Floyd, Johnson, Lawrence, and Pike, which bordered what would become West Virginia, three times as many men enlisted in the Union army as in the Confederate. Suggesting that slave ownership was not a significant determinant of loyalty, both Union and Confederate enlistments in these counties owned slaves in similar numbers.[14]

After the war, however, many Kentucky mountain whites marked themselves as distinct from their lowland counterparts when their loyalty to the government during the war translated into voting Republican. During the fifteen years that followed the war, the state's mountain counties proved to be the state's only major white base of Republican strength. In some places, the contrast in political geography was striking. In 1865, when Lincoln garnered only 30 percent of Kentucky's vote, over 90 percent of Whitley County and Johnson County voters cast their ballots for him. Overall, however, political sentiment was uneven and varied from county to county. In the Big Sandy region, for instance, between 1865 and 1872, Johnson County, which prior to the war had been the most Democratic county, became solidly Republican by a two-to-one margin, Floyd and Pike Counties remained marginally Democratic, and Lawrence County residents cast ballots in numbers similar to those before the war.[15]

Eastern Kentuckians' propensity to vote Republican, however, by no means translated into racial egalitarianism. Despite their purported ignorance of African Americans, they were just as attuned to racial issues as other white Kentuckians, and their loyalty to the Republicans was contingent upon the party's moderate conservatism. In 1869, when the Republican state convention endorsed the Fifteenth Amendment, many mountain counties "revolted" from the "radical program," and some previously staunchly Republican counties supported Democratic candidates. Furthermore, Republican voting in the mountains showed its most marked increase when the state party toned down its antagonistic anti-Confederate rhetoric in 1870 and 1871, choosing instead to campaign on such issues as internal improvements and education.[16]

Appalachia did boast significant Unionist war memory. In 1884, the citizens of Vanceburg constructed a monument that is among the strongest representations of Union war memory in the state. A Federal soldier, from his perch in front of the Lewis County courthouse, looks northward down upon the Ohio River. Leaving no question as to the town's convictions, the inscription reads: "To communicate the bravery and patriotism of our soldiers who lost their lives in the war for the preservation of national unity . . . the war for the Union was right, everlastingly right, and the war against the Union was wrong, forever wrong." Local historians contend that the Vanceburg monument may be the only pro-Union, publicly funded monument dedicated to the general Union cause in a public space below the Mason-Dixon Line. In spite of a variegated pattern of Civil War participation and postwar political alignments—and racial attitudes that, on the whole, diverged little from their lowland counterparts—by the 1880s eastern Kentucky had developed wartime and postwar narratives distinct from those of the rest of the state.[17]

Berea College became one of the most influential ongoing sources of Unionist identity for Appalachian Kentucky. Located in the foothills of the Cumberland mountains, the small college was founded in 1855 by Kentucky's two most famous abolitionists, John Fee and Cassius Clay, with a mission to educate free African Americans and southern mountain whites. The school shut its doors during the upheaval of the Civil War, and when it reopened them, school officials began to emphasize the educational needs of the "hardy and loyal men" it served.[18]

In promotional pamphlets aimed at northern philanthropists, the school strategically set its constituency apart from the rest of Kentucky's population, implicitly pitting the mountain yeomanry against the advantaged heirs of slavery. One brochure argued that in the South education was a privilege that had always been "monopolized by the wealthy class of planters." Underscoring the mountaineers' service to the nation, the tract noted that several counties proximate to the school had surpassed the draft quota and inquired: "Can any part of the North show so good a record?"

"Now that these men, their ideas enlarged and energies developed by the War, are asking for the key to knowledge, their wants must be met," college promoters reasoned. "Having periled their lives for the Union, the least their grateful countrymen can do, is give them those Christian Seminaries necessary to the full development of their manhood." In another pamphlet, college boosters described Berea's educational mission in terms of the "three distinct classes in Kentucky, namely: the inhabitants of the Blue Grass (ex-slaveholders), the colored people (confined almost entirely to the same region), and the mountain people."[19]

The idea of an Appalachia unbesmirched by slavery was a common theme in Berea promotional efforts. In 1870, Berea president Charles Fairchild gave a speech to the American Missionary Association in which he emphasized that it was mountain whites who "made an antislavery church and school in a slavery state," implying that the rest of the state was proslavery. He admonished his listeners to "remember that this whole section was loyal in the battle for a united country unstained by slavery." An 1888 pamphlet remarked that "the mountain people have been almost entirely separate from slavery and slaveholders, and have had little interest in them, and have been, in the main independent of them." Once again reiterating the commonwealth's Confederate identity, college promoters argued that mountaineers had played a special role in the Civil War course of the state:

> Had Kentucky been a wholly slaveholding State, it would have been wholly a Rebel State; but it was neutral, not because its individual men were neutral, but because its zealous Rebel element was neutralized by [a] Union element just as zealous. The mountain men were nearly all for the Union, and some counties furnished more Union soldiers than they had men liable to enter military duty. A few mountain men were violent Rebels, and a few slaveholders were ready to sacrifice everything for the Union. But the grand division was between the mountains and the plains; and there is the same division still. The mountain counties are generally Republican, some of them almost exclusively so; and the Blue Grass counties are Democratic, their white population almost entirely so. Thus, though the mountain people were not Abolitionists, and had no special sympathy with the colored people as slaves, there are now several bonds of union between them.

Thus had the Kentucky mountaineers' exceptional and virtuous (yet safely nonradical) racial views kept the state out of the Confederacy.[20]

The college's efforts to link the Kentucky mountains to the Unionist cause heightened when William Goodell Frost became the Berea president in 1892. When Frost, formerly the president of Oberlin College, arrived at Berea, he found the school at a crossroads. With dwindling financial means and stalled enrollment of both African American and white students, Frost decided to redirect the college's recruitment efforts toward mountain youth. He traveled tirelessly in pursuit of northern funding, speaking to audiences in the Midwest and Northeast, often drawing on the now-common theme of Appalachian distinctiveness and deprivation. He also wrote prodigiously in support of his new educational mission, publishing articles in magazines such as *Atlantic Monthly*, *Outlook*, and *American Review of Reviews*. With his extensive efforts to raise public awareness of Berea's mission and to raise funds for its work, Frost presented northern audiences with an expansive vision of the southern mountains.[21]

Declaring Appalachia the "ward of the nation," Frost emphasized the geographical and metaphorical remoteness of the region, once stating: "It is a longer journey from northern Ohio to eastern Kentucky than from America to Europe; for one day's ride brings us into the eighteenth century." He argued that education was integral to waking mountaineers from their Rip Van Winkle–like sleep. The mountaineers were not unredeemable, however. "They are not a degraded people," Frost once told a New York City audience, "they simply need to be graded up."[22]

Significantly, in return for financial and educational aid, Frost believed that Appalachians had something to offer America: a repository of unmitigated whiteness. Once they were uplifted, their hearty Anglo-Saxon Protestant stock would counterbalance the rising tide of "undesirable foreign elements." If taught the lessons of civilization and modern progress, mountaineers could contribute to the ranks of solid white citizenry in the country. Moreover, with their "central location in the heart of the South," they could exert positive influence over their poor southern lowland neighbors, who, Frost argued, had been "degraded by competition with slave labor," were "totally unenlightened," and "threatened to undo the progress of the last twenty years." Arguing that poor whites rather than "former slave-holders" were responsible for lynching and the general problems of the South, Frost believed that "the 'old colonel' [was] losing his grip and the uneducated white masses are gaining the upper hand." Thus would mountaineers serve as a radiant force of loyalty in a region that some northerners felt to be errant in its nationalism.[23]

Frost's most widely read and influential tract was "Our Contemporary Ancestors in the Southern Mountains," which appeared in the *Atlantic*

Monthly in 1899. Here he revived the old notion of mountain loyalty, arguing that it was not just the mountaineers' backwardness and need that granted them "large claims upon our interest and our consideration," but their deservedness as fine citizens of the nation, whose "old-fashioned loyalty" had "held Kentucky in the Union." "The feeling of toleration and justification of slavery, with all the subtleties of states rights and 'South against North,' which grew up after the Revolution did not penetrate the mountains. The result was that when the civil war came there was a great surprise for both the North and the South. Appalachian America clave to the old flag." When Theodore Roosevelt spoke on behalf of the college at Boston's Trinity Church in 1897, he drew on the same arguments of loyalty. "When the full history of the war is written we shall realize more than we do our debt to the loyal people of the South," he avowed, stating that "there [was] a larger proportion of descendents of revolutionary soldiery in Kentucky than in any other state," who could "overflow from their mountains and re-enforce the nation." "In helping Berea we are putting in our efforts where they will count to the utmost for the cause of true patriotism," he proclaimed.[24]

The theme of Kentucky mountain Unionism also pervaded many of William Frost's public appearances. At one fund-raising event in Columbus, Ohio, he recounted the story of how the 8th Kentucky Regiment, composed primarily of mountain whites, had supplied the American flag, handmade by Estill County women, that was planted on Lookout Mountain after Union battle victory. After his speech, Frost unfurled an identical flag before the audience as the Berea glee club sang both "negro" and mountain music. On another occasion, Frost declared: "It is a monument of the progressive sentiment of Kentucky—not the Kentucky of the bourbons, but the Kentucky of Clay, the Kentucky that stood for the union, the Kentucky that gave birth to Lincoln."[25]

Another fund-raising tool in Berea's arsenal was the *Berea Quarterly*, a journal the school published between 1895 and 1916. The *Quarterly* served as both a chronicle of Appalachian history and a promotion of the inhabitants' praiseworthy qualities. Many articles blended history and merit, and, as Shannon Wilson has noted, the publication became part of "a serious effort by Berea to present documentary evidence of the worthiness of Appalachian southerners and their need for educational support, based primarily upon their contributions during the Civil War." In the process, the *Quarterly* became another force for redefining the geography of Kentucky's wartime sympathies. One of the first issues of the quarterly published an article entitled "The Mountain People in the Struggle for the

Union," which argued that Kentucky mountaineers enabled Kentuckians in the rest of the state to "hold the state firmly in the Union, in spite of the fact that a majority of those who represented the wealth and the education of the middle and western parts sympathized with the Rebellion." Other articles drew attention to the contrast with "Confederate" Kentucky by focusing on the antislavery roots of the school. In "Crossing the Lines of War," the Reverend J. A. R. Rogers offered a firsthand account of the return of Berea officials to the state in 1862, following their expulsion shortly after John Brown's raid.[26]

William Barton confronted the state's emerging Confederate identity head-on in an 1897 article entitled "The Cumberland Mountains and the Struggle for Freedom." Recognizing that the state received "full credit in the popular mind" for sympathizing with the South, he reiterated that "more than twice as many soldiers from Kentucky went into the Union army" but that they were mostly from the "loyal portion only." "It is not too much to say that while the state had a very strong secession sentiment and sent more than a fourth of its troops she raised into the Confederate army," he continued, "she should be [remembered] as a loyal state, and that which held her for the Union, politically as well as in the result of her military operations[,] was the loyal sentiment of her own people, scattered throughout her area, but most of all those in the mountainous section of the state."[27]

The biggest historical sleight of hand that Berea boosters attempted, however, was their effort to remake Abraham Lincoln into a mountaineer. Despite the fact that the beloved president was born in Hodgenville in the central part of the state, college promoters granted him an Appalachian heritage enhancing the already Unionist identity of the region. They did this by linking the conditions of Lincoln's early life to those in Appalachia and then conflating them. As early as 1888, Berea made misleading connections between the two in promotional literature: "No truer type of manhood can be found than is found in the mountains of Kentucky—the same region that gave birth to Abraham Lincoln." By 1901, the college's letterhead read: "In Lincoln's state—for Lincoln's people." One *Quarterly* writer asserted that Berea's "first and largest endeavors have been for the young people of the class and circumstances from which [Lincoln] came."[28]

William Frost argued that Lincoln was an example of "the few representatives of this obscure people who have made their way to regions of greater opportunity" and who "have shown no mean native endowment." Like Lincoln, whose "great career hinged upon the fact that his mother had six books," mountain youth could, with the help of a Berea education, step out of their backwardness and contribute great things to the country. "The principal building of Berea College is named after this greatest American, and we expect to find other similar outcroppings from the same strata." In another article, entitled "The Southern Mountaineer: Our Kindred of the Boone and Lincoln Type," Frost asserted, "Abraham Lincoln provided a personal embodiment of the qualities attributed to mountain people— loyalty, patriotism, bravery, plainness, and lack of opportunity." Nearly a quarter century later, in an address entitled "Abraham Lincoln, Kentucky Mountaineer," William Barton declared that "Abraham Lincoln's ancestry was the common ancestry of the people of the Kentucky mountains . . . un-mixed Anglo-Saxon." "Lincoln experienced mountain-like conditions at the time he lived," he argued, adding that if he had been living then and "were a young man in the hills of Kentucky[,] who can doubt that he would strain every effort to become a student at Berea?"[29]

As a native Kentuckian, the Great Emancipator was a figure uniquely suited for Berea's mission of biracial education. At a 1901 celebration of Lincoln's birthday in Carnegie Hall, William Frost spelled out this connection: "Abraham Lincoln did not spring from the so-called 'poor whites' of the South. The old South had its small class of aristocratic slave-holders, and it had its 'poor whites,' people who lived in the midst of slavery, and were degraded by the competition with slave labor. But there was another class of people, in Lincoln's childhood widespread, but later confined to the mountains, a true yeoman class, who owned land but did not own slaves, and it was among these that our greatest president had his parentage." And while the rest of the nation had forgotten about these mountaineers in the years before the Civil War, "Lincoln alone of the statesmen of North or South knew that they were there, and he counted on them to stand for the Union."[30]

Apart from its educational mission, Berea College also became one of the state's foremost sites of Unionist memorial activity in the state. In 1890, the college served as the home of the James C. West Post of the Grand Army of the Republic, which drew members from all over eastern Kentucky. In 1905, a Ladies Auxiliary chapter formed at Berea as well. In this capacity, the college hosted Memorial Day celebrations and Fourth of July picnics, which had broad participation by Berea students and drew large crowds from the region. For such celebrations, the college suspended classes "for sacred patriotism." In 1915, the West Post celebrated the fiftieth anniversary of Lee's surrender.[31]

No one, however, more effectively convinced more Americans of mountain Kentucky Unionism than John Fox Jr. in his best-selling 1903 novel, *The Little Shepherd of Kingdom Come*. Born in 1863, near Paris, Kentucky, Fox was a bright but directionless young graduate of Harvard who worked briefly as a reporter for the *New York Sun* and the *New York Times*. In 1885, Fox returned to Kentucky to help his older brother, James, with his fledgling coal-mining venture located in Jellico, a town on the Kentucky-Tennessee border. Once there, Fox began to "[drink] in like a sponge the peculiar mountain-race and its beautiful natural environment." Here, in the midst of booming industrial Appalachia, Fox decided to devote his career to writing about his native state. He wrote his friend Micajah Fible, a Louisville native and Harvard classmate, "I don't want to write about anything else than Kentucky. . . . I want to be steeped in its history, have its people, their characters, their personalities, their modes of life, and thought in my brain. . . . This is my plan." Fox's interest in the Civil War and American sectionalism also figured into his early plans. "I mean to confine my thought and observation to the Northern-Southern character— vice-versa and the individual character of each people and I want to vacillate between the two sections," he declared to Fible in 1886.[32]

By the turn of the century, Fox had successfully parlayed his mentor James Lane Allen's idea of "two Kentuckys" into several well-known short stories in major magazines. In 1892, *Century* magazine published "A Mountain Europa," a romantic tragedy about a mountain lass and the outsider who falls in love with her, followed by "A Cumberland Vendetta," which chronicled the fictitious Stetson-Lewallen feud in 1884. These two stories won him both exposure and admirers, including Theodore Roosevelt. Fox drew even more public recognition from "On Hell-fer-Sartain Creek," a short piece about moonshining in the Kentucky mountains, published in *Harper's* in 1894, and *The Kentuckians*, serialized in the same publication in 1897.[33]

Fox's stories often incorporated Civil War divisions in the state as both a factor in and product of the differences between highland Kentucky and lowland Kentucky. In a 1901 essay entitled "The Southern Mountaineer," Fox asserted that it was the outbreak of the Civil War that actually prompted the rest of the world to unearth the mountain dwellers. "The American mountaineer was discovered," he declared, "at the beginning of the war, when the Confederate leaders were counting on the presumption that Mason and Dixon's Line was the dividing line between the North and South." They were mistaken, of course, and "then the South began to realize what a long, lean, powerful arm of the Union it was that the Southern Mountaineer stretched through its very vitals; for that arm helped hold Kentucky in the Union by giving preponderance to the Union sympathizers in the Blue-grass." Had it not been for their crucial role in stymieing Confederate unity through their loyalty to the Union, Fox contended, they might still be forgotten. "The North has never realized, perhaps, what it owes for its victory to this non-slaveholding Southern mountaineer," he wrote.[34]

Fox's most protracted and enduring effort to describe the geographical Civil War allegiances in Kentucky came in the 1903 sentimental best seller *The Little Shepherd from Kingdom Come*. *Little Shepherd* told the story of Chad Buford, an orphan who descends from his home in the heart of the Cumberland mountains to the valley of Kingdom Come, where the Turner family takes him in. Here Chad flourishes, among people who were "rude, rough, semi-barbarous if you will, but simple, natural, honest, sane, earthy." In the valley, Chad encounters enslaved African Americans for the first time in his life. "Dazed" by their appearance, Chad asks his new acquaintance, Tom, "Whut've them fellers got on their faces?" Laughing, Tom replies, "Lots o' folks from your side o' the mountains nuver have seed a nigger.... Sometimes hit skeers 'em." Unruffled, Chad replies, "Hit don't skeer me."[35]

Chad's world changes drastically when, on a trip to the "settlements," as the mountain folk call the Bluegrass region, Chad gets lost in the state capital of Frankfort. While making his way back to the mountains on foot, he meets Major Calvin Buford, who, convinced that Chad may be a distant relative of his, takes the mountain youth to Lexington to live with him as a member of his own family. Chad finds life in the city, the "aristocratic heart of the bluegrass," utterly different from anything he has ever known. In Lexington, Chad's rough-hewn ways come into conflict with the genteel conventions of Bluegrass culture, but, blessed with innate charm and ability, he succeeds in winning the admiration of nearly everyone he meets. During his time in Lexington, Chad begins to conform to the refined but normative behavior of lowland Kentuckians. He learns to say "sir" and "ma'am" and that it is bad form for young boys to chew tobacco and drink whiskey. He begins to doff his cap when he passes a lady. Eventually, the major's hunch regarding the boy's pedigree proves correct, and Chad, who was once thought to be illegitimate, turns out to be of refined parentage. He transforms from a mountain waif into a "highbred, clean, frank, nobly handsome" man, embodying "the long way from log-cabin to Greek portico"—the progress of man from semibarbarity to civilization.[36]

As mounting sectional tensions begin to invade the commonwealth, however, Chad's life grows unsettled. People all around him must decide whether to follow Kentucky's "convictions" and side with the Union, or the state's "kinship and sympathies," which rest with the South. Kentucky, it seems, is destined to contend with a dual identity. Once home to both Abraham Lincoln and Jefferson Davis, the state had "given birth to the man who was to uphold the Union—birth to the man who was to shatter it." Meanwhile, Chad's life embodies both, as "fate had given [him] the early life of one, and like blood with the other." *Little Shepherd* becomes not just the story of Chad's personal struggle to discern the path the impending sectional crisis will force him to take, but a chronicle of Kentucky's internal divisions. "In no other state in the Union was the fratricidal character of the coming war to be so marked as in Kentucky," asserts Fox; "in no other State was the national drama to be so fully played to the bitter end."[37]

In Fox's hands, Kentucky's Civil War experience is compellingly tragic. The Bluegrass region, though dominated by those ready to defend the slave foundation of their gracious lifestyle, is cleaved open by fratricidal struggle, as men who have worshiped alongside, done business with, and lived next to one another, align against one another in war. Often too, they have "slept in the same cradle, played under the same roof." Chad sees this process firsthand when his close companion Harry Dean, who had come under the influence of his "homegrown abolitionist" uncle, joins the Union war effort, even though it will mean taking up arms against his own father and brother.[38]

Kentucky's mountains, marked by near "uniformity" of Union sentiment, offer a sharp contrast to the divided Bluegrass. The basis of this Unionism is an innate patriotism that had never been corrupted by slavery, an institution, according to Fox, unknown to mountaineers. Having little knowledge and even less vested interest in the institution frees them from the politics surrounding it. To these mountaineers, Fox explains, slaves are seen only in their biblical context as "hewers of wood and drawers of water." Before coming to the Bluegrass, Chad had read *Uncle Tom's Cabin*, and he smiled incredulously at the tale, for "the tragedies of it he had never known and he did not believe." Although some valley folk, like Chad's first adoptive family, the Turners, own slaves and decide to fight for their human property, "as they would have fought for their horses, their cattle, or their sheep," most "Southern Yankees," stated Fox, "knew nothing about the valley aristocrat, nothing about his slaves, and cared as little for one as for the other."[39]

Fox's mountaineer, incarnate in Chad Buford, presents an alternative Kentucky Civil War character. Unsullied by connections to slavery and unencumbered by radical abolitionism, he is a white southerner with no sectional and racial baggage, a holdover from a time when Americanism was purer and simpler. "Unconsciously," Chad "was the embodiment of pure Americanism," who "like all mountaineers . . . had little love of State and only love of country. . . . [He] was first, last and all the time, simply American." This identification, furthermore, is not based upon reason but is instinctual. Just as Appalachian people are arrested in their development in other ways because of their isolation, so are they in politics. They had crossed over the mountains in the late eighteenth century, taking their Revolution-era politics with them, and there in this isolated land they had incubated without change for almost a century. Mountaineers had, since 1776, known only one flag and, claimed Fox, "never dreamed there could be another." Chad "was an unconscious reincarnation of that spirit, uninfluenced by temporary apostasies of the outside world, untouched by sectional prejudice of the appeal of the slave." Therefore Chad, the pure American, ultimately sacrifices his relationship with nearly everyone he loves for his primordial loyalty to the Union and rides off to join the Union army, albeit astride a horse named Dixie.[40]

In *Little Shepherd of Kingdom Come*, John Fox Jr. essentially defines the geography of Kentucky's Civil War experience for his readers. Although Fox acknowledges that both slaveholding and Confederate sentiment exist in Appalachia, his mountaineers side overwhelmingly with the Union. Fox also reinforces the perception that the Bluegrass was, with the exception of the occasional rabid abolitionist, the embodiment of the Confederacy. Whether in the mountains or the lowlands, Fox makes little provision for the patchwork of loyalties but instead portrays Kentucky as a state with essentially two ways of life, mountain and Bluegrass, and two corresponding sectional sentiments. Slaveholding almost always corresponds with the Confederacy and antagonism toward or ignorance of slavery with the Union. Mirroring the nuances of Kentucky's real-life, racially contingent brand of loyalty, however, Fox makes clear that Chad is no racial egalitarian. When the Union army begins to recruit black troops in 1864, "no rebel fe[els] more outraged than Chadwick Buford." Once African Americans join the fight, Chad "[feels] like tearing off with his own hands the straps which he had won with so much bravery and won with so much pride." In the end, however, "the instinct that led him into the Union service ke[eps] his lips sealed when his respect for that service, in his own State, was well nigh gone—ke[eps] him in that State where he thought his duty lay."[41]

Equally significant in *Little Shepherd* is the divergent manner in which the mountains and the Bluegrass recover from the upheaval of war. In the mountains, wartime divisions quickly spawn feuds, "a reign of forty years' terror." In civilized Lexington, however, mutual admiration for former enemies prevails among people. Chad sees his old nemesis and former Confederate Richard Hunt and realizes that he "was a man who knew no fight but to the finish," who, steeped in the code of honor, "would die as gamely in a drawing-room as on a battlefield." He was, in Chad's mind, "as good an American as Chadwick Buford or any Unionist who had given his life for his cause!" In Fox's estimation, Union loyalty is the highest form of nobility, but the Confederacy is honorable as well. He celebrates Morgan's men and their swashbuckling deeds, and when the war ends he dubs them the "pall-bearers of the Lost Cause."[42]

When all was said and done, according to Fox, "the hatchet in Kentucky was buried at once and buried deep." "Son came back to father, brother to brother, neighbor to neighbor." Tellingly, Fox credited the removal of "political disabilities" from Confederates to the fact that "sundered threads unraveled by war, were knitted together fast." That, according to Fox, who clearly spoke for *white* Kentuckians, was "why the post-bellum terrors of reconstruction were practically unknown in the state." As for Kentucky's African American citizens, Fox wrote that they "scattered, to be sure, not from disloyalty so much as a feverish desire to learn if they could really come and go as they pleased." After learning that their freedom was real, "most of them drifted back to the quarters where they were born." The Deans' black "mammy" stayed with them, "un-tempted by the doubtful fruits of freedom." In a reunion of hearts, Chad reconciles with his true love, Margaret Dean, helping to remove her stars and bars, tattered and weathered, from their wartime perch at the front gate of the family home. As they plan their future together, Margaret repeats the words of a fellow Confederate: "Every man, on both sides, was right—who did his duty."[43]

In Chad Buford, John Fox Jr. put forth an alternative picture of Kentucky Civil War loyalty, creating a literary counterpoint to the notion, built over the previous forty years, that Kentucky was entirely Confederate in sympathy. The Kentucky mountaineer, with all of his crude manners and improper English, had a simplicity and integrity to be admired. The American reading public agreed. *The Little Shepherd of Kingdom Come* appeared in serialized form in *Scribner's* magazine between January and August 1903, and in September of that year *Scribner's* published it in novel form. An instant success, by the end of the year the publisher had sold 50,000 copies. Readers all over the country devoured the work, reading it over and over again, delighting in the romance of both the novel's plot and its setting. One fan from New Hampshire wrote Fox that the book caused him to wish he "had been born in Kentucky instead." *Little Shepherd* climbed the ranks of the best-seller list in 1903 and remained there in 1904, enjoying sales "unheard of" for the time. Fox reaped financial and critical awards for the book and by one estimate made $100,000 from the serialization and the multiple editions of the book.[44]

Just as the discovery of Appalachia charted a new landscape of Civil War memory, it also shifted the geography of Kentucky violence. By the last decade of the nineteenth century, along with celebrating the racial purity of the mountaineer, the region's chroniclers began to dwell on their depraved lawlessness, indicting in particular the customs of moonshining and feuding, as well as "bushwhacking, inbreeding, and indiscriminate violence." As historian Anthony Harkins has explained, mountaineers became "not just out of step with" but "actually a threat to civilization." Although this kind of violence was seen as characteristic of the southern mountains in general, James Klotter notes that of the "dozen or so major feuds, most were associated in some way with the state of Kentucky."[45]

Newspaper accounts all over the world described "the old feudal spirit that ha[d] so long poisoned the blood of the State of Bourbon and Bluegrass," and local-color literature began to reflect this special connection between feuding and the Kentucky mountains. The eastern Kentucky lawlessness spawned a new character type: the "Kentucky desperado," quite different from his still-worrisome lowland counterpart. Unlike the central Kentucky assassin who at least cloaked his actions in pretenses of yesterday's gentility, the mountaineer, nearly always operating under the influence of moonshine, was more likely to "l[ie] in an ambush and [fill] his enemy with buckshot." James Lane Allen cast the Kentucky mountains as a place where "quarrels [are] frequent and feuds deadly" and "personal enmities soon serve to array entire families in an attitude of implacable hostility," quickly escalating into "war[s] of extermination," thereby rendering mountain people "turbulent, reckless, and distressing."[46]

In 1901, John Fox Jr. wrote that "nowhere is the feud so common, so old, so persistent, so deadly, as in the Kentucky mountains," where nearly every county could claim a past or ongoing conflict. He elaborated: "It is the feud that most sharply differentiates the Kentucky mountaineer from his fellows, and it is the extreme isolation that makes possible in this age such a relic of mediaeval barbarism. For the feud means, of course, ignorance, shiftlessness, incredible lawlessness, a frightful estimate of the value of human life; the horrible custom of ambush, a class of cowardly assassins who can be hired to do a murder for a gun, a mule, or a gallon of moonshine."[47]

Fox and many other writers blamed the feud on the mountaineers' supposed primal instincts, which thrived in the region's geographic isolation. The feud embodied the dark side of the mountaineer's racial purity, "an inheritance" from Scotland, "a race instinct, old-world trait of character, or moral code" that had gone into the mountains with backwoodsmen and had taken root in their isolation. Whereas southern violence had been a regional pathology for decades, late nineteenth-century commentators often attributed mountain violence specifically to Old World ways, to "clan responsibility" or a "sacred obligation" for personal justice. Although an uncivilized lack of regard for life had always characterized Kentucky violence, the supposed isolation of the mountains gave new credence to the survival of an individualistic "pioneer organization of society," compounded by the fact that local law enforcement and juries were steeped in the same culture and rarely compelled to convict killers. Although Kentuckians as a whole continued to bear the attribution of violence, it became increasingly seen as a symptom of Appalachian arrested development.[48]

Appalachian scholar Altina Waller notes that this was a notion that was first denied but eventually embraced by Henry Watterson and other central Kentucky boosters. At a time in which he and other New Departurists were trying to make the state look as attractive as possible to potential economic investors, Watterson found the Appalachian pathology a useful smokescreen for violence in the rest of the state, as it helped to redirect the nation's attention from Kentucky violence to eastern Kentucky violence. "For Henry Watterson and his readers in Bluegrass Kentucky," Waller asserts, "it was undoubtedly a relief to focus on the suppression of violence in mountaineer culture that industrialization would soon bring about than to confront the uncomfortable reality of increasing racial violence in their own backyard." With this geographic shift of violence from the South to the mountain South, she adds, "northerners could be distracted from the daily racial and political violence that continued to increase in the last two decades of the century."[49]

This theme appeared in fiction as well. In *The Kentuckians*, John Fox Jr. portrayed the Bluegrass and mountain sections as arrayed against one another over the subject of lawlessness. The plot of the novel revolved around the political drama in Frankfort as lawmakers decided how best to deal with feuds. "The reputation of the State was at issue, and civilization in the Bluegrass was rebuking barbarism in the mountains." As the book's antagonist describes, Bluegrass residents came to see the "scathing mountain lawlessness as a red blot on the 'scutcheon of the state." Feuding "had stained the highland border of the Commonwealth with blood, and abroad was engulfing the reputation of the lowland blue-grass."[50]

The discourse surrounding mountain violence only added to the idea that there were "two Kentuckys" and two types of Kentuckians. In a 1900 article entitled "The Kentuckian," published in *Century*, John Gilmer Speed asserted that "in most instances these private quarrels which lead to murder are among mountaineers, who are in no sense the kind of Kentuckians whose characteristics I'm discussing." He argued that before industrial development began other Kentuckians "paid no heed to these people and their quarrels, but unwisely perhaps, left them to their own devices, upon the theory that the more they killed of one another, the better off the world would be." He then blamed "newspaper extravagance" for making feuds between "mountain outlaws appear to be an affair between Kentucky gentlemen."[51]

This shift in the geography of violence coincided with the realization that the coal fields and timber of the state were the commonwealth's new economic frontier. In fact, as Watterson ultimately argued in the pages of the *Courier-Journal*, it would be investment, development, and ensuing civilization that would break the cycle of ignorance and lawlessness. Mountain redemption would come in the form of railroads, schools, and churches. Watterson was not the only person to see industrialization as the answer to curtailing the violence. The *New York Times* reported that the springing up of thousands of miles of railroad track in eastern Kentucky would, in addition to transporting the mineral resources, "gradually civilize an area given over to outlaws." "The new roads will serve as missionaries to transform gradually but surely the character of the secluded villages, and put an end to the feuds and vendettas in which the energies of the isolated people have been expended," the paper predicted.[52]

Journalists and writers attributed mountain violence to several factors, one of which was the Civil War. Like Charles Dudley Warner, they usually cited "the habit of carrying pistols and knives, and whiskey," and general "want of respect for law." Almost always, however, observers blamed the Civil War for channeling mountaineer instincts in a negative direction. Some pointed to the local warfare distinctive to the Kentucky mountains—civilian suffering at the hands of bushwhackers and the informal partisan bands of Union or Confederate sympathy composed of "native ruffians, banditti, deserters, guerrillas, and desperate people," which plagued eastern Kentucky and other areas of Appalachia. Citing the prevalence of this warfare, one local told Warner that "lawlessness" had "only existed since the war; that before, the people, though ignorant of letters, were peaceful." Warner himself asserted that "the habit of reckless shooting, of taking justice into private hands, [was] no doubt a relic of the disorganization during the war."[53]

Importantly, while guerrilla warfare had plagued all of Kentucky during the Civil War and gave rise to much of the state's immediate postwar violence, by the 1880s and 1890s many chose to remember ferocious civilian conflict as a particularly Appalachian phenomenon. Berea College professor Elijah Dizney, for example, proclaimed the Civil War to be "the most fundamental and precipitating cause" of the feuds, which were "mostly unknown" before it. "Every county in Eastern Kentucky has its tales of blood-curdling deeds. . . . The whole story of the disorder of the Home Guards, guerrilla bands of Confederates, and 'swamp companies' which plundered both sides, would be a natural introduction to the history of Kentucky feuds," he claimed, adding that "it should be noted too that the principals in these feuds were during the Civil War boys whose imaginations were filled with all these horrors." Likewise, William Goodell Frost explained that although the feud was based in ancient Old World traditions, it seemed "to have been decadent when the confusions of the civil war gave it a new life." In "Civilizing the Cumberland," John Fox Jr. wrote that "but for the war that put weapons in his Anglo-Saxon fists, murder in his heart, and left him in his old isolation," the mountaineer would have respect for the law. The connection between the Civil War and feuding only increased with the rise in public consciousness surrounding the most famous feud of them all, which pitted West Virginia Confederate "Devil Anse" Hatfield and his family against that of Kentucky Unionist Randall McCoy.[54]

In reality, some of the earliest incidents of Kentucky violence that the press categorized as feuds did seem to grow out of Civil War and Reconstruction tensions. Familial conflicts sprung up in Breathitt, Garrard, Owen, and Henry Counties, where feuding parties disagreed over the issue of black suffrage. In the Rowan County Tolliver-Martin feud, the Tollivers were mostly Democrats and the Martins were Republicans. Recent scholarship on feuds blames mountain unrest on the anxiety over regional modernization and industrialization, casting the violence as "politically motivated struggle" related to economic development, agricultural decline, and land pressures. Just as for other southerners, Appalachian scholars suggest, violence was an exercise in power for those who felt their old ways of life threatened. Yet, for late nineteenth- and early twentieth-century observers, it was easier to blame a combination of mountain pathology, moonshining, and wartime grudges.[55]

Thus, the Civil War memory of Appalachian Kentucky was full of contradictions. At the same time as the region's supposed overwhelming loyalty to the Union was often given as proof of the mountaineer's merit, observers often blamed the Civil War for triggering the mountaineer's worst instincts. The war that gave eastern Kentuckians a favored status in the nation was also blamed for their corruption. Paradoxically, as people like William Frost held up Kentucky mountaineers as the vanguard of reunion and the hope of the New South, others cited their divided loyalties as the cause of regional brutality. The perceived normality of the Confederate portion of Kentucky—an area capable of peaceful reunion—exacerbated Appalachian Kentucky's growing lawless reputation. Moreover, this perception that made Unionism seem an anomaly not only legitimized the state's Confederate identity but made it look like the preferable, more civilized one.

A Place Full of Colored People, Pretty Girls, and Polite Men

LITERATURE, CONFEDERATE IDENTITY,

AND KENTUCKY'S REPUTATION, 1890–1915

At age five, Lloyd Sherman, or the "Little Colonel" as her friends and family affectionately call her, moves from New York to Kentucky. Upon her arrival in Lloydsboro, "one of the prettiest places in all Kentucky," she encounters her maternal grandfather, Colonel Lloyd, who, "from his erect carriage to the cut of his little goatee on his determined chin," is reminiscent of "what Napoleon might have looked like had he been born and bred a Kentuckian." Charmed by the old man, little Lloyd discovers that her grandfather is estranged from her mother, thanks to the latter's decision years earlier to marry a northerner, Jack Sherman. Thirty years have passed since the Civil War, but the colonel, who sacrificed his right arm and his beloved son to the Confederate cause, still "hates Yankees like poison." Nonetheless, the irrepressibly charming Little Colonel inspires reconciliation between father, daughter, and son-in-law. Theirs becomes a reunion not only between family members but also between North and South. The joyous turn of events prompts the Little Colonel to drawl gleefully, "Isn't this a happy mawnin'?"[1]

Lloyd Sherman is the protagonist of Annie Fellows Johnston's children's book, *The Little Colonel.* Written in 1895, the book gained a wide following, and by 1912, Johnston had added eleven more books to the series. More than just a "phenomenon in popular literary culture," Johnston's books became part of a wave of popular romantic literature that streamed out of the state around the turn of the century. These Kentucky authors joined the larger, regionwide trend led by authors such as Thomas Nelson Page and Joel Chandler Harris in romanticizing the antebellum South. As David Blight has noted, "The age of machines, rapid industrialization, and labor unrest produced a huge audience for a literature of escape" into the South of plantations and slavery. Once "all but 'lost,'" notes Blight, the region "was now the object of enormous nostalgia."[2]

Johnston, along with widely read Kentucky authors like James Lane Allen and Irvin Cobb, set her stories in the commonwealth and specifically rooted them in an antebellum, slave-based past whose vestiges lived on in benign African American and Confederate-sympathizing white characters. By writing about the commonwealth as a place where Old South values prevailed and as a home to people intimately connected to the Confederate experience, Johnston, Allen, and Cobb, all of whom developed a national reputation, helped further the perception of Kentucky as a Confederate state.

Furthermore, this literature offered an alternative vision of Kentucky at a time when national newspapers were full of the misdeeds occurring in the state. Indeed, by the time Johnston, Allen, and Cobb gained literary notoriety, life in Kentucky was anything but a "happy mawn'in." Between the end of the Civil War and the early twentieth century, the state's reputation declined markedly. Once known for its prominence in national politics during the antebellum era, Kentucky became better recognized for its political corruption and strife. When William Goebel was gunned down in the courtyard of the state capitol in 1900, the commonwealth attained the dubious distinction of having the only governor to die by assassination while in office. Coming on the heels of a contested gubernatorial election, the catastrophe virtually launched a civil war within the state and left an enormous blight on Kentucky's already-tarnished character. Following the assassination, the state was, as *Collier's Weekly* put it, "on trial," along with Goebel's accused murderer.[3]

In 1904, as feuding continued to keep the eastern portion of the state in the national spotlight, violence erupted on the opposite side of the state. When tobacco prices plummeted, to lower than production costs, western Kentucky farmers organized into the Planters Protective Association in an effort to pool their crops. By 1906, when some local planters resisted joining the association, scores of armed, mounted men, known as night riders, resorted to violent coercive tactics, burning tobacco barns and company warehouses and threatening, whipping, and shooting those who opposed them. Often the victims were African Americans who farmed small plots of the leaf and could not afford to hold their crops off the mar-

State seal of Kentucky as it was revised by a cartoonist after Governor William Goebel's assassination. *Minneapolis Journal*, February 1, 1900. Courtesy of Special Collections, University of Kentucky Libraries.

ket. Night riders raided towns throughout western Kentucky, including Hopkinsville, Princeton, and Russellville.[4]

By 1908, the vigilante violence had spread to the tobacco farms of the Bluegrass. Republican governor A. O. Stanley eventually sent the National Guard to quell the disorder. The worst violence lasted for only three years, but the effects on the state and those that lived there were long lasting. Robert Penn Warren, who grew up in the small town of Guthrie, a center of tobacco discord, later recalled, "There was a world of violence that I grew up in. You accepted violence as a component of life. . . . You heard about violence and you saw terrible fights . . . [and] there was some threat of being trapped into this whether you wanted to or not." Untold numbers of farmers succumbed to exile, or simply left Kentucky of their own accord, to grow tobacco in other states such as Missouri, Indiana, and Ohio.[5]

The Black Patch disorder damaged Kentucky's reputation, refreshing and solidifying the notion, accrued over the past half-century, that it was a treacherous and violent place. The *Philadelphia Inquirer* noted that "in Kentucky life was less sacred than in almost any other part of civilization," and the *Washington Times* suggested that Kentucky was in need of a "'flying squadron' of military police to keep peace within her borders," something that might help improve "the standing of the State abroad."[6]

The first years of the new century held little promise for the Bluegrass State. As one historian noted, "Kentucky entered the twentieth century under a cloud which never lifted. The state's dark image of violence severely hindered development, retarded growth, and limited the state's ability to compete with other regions. Citizens seemed in a constant siege from without and deeply divided within." In 1908, a *Chicago Tribune* column conducted a virtual tour of the Frankfort Cemetery, taking note of the multiple residents who had died as the result of dueling, murder, and assassination. "This list of crime and murder might be repeated from every cemetery in many parts of the State. The condition has existed since the founding of the Kentucky commonwealth and shows no sign of passing away."[7]

Yet, within the public mind, Kentuckians presented a multidimensional image. "A most interesting book could be written upon the character of the average Kentuckian," remarked a Chicago writer. "His courage is a proverb and his lawlessness a byword. His hospitalities are boundless and his courtesy extreme; his vindictiveness is violent and his enmity eternal. No state in the Union offers such extremes of moral worth." The dual nature of life in Kentucky mirrored the "paradox of the New South"—as C. Vann Woodward described it, "the contrast between the earnestly professed code of shopkeeper decorum and sobriety and the continued adherence to a tradition of violence." Kentuckians parodied this duality in dozens of songs and poems in the early twentieth century, many of which were reprinted in local newspapers. Some had choruses that claimed that Kentucky was "not what she ought to be." Another "fugitive rhyme" that circulated toasted the state with humorous irony:

> Here's to ole Kentucky, where you never have the blues,
> Where the Captain kills the Colonel and the Colonel kills the booze.
> Blood it flows like water and bullets fly like hail,
> Every pistol has a pocket and every coat it has a tail.
> You start out in the morning to give your health a chance
> And they bring you home at midnight with buckshot in your pants;

They always hang the jury, but they never hang the man,
You call a man a liar and then get home if you can.
The owl's afraid to holler and the birds don't dare to sing
For it's hell in old Kentucky, where they shoot 'em in the wing.[8]

Against the backdrop of the state's misery and shortfalls emerged a mass of literature about Kentucky that looked back nostalgically at purportedly better days. These literary backward glances, moreover, often invoked Confederate characters through whom the graciousness of the past was channeled. James Lane Allen, a Lexington native who became even better known for his fiction than for his local-color sketches and the most critically acclaimed author from the Bluegrass State, wrote romantic stories that focused on human nature and the tension between modern and past ways of life.[9]

One of Allen's popular tales, "Two Gentlemen of Kentucky," is a somber short story about aging Bluegrass colonel Romulus Fields and his faithful black body servant, Peter Cotton, who remains with him even after emancipation. The war and the societal changes it wrought have come upon the colonel like a "killing frost," and Allen writes that "the whole vast social system of the old regime had fallen, and he was henceforth but a useless fragment of the ruins." Lacking a purpose on the old family estate, Romulus Fields and Peter Cotton move to Lexington, where they venture into the hardware business. The colonel, however, too kindly to succeed in the world of New South mercantilism, gives away more merchandise than he sells and must soon close the store.[10]

The colonel often "dwel[ls] fondly upon scenes of the past." In these reveries, "the silent fields around him seemed again alive" with singing slaves, with visions of "one little negro" blacking his shoes while another tended to his horse and still another brought a thirst-quenching beverage. Allen assures readers, however, that, "convinced that slavery was evil, yet seeing no present way of removing it, he had of all things been a model master." It is because of this, no doubt, that Peter Cotton, with an "inner sun upon his tranquil heart," remains with his former master even after emancipation, refusing a salary.[11]

"Two Gentlemen" is a tale of decline and sad nostalgia, but it is also a morality tale about days when race relations were easier. The two men, one kindly respectful and the other reverently loyal, "kept up a brave pantomime of their obsolete relations." "To a few deepseeing eyes," Allen wrote, "the colonel and Peter were ruined landmarks on a fading historic landscape, and their devoted friendship was the last steady burning-down of that pure flame of love which can never again shine out in the future of the two races." "The sun of their day had indeed long since set," but "they were still radiant with the glow of the invisible orb." The story ends in quiet sadness as the colonel passes away, with Peter following him as faithfully into death as he had served him in life. The two are buried side by side.[12]

Annie Fellows Johnston's Little Colonel presented a more happily nostalgic literary creation of Kentucky's Confederate past. Johnston, a native of Evansville, Indiana, first encountered and embraced Louisville's fondness for days gone by in Pewee Valley, a tiny town eleven miles east of the city. Founded in 1870, Pewee Valley was a community of summer residences where Louisville's wealthiest families escaped the heat of the city. Johnston first traveled there in 1893, shortly after the death of her husband, William Johnston. During their brief marriage, her husband had encouraged Johnston to submit the occasional story to children's magazines. After his death, however, the twenty-nine-year-old Johnston turned to writing as a way to support herself and her husband's three children from a previous marriage.[13]

Johnston later wrote in her autobiography, *The Land of the Little Colonel*, that upon her arrival in Pewee Valley she "felt as if [she] had stepped back into a beautiful story of ante-bellum days. Back into the times when people had leisure to make hospitality their chief business in life, and could afford for every day to be a holiday; when there were always guests under the spreading rooftree of the great house, and laughter and singing in the servants quarters." For Johnston, Pewee Valley was the sort of sleepy southern town where the post office was the center of the community. In front of it passed a steady stream of summer residents in their "old family carryalls loaded with children in the care of their black mammies," as well as "pretty girls and their escorts on horseback," who "drew rein in the shade of the locusts arching the road." Pewee Valley was so reminiscent of the Old South, Johnson explained, that "one half expected to find 'Mars' Chan' and 'Meh Lady' among [the residents], for the families represented [there] were sprung from the old Virginia stock and showed their birth and breeding both in feature and in charm of manner."[14]

The people and the environment of Pewee Valley provided a ready subject for Johnston's pen. Explaining her creative formula in her autobiography, she wrote: "The Land of the Little Colonel, like 'all of Gaul,' is divided into three parts. One lies in the State of Kentucky, one in the Country of Imagination, and one in the dear desmesne of Memory." Inspired by real people and an actual place, Johnston constructed a series of

Annie Fellows Johnston and Hattie Cochran, her model for the Little Colonel, stand outside of The Beeches in Pewee Valley. Kate Matthews Collection, ULPA 1980.24.038n. Special Collections, University of Louisville.

stories from multiple layers of reality and fiction. Setting her tales at the turn of the century, Johnston beckons readers back to an imagined ante-bellum existence. The beautiful and affluent town of Lloydsboro provides an enchanted backdrop for romantic and idealized characters. The Little Colonel, her family, and her friends lead enviable lives of leisure filled with house parties, boarding school high jinks, and European voyages. They enjoy a gentle existence buffered from insecurities by a stable social arrangement that entails powerful yet chivalrous men and well-behaved, maternal women. Most important, however, this safe, unburdened or-der rests upon the deference and servitude of faithful, contented African Americans.

As fanciful as her stories seem, however, Johnston relied heavily on what she saw as the real essence of life in Pewee Valley for her inspiration. She modeled most of her characters, for instance, on real-life residents of Pewee Valley and Louisville. On her first visit to the small town, Johnston met Miss Hattie Cochran, the little girl who soon became her inspiration for the Little Colonel. She first encountered the "child of delicate flower-like beauty" one day as Hattie, accompanied by her grandfather, pushed a ragged-looking parrot in a doll carriage. The grandfather was an eccen-tric Confederate colonel, George Weissinger, whom Johnston described as a larger-than-life fixture in the town. Clad in white duck in the summer and a dignified military cape in the winter, he was greeted deferentially by all who met him. Johnston decided to write about the pair when a local woman described Hattie Cochran as "her grandfather all over again" in her "temper, lordly manners, imperious ways and all." Likewise, Johnston based the Little Colonel's nanny, Mom Beck, on Rebecca Porter, who worked for a family in Pewee Valley and had been a slave in Virginia be-fore the Civil War.[15]

Through her local-color descriptions, Johnston evokes visions of the Old South and, by extension, of the Confederacy. Like other writers of the genre, Johnston illuminates Lloydsboro's unique lifestyle and environs richly. Many of the large houses there have wide porches and white col-umns shrouded by Virginia creeper and bear stately sylvan names such as "Oaklea" and "The Beeches," taken from titles of actual residences in Pe-wee Valley. "The Locusts," home to the Sherman family, was no exception, with its "pewees in the cedars and robins on the lawn; everywhere the cool deep shadows of great trees and wide stretches of waving blue-grass."[16]

The white characters around whom Johnston's stories revolve present an equally appealing picture of graceful gentility as they go about lead-ing lives of wealth and privilege. Lloyd's father, Jack Sherman, becomes wealthy through his work with a mining company in the West and other male characters have legal and military careers, but the wealth of most Lloydsboro families is buttressed by long-standing family fortunes. Their money and social stature allows Johnston's characters to make leisure and holiday their prime pursuits. Johnston's characters look their part. Lloyd and her closest friends often appear in a "flutter of white dresses and gay ribbons," while her grandfather, befitting an old Confederate colonel, dons white "from May till October."[17]

The fictional world of the *Little Colonel* both reflects and magnifies the Confederate atmosphere of real-life Pewee Valley. Johnston achieves this by employing concepts that Gilded Age citizens commonly associated with the former Confederacy. She wrote for readers who accepted the idea of black inferiority and who increasingly viewed slavery nostalgically as a benign institution. Additionally, the idea of the South as a persistently agrarian society and a region of refined domestic comfort only heightened the "romance of reunion" for white Americans who looked apprehensively at the increasingly urban industrial and ethnically diverse nation in which they lived.[18]

Johnston's African American characters formed the cornerstone of this nostalgia. Although the events about which Johnston writes take place three and four decades after emancipation, the existence that she creates for her black characters has changed very little since antebellum times. The servants who work at "The Locusts" still live in cabins on the premises. African Americans appear in the books only in positions of servitude, faithful and obedient to their white employers, many of whom they served before the Civil War. Lloyd's governess, Mom Beck, for instance, had been her mother's nurse in antebellum days. Johnston's characters also claim a sort of de facto ownership of their servants. Lloyd once explains her participation in the wedding of Sylvia, a young black woman, by telling a friend, "You see, Sylvia's grandfathah was the MacIntyre's coachman befoah the wah, and her mother is our old Aunt Cindy. She considahs that she belongs to us and we belong to her."[19]

Annie Fellows Johnston's portrayal of African Americans undergirds the mood of leisure and privilege in the *Little Colonel* books. The deference and service of African Americans uphold the superiority and social status of whites. They grant femininity to women whom they unburden of cooking and child care, leisure to the children who are not bothered with chores, and power to the men who are wealthy enough to employ them.

By means that are sometimes understated, African Americans serve to maintain social and racial order. Furthermore, Johnston's African

Photograph of Rebecca Porter, the real-life model for Mom Beck in *The Little Colonel* series. The photograph of Abraham Lincoln and his son, Tad, positioned behind Porter represents an interesting counterpoint to the Confederate-dominated Civil War memory in Johnson's books. Kate Matthews Collection, ULPA 2007.14.057.p. Special Collections, University of Louisville.

American characters venerate white men of their own volition. One of the "pickaninnies" who resides at "The Locusts," for instance, is named Henry Clay, in honor of the prominent Kentucky statesman. Another, less subtle, show of deference comes during Sylvia's wedding, when the black congregants wait until all of "the white folks passed out" of the church before exiting.[20]

The Little Colonel learns about racial order at a young age when her grandfather excoriates her for cavorting with two black children. Even as she dominates them, ordering them around in play, Colonel Lloyd rages, "What does your mother mean by letting you run barefooted around the country just like poor white trash? An' what are you playing with low-flung niggers for? Haven't you ever been taught any better? I suppose it's some of your father's miserable Yankee notions." Here, a breach of social and racial order is equated with northern mores. By age twelve, however, Lloyd has learned racial protocol. Upon her return from Europe, she introduces her souvenir, a Saint Bernard, to "her little black admirers." She orders them to fetch the dog some food and water, adding, "If you all fly around him and wait on him right good, he'll like you lot's bettah." In the land of the Little Colonel, even a dog deserves the deference of African Americans.[21]

In spite of their subordinate status, Johnston's African Americans never appear dissatisfied with their second-class citizenship. Cast as simpleminded and superstitious, they remain content in their servitude, harboring no greater aspirations. Although Johnston wrote the *Little Colonel* series during a time in which Kentucky African Americans were steadfastly fighting to overturn existing and newly emerging Jim Crow legislation, her black characters seem to relish and reinforce the oppressive social customs. At one Lloydsboro social engagement, "two or three darkies, with banjoes and mandolins," contribute "to the general festivities by a jingling succession of old plantation melodies." Johnston also writes about Waffles, a black cook who had traveled west with his employer. Upon departing Arizona for Kentucky, he happily whistles "Going Back to Dixie." Johnston's picture of race relations in turn-of-the-century Kentucky was so enticing to her white readers that Anne Firor Scott has written that reading *The Little Colonel* as a child made her regret that she "had not been born in slavery times."[22]

Beyond "a place full of colored people, pretty girls, and polite men," as one of her characters describes the state, however, Annie Fellows Johnston posits that Kentucky is not only southern but a place loyal to the

Confederacy. Several times, she mentions the presence of a Confederate veterans' home in Lloydsboro, inspired no doubt by the actual Kentucky Home for Confederate Veterans, established in Pewee Valley in 1902. Johnston portrays Lloyd's father as a regular visitor to the home, despite his status as a native northerner. Johnston's characters often display a sectional partisanship that goes beyond the obvious link between the old colonel and the Confederacy. Lloyd, despite her father's northern roots, also shows herself to be a proponent of the late southern cause to such an extent that, in one instance, she is surprised when confronted with her own emerging nationalism in the wake of the Spanish-American War. When Mrs. Walton, a family friend, describes Lloyd as patriotic, the Little Colonel is taken aback, exclaiming, "I always took grandfathah's side, you know because the Yankees shot his arm off. I hated 'em for it, and I never would hurrah for the Union. I've despised republicans and the North from the time I could talk."[23]

In spite of the occasional reference to the theme of reunion, Johnston consistently returns to sectionalist dialogue throughout the *Little Colonel* series. She was one of several authors, Thomas Nelson Page and Joel Chandler Harris among them, who spawned in their readers what Paul Gaston has called "a national lovefeast for the Old South." Harking back to a racially innocent golden age of landed aristocracy, Johnston's portrayal of life in the Bluegrass State shared the same visions of the Old South that buttressed the Lost Cause movement. Furthermore, Johnston never once alludes to Kentucky's divided Civil War loyalties. She simply chooses to forget or to ignore, as did many white Kentuckians, that Kentucky had remained loyal to the Union. None of Johnston's characters are Union veterans, or even offer up memories of the federal wartime experience. Thus, by placing Kentucky squarely within a larger Old South–Lost Cause narrative, Johnston offers only part of Kentucky's Civil War legacy. Taking a cue from the real people who served as her inspirations, she creates a Kentucky whose allegiances and whose historical memories are entirely Confederate.[24]

By the time Johnston died in 1931, her books had sold over 1 million copies. According to *Publishers Weekly*, the number of copies of the lowest-selling book in the series was 81,000; the highest was 136,000. By the mid-twentieth century, the number had climbed to 2 million. One writer has called the popularity of the books among children of the early twentieth century "a kind of religious fervor." Several of Johnston's acquaintances noted that the author was more proud of the responses her books provoked in their readers than of their sales figures. The stories touched a chord in readers across the country, and after the translation of several books into foreign languages they became popular among children around the world. The response from impressionable young readers was overwhelming. In 1913, a children's magazine even surmised that "Mrs. Johnston probably receives more letters from appreciative readers than any other author in the United States." The immense popularity of the series meant that Annie Fellows Johnston brought the idea of a Confederate Kentucky to people all over the world.[25]

The popularity of *Little Colonel* reached its height in 1935 when Paramount Studios made the book into a motion picture. Starring Shirley Temple, the most popular film star of the day, the film was a commercial success, in Kentucky and elsewhere. Overflowing crowds broke the attendance record at Louisville's Rialto theater on the day the film opened. The crowd of 15,000 children and parents required the labor of three box offices and four ticket sellers. The *Louisville Times* reported that "thousands of children from dozens of communities near Louisville came on interurbans, in private conveyances, and school busses to see what Hollywood has done to one of the most lovable characters ever created by a Kentucky author." The paper added that this was "proof that interest [in the *Little Colonel*] has not declined with the years."[26]

The film touched off a flurry of commercial activities associated with the *Little Colonel*. Since 1909, fans of the series had enjoyed Little Colonel paper dolls and *The Little Colonel Good Times Book*, diaries in which they recorded their life's pleasures. The advent of the movie, however, prompted Louisville stores to open Little Colonel shops for juniors and to offer free admission to the film with a purchase. Nationally, the marketing of the movie included a Little Colonel fashion show in a New York hotel and a Little Colonel shop in Macy's department store. "Little Colonel, Incorporated," granted licenses to twenty-five firms to manufacture Little Colonel clothing and other merchandise, including dresses, hats, shoes, pocketbooks, handkerchiefs, jewelry, toothbrushes, toys, games, dolls, and watches.[27]

The film was an undeniable commercial success, but several local film columnists decried the plot's divergence from the book. The acid-penned critic from the *Courier-Journal* claimed that the movie was "a true Hollywod [sic] conception and as little like the originally universally popular stories as Lionel Barrymore is like a Kentucky colonel except as he is pictured on liquor labels." He added a disclaimer, however: "Of course, in my day I have seen the Kentucky colonel's physiognomy change considerably." He also noted that the movie, unlike the book, was set in 1870, portraying "a South of the era of military drama of heroic statute." A critic for the *Louisville Times* was kinder, asserting that the film "seemed to be representative of the traditions of the State." Like the *Courier-Journal* critic, he believed Lionel Barrymore's portrayal of the colonel to be stereotypical and "a composite of all the mint-juleped Kentucky Colonel's of fiction."[28]

The critics' preoccupation with the portrayal of the colonel reflects their recognition of the icon's powerful representation of their state. As the *Courier-Journal* writer intimated, however, like so many of Johnston's other characters, the "Kentucky colonel" was a stereotype with a factual basis. Kentucky native and distinguished journalist Arthur Krock once noted that although the city of Louisville "had its quota of distinguished soldiers on both sides [of the Civil War]" it was the characteristic features of the city's numerous former Confederates that became the hallmarks of the prototypical Kentucky colonel. Their signature look: "long-legged, slender, tall, mustachioed and goateed," and the intense rhetorical devotion to the Confederacy they delivered in a soft "Bluegrass accent" soon came to stereotype much of the state's population. Only the emerging image of the feuding mountaineer challenged its personification of Kentucky. This icon became more than just a set of physical characteristics, however. As one historian has noted, many people in the late nineteenth century "trusted Kentucky colonels as the repositories of not only mint juleps but of old-fashioned virtues." The colonel icon itself came to represent both the gracious lifestyle and the conservative white values of the Old South. The Kentucky colonel was nothing less than a cultural expectation for outsiders. In 1905, a Boston couple attending horse races in Lexington stopped a local man, General H. W. Gentry, and asked if he might pose for a photograph so that they might have an image of "some typical southern gentleman of renown" to take home with them.[29]

Other Kentuckians took issue with Johnston's glorified Bluegrass colonel. Irvin Cobb, a journalist and writer for the *Saturday Evening Post*, sought to transcend the typical literary characterizations of southerners. The son of a Confederate veteran, Cobb shied away from both those "drawn from a more or less top stratum of southern life, or else from a bottom-most stratum—either he purported to be an elderly unreconstructed gentleman of highly aristocratic tendencies residing in a feudal state of shabby grandeur and proud poverty on a plantation gone to seed; or he purported to be a pure white of the poorest." He wrote about his signature character, Judge Priest, in a series of over twenty-five widely read short stories, set in his western Kentucky hometown of Paducah.[30]

In *Back Home* and in subsequent volumes, Cobb reminded readers that most southerners were not "venerable and fiery colonels with frayed wrist bands and limp colors." Nor were they "snuff-dipping, ginseng-digging clay eaters." They were instead "just such folk as allowing for certain temperamental differences—created by climate and soil and tradition and by two main contributing causes: the ever-present race question and the still living and vivid memories of the great war." He desired more than anything else "to set down on paper, as faithfully as [he] might, a representation of [Kentuckians] as [he] knew them." Furthermore, Cobb sought to capture another kind of Kentuckian, distinct from the Bluegrass or mountain variety, from the western portion of the state "that gave to the nation among others, Abraham Lincoln and Jefferson Davis." The product of Cobb's revisionism was the "cracker barrel sage," Judge Priest, who, rather than donning crisp white suits, appears "paunchy and rumpled in a worn black alpaca coat and baggy white linen trousers."[31]

The Judge Priest stories are a mixture of trickster tale and morality play, as the good-natured and morally centered judge outwits his nemeses through feigned ignorance. Though he represents a more down-to-earth portrait of a Kentuckian, he is as Confederate as the more-rarified colonels he is contrasted with. He smokes cigars and drinks bourbon liberally, frequently recollects war battles, and continues to thwart wayward Yankees. His closest associates are also typical of southern literary characters, including a fellow nostalgic Confederate veteran, who still wears his forty-year-old army-issue jacket, and Jeff, an African American "manservant, valet, and guardian," who speaks in dialect. Adding a layer of complexity that evaded most white local-color writers, however, Cobb allows that Jeff was happier in freedom than under slavery. Despite the fact that on one occasion Jeff marches alongside Judge Priest in a Confederate veterans' parade, his "private personal convictions," Cobb notes, "were not with the late cause which those elderly men in gray represented."[32]

Likewise, the popularity of John Uri Lloyd's 1900 novel, *Stringtown-on-the-Pike: A Tale of Northernmost Kentucky*, came in part from his diverse collection of characters. Lloyd sought to capture Civil War–era life in tiny Stringtown, modeled after the town of Florence, which lies just across the Ohio River from Cincinnati. Although this northern Kentucky community lacks the pastoral romance of Pewee Valley or a Bluegrass plantation, in Lloyd's writings it boasts its fair share of stock characters indigenous to the commonwealth: "Kentucky Gentlemen," superstitious African Americans, and run-of-the-mill poor whites. The most reprehensible character in the novel is a feuding mountaineer, known only as "Red Head," who is so despised and distrusted in Stringtown that even local African Americans refer to him as "East Kaintuck scrub stock." The *New York Times* lauded the diversity of characters, claiming that "no two have the same manner, and the spice of variety is of high quality, though all the tales smack strongly of Kentucky soil." Lloyd, perhaps more than any other white chronicler of postwar Kentucky, tried to make his African American characters multidimensional. He tells much of *Stringtown-on-the-Pike* through the eyes of Cupe, a former slave who remains a loyal servant to the man who has freed him. Although Cupe speaks in dialect and is beset by ignorance and a seemingly endless number of superstitions, locals come to rely upon his "sign reading," and by the end of the novel his folk wisdom proves superior to modern empirical evidence.[33]

Like some other turn-of-the-century Kentucky authors, Lloyd stressed community discord during the Civil War. *Stringtown-on-the-Pike* is filled with stories of Federal troops seeking out rebel traitors, southern sympathizers stealing south in the night to join the Confederate army, and a father who grieves the death of his sons, one who died in a gray uniform and the other in blue. A reviewer from the *New York Times* commended Lloyd's treatment of his wartime setting, claiming: "The temptation to make a war story and to display partisan feeling has been resisted, as has also the common tendency to 'high color' for everything that war touched in the border states." Though Lloyd's novel was patently fictional, early twentieth-century reviewers and readers alike took satisfaction in its apparent historical veracity and realism. "It is easy to imagine," praised one reviewer, "[that the book] is the outcome of actual occurrences which memory has cherished through many years and finally committed to paper for the sole pleasure of telling." Another man who visited the Florence area in the author's company was delighted to find that the residents "seemed as if they had stepped out of Lloyd's books." He found them to be "warm-hearted, true, loyal to tradition and to Kentucky, hospitable but independent, careless alike to form and conventionality, they cared not whether they were living in the last century or the present." In short, they seemed the very picture of "living history."[34]

Although it was white authors who most often mined Kentucky as a nostalgic setting for their fin de siècle literature, the most famous African American author of the day also turned to the Bluegrass State for his story lines. Paul Laurence Dunbar, "poet laureate of the Negro Race," as Booker T. Washington anointed him, regularly cast Kentucky as a setting and Kentuckians as characters in his poems and short stories. Dunbar's father, Joshua, and mother, Matilda, were born into slavery in the Bluegrass State. Joshua escaped to Canada and later returned to the United States during the Civil War to enlist in the 55th Massachusetts Regiment. He and Matilda met and married in Dayton, Ohio, after the Civil War, where Paul was born in 1872.

Though he lived his entire life in the North, Dunbar drew the inspiration for much of his writing from the stories his father and mother told him about their days in bondage in Kentucky as he built a literary reputation for his ability to capture black southern rural folkways and present them to a white reading public. In one of his early collections, *Folks from Dixie* (1898), for example, Dunbar sets five of the volume's twelve stories in the commonwealth.[35]

As might be expected, as an African American author, Dunbar had a more nuanced take on Kentucky's Civil War and Reconstruction era history than did his white counterparts. His writing conveys both a fondness for the state and a recognition of its heritage of slavery and poor treatment of African Americans in the postwar period. Nearly all of his Kentucky-based tales take place after the Civil War, and, although slavery no longer exists and African Americans are free, they bear a real attachment to the charms of southern life often associated with the Old South. Dunbar's poem "After a Visit," for example, offers evidence that African Americans as well as whites associated "Old Kentucky" with hospitality and pleasantries:

I be'n down in old Kentucky
Fur a week er two, an' say,
'T wuz ez hard ez breakin' oxen
Fur to tear myse'f away.
Allus argerin' bout fren'ship
An' yer hospitality—
Y' ain't no right to talk about it
Tell you be'n down there to see

Wife, she sez I must be crazy
'Cause I go on so, an' Nelse
He 'lows, "Good gracious! Daddy,
Cain't you talk about nuthin' else?"
Well, pleg-gone it, I'm jes' tickled,
Bein' tickled ain't no sin;
I be'n don in ole Kentucky,
An' I wan o' go ag'in.

Despite the many factors that drove African Americans out of Kentucky after the Civil War, Dunbar suggests that there were attractions that called them back, if only to visit.[36]

Dunbar did, however, present issues of slavery and historical memory with more subtlety than did his white counterparts. In his short story "A Family Feud," he describes his character "old Aunt Doshy," who had been a house servant in "one of the wealthiest of the old Kentucky families," as "inordinately proud of her family" and "never weary of detailing accounts of their grandeur and generosity." Acknowledging the ability of time to obscure the harshness of the past, Dunbar asked: "What if some of the harshness of reality was softened by the distance through which she looked back upon them; what if the glamour of memory did put a halo round the heads of some people who were never meant to be canonized?" The tale continues as Aunt Doshy reminisces about another house slave, Aunt Emmerline, who oversteps her bounds in order to reunite two feuding families and to save the relationship between her alienated master and his son. Although Dunbar never romanticizes slavery as an institution, he certainly portrays a fondness and kindness between master and bondswoman similar to that portrayed in plantation school literature. Furthermore, the fact that many of his Kentucky-based stories feature free blacks who had been house servants and had had close, amicable relationships with their masters underscored the widespread popular recollection that slavery had been a kinder, gentler institution in the commonwealth.[37]

The theme of formerly enslaved Kentuckians and their struggle to both remember and forget the painful aspects of their past was one that Dunbar explored in another short story, "Nelse Hatton's Vengeance." In this tale, Hatton is a former Kentucky slave, now a well-respected and financially comfortable resident of a small Ohio town. One day, a disheveled white "tramp" shows up at his doorstep asking for assistance. After Hatton invites his unfortunate visitor in for a meal, the latter explains in bitter tones that he is returning south after "five years of fruitless struggle" in the North, which is not "the place for a man with blood in his veins." Referring to old sectional animosities, he explains, "I thought that I was reconstructed; but I'm not." He adds, "My State did n't need it, but I did." This comment leads the two men to discover that they are both native Kentuckians. The white visitor is not surprised, saying, "There's no mistaking our people, black or white, wherever you meet them. Kentucky's a great State, sir. She did n't secede; but there were lots of her sons on the other side. I was; and I did my duty as clear as I could see it." Hatton replies: "That's all any man kin do . . . an I ain't a-blamin you. I lived with as good people as ever was. I know they would n't 'a' done nothin' wrong ef the'd 'a' knowed it; an' they was on the other side."[38]

As the conversation continues, the two men discover that they are former master and slave. Hatton's generous spirit is, not surprisingly, challenged by this revelation as he struggles with the memories of the cruelties his former master inflicted upon him. Although he briefly considers wreaking vengeance and violence upon his visitor, Hatton is moved to sympathy by the diminished circumstances of his former oppressor. In pity and perhaps with not a little satisfaction that the bottom rail is now clearly on top, he vows instead to send the disheveled white man back to Kentucky "a gentleman." He sends him away in his best suit with a pocket full of money, charging him to "go home—go home; an' ef there's any of the folks a-livin', give 'em my love, Mas' Tom."[39]

Along with Nelse Hatton, several of Dunbar's Kentuckians were, like his own parents, expatriates who left the state after the war to seek better economic opportunities and less oppression. Kentucky, however, is never far from their minds or their hearts. In his tale "The Finish of Patsy Barnes," Eliza Barnes resettles in Ohio with her son Patsy, who misses his old home and its horses and stables so much that he dreams of fleeing back to the Bluegrass. Dunbar portrays his African American Kentucky natives as attached to their home state and privy to its charms while simultaneously underscoring the state's troubling past. More than his white counterparts, Dunbar's black Kentuckians bear the emotional scars left by their time in slavery and endure indignities in both the post-Reconstruction South and the supposedly more egalitarian North.[40]

Though Dunbar usually managed to explore themes of racial injustice in subtle, nuanced tones that did not detract from the feel-good nature of his stories, he was not afraid to offer more direct critiques of practices like lynching. In "The Tragedy at Three Forks," residents of a central Kentucky town seethe with anger when the home of a local white family burns to the ground. Blame quickly turns racial: "Look a here, folks, I tell you that's the work o' niggers. I kin see their hand in it," asserts one white resident. The county paper screams: "NEGROES! UNDOUBTEDLY THE PERPETRATORS OF THE DEED!" Townspeople wrongly accuse two innocent black itinerant laborers of the arson, and the county attorney forces them to confess to the crime. They meet their demise, "dancin' hemp" at the hands of a frenzied lynch mob. For added complexity, Dunbar tells the story through the eyes of the white teenage girl who actually set the fire. Many of Dunbar's short stories contain an optimism that more than counteracts his understated critiques of the turn-of-the-century racial status quo, but "The Tragedy at

Paul Lawrence Dunbar's "Nelse Hatton," rendered by E. W. Kemble, in *Folks from Dixie*. Dunbar's African American Kentuckians carried both nostalgic and painful memories of their enslavement in the Bluegrass State. Courtesy of Special Collections, University of Kentucky Libraries.

Three Forks" serves as a rare, unsparing look at one instance of a fevered miscarriage of justice in a small Kentucky community.[41]

Dunbar's writings enjoyed wide popularity and great critical acclaim among white and black readers during the course of his short career. His writing made use of the same literary conventions such as "negro" dialect that literary critic and Dunbar admirer William Dean Howells referred to as "delightful personal attempts and failures for the written and spoken language," which could also be found in the stories of Annie Fellows Johnston, Thomas Nelson Page, and Joel Chandler Harris. Illustrated by artist E. W. Kemble, his books included images such as the turbaned Old Aunt Doshy and a Sambo-like Nelse Hatton that seemed at odds with his nuanced, well-rounded, written characterizations of them. In short, his books tapped into literary tropes that so often portrayed African Americans as pleasantly ignorant, submissive, and satisfied with their second-class status, while simultaneously offering up what Howells described in his introduction to Dunbar's *Lyrics of Lowly Life* as the uncanny ability to "feel the negro life aesthetically and express it lyrically . . . and to have represented him as he found him to be with humor, with sympathy, and yet with what the reader must instinctively feel to be entire truthfulness." This quality was what made Dunbar's writings so accessible to and popular among his white and black readership alike, until some members of the New Negro movement began to criticize them in the 1920s for painting too roseate a picture of black southern life. Dunbar offered a more complicated assessment of the antebellum, Civil War, and postemancipation eras in Kentucky, but his portrait of the state certainly bore its own sense of nostalgia and charm.[42]

It is clear that Kentuckians, and not just outsiders, found comfort in the literary scenes of their past. When Harrodsburg native Hannah Pittman published her novel *The Belle of the Blue Grass Country* in 1906, the *Lexington Leader* lauded the author's depiction of immediate postwar scenes of the Bluegrass region, including local customs of horse races, barbeques, fairs, and stagecoach travel. More important, the paper noted, the book was "especially rich in memories of the Negroes just after the war, before freedom had time to destroy that intimate and so often loving relationship of master and servant, now often usurped by the 'high faluting,' colored ignoramus and the omnipresent servant problem." "It is excellent," surmised the *Leader*, "that those who knew the old time 'darky' should preserve his good qualities in such charming prose."[43]

Even as the nation took issue with the decline of contemporary, lawless Kentucky, readers across America escaped modern confusion in the glories of its supposedly Confederate past. Once maligned, the state's Confederate identity, and the romantic and secure past with which it was inextricably intertwined, appeared to be the antidote to the commonwealth's contemporary ills. This nostalgic reflection became one of the few positive associations ascribed to Kentucky. Alluding to the fleeting nature of that manufactured existence, however, Annie Fellows Johnston warned readers of her 1929 autobiography that the Pewee Valley of Cavaliers and Confederates had disappeared: "A thousand times I have been asked, 'Is Lloydsboro Valley a real place?' and this is always my answer: You will find it on the map of Oldham County under the name of Pewee Valley, but you will never find it along any road whatsoever where you may go on a pilgrimage, for the years have stolen its pristine charm and it is no longer a story-book sort of place."[44]

However fleeting the basis for *The Little Colonel* may have been, the stories themselves proved incredibly resilient. Despite the fact that the books went out of print in the mid-twentieth century as their racial politics became less acceptable, they retained a place in the public imagination. Thousands of fans from around the world came to visit the little town of Pewee Valley even as late as 1968, when an elderly woman from Selma, Alabama, rode up to "The Beeches" in a taxi to fulfill her childhood dream of visiting the Little Colonel's home. To her, as to many children, the *Little Colonel* stories were all the more realistic because they had an actual point of origin. Like other visitors, she remembered that the land of the Little Colonel—filled with moonlight, magnolias, Confederates—was in Kentucky.[45]

Whether about debonair colonels, Bluegrass belles, or lackadaisical black servants, nostalgic literature that came out of Kentucky in the early twentieth century further linked the state with both a southern and a Confederate past. Genuine or not, these individuals seemed real to readers, if only in their imaginations. Annie Fellows Johnston expressed this conviction herself when she wrote of her *Little Colonel* characters: "If they haven't all lived as and where the stories depict, they have at least lived in somebody's personal experiences and Memory shows them many a time, trudging through the scenes of my own past."[46]

A Manifest Aversion to the Union Cause

WAR MEMORY IN KENTUCKY, 1895–1935

In July 1895, only months before the Grand Army of the Republic (GAR) encampment came to town, Louisville's Confederate community unveiled its monument to the southern dead. The massive seventy-foot statue crowned with an eight-foot-tall bronze infantryman was the product of an eight-year effort by the Kentucky Women's Monument Association, a group headed by a group of elite Confederate women. To fund its endeavor, the monument association hosted many social events, including "lawn fetes," bazaars, a "kindersymphony," and even a stage production of *Ben-Hur*, based on the novel by Federal army general Lew Wallace. Although the fund-raising events featured clear sectional overtones, an 1890 article in the *Louisville Courier-Journal* urged all Louisvillians to attend one of the association's musical programs, casting the effort to build the monument as one of civic pride. "This is one of the few cities of its size which has no commemoration of the civil war," stated the newspaper. "Those in charge of the movement to erect the monument should receive public support not simply for that cause, but further with the idea that they will arouse a public spirit in the city that will lead our people to erect other monuments."[1]

Only a year later, more than 3,500 people gathered in Nicholasville, Kentucky, a small town just south of Lexington, to dedicate a more modest Confederate monument. Jefferson Oxley, a Confederate veteran, and his fellow members of the Jessamine County Memorial Association had initiated their effort in 1880. After sixteen years of low-yield fund-raising, they scraped together the nearly $1,500 necessary to purchase an unclaimed bronze figure of a Union soldier that a monument company sold them for a reduced price. In a move that could be seen as representing the course the state had followed for the past thirty years, the monument association had the Federal figure altered to appear to be Confederate and placed it atop an eleven-foot granite pedestal that sat on the lawn of the Jessamine County courthouse.[2]

PARTISANS OF THE southern cause erected monuments, sometimes imposing, sometimes modest, to the Lost Cause between 1895 and 1925 in greater numbers than ever before. From Fulton on the Mississippi River to Owingsville in the Appalachian foothills, twenty-seven Confederate monuments sprang up on courthouse lawns, in town squares, and in cemeteries across Kentucky. By contrast, in the same time period, white Union partisans built only three monuments. The lopsided numbers are indicative of the way that the Confederate war memory, through organizations, national reunions, and other means, came to dominate Kentucky's historical landscape well into the twentieth century. Within a memorial climate that increasingly focused on forgetting past grievances and reuniting with old enemies, the Lost Cause won the day. Yet the monuments and public displays obscured the strident efforts of other Kentuckians who sought to subvert Confederate historical interpretation and clarify the Union war record. Although their efforts were less successful and therefore ultimately less memorable, they stand as testimony to the active historical conversation surrounding Kentucky's role in the Civil War into the twentieth century.[3]

After 1895, the prevailing theme in Civil War memory in Kentucky matched the national mood of white reconciliation that was so evident at the Louisville GAR encampment. Like many Americans, Kentucky whites symbolically "forgot" past grievances and promoted sectional reconciliation. With its emphasis on nationalism, the Spanish-American War aided Kentuckians in this process. A Lexington paper described the unifying effects of the war when it described Memorial Day 1899 as "particularly significant." "Southern blood having been spilled in the defense of the flag," reasoned the paper, "the Southland will now and hereafter lay claim to her share of the day's sorrows and glories." The frequent soldiers' reunions around the turn of the century regularly featured symbolic crosspollination between Confederate and Union veterans, with both sides routinely inviting the other to participate. In 1898, for example, the surviving members of Morgan's command traveled en masse to the national GAR encampment in Cincinnati, where the 7th Ohio Cavalry, whose members Morgan's men had captured during the war, hosted them as special guests.[4]

Several years later, Morgan's men returned the favor when they invited Colonel Theodore Allen of the 7th Ohio to camp with them for several days at one of their reunions. After Allen's first night in the camp, one of the Confederate veterans woke him and, proffering a bottle of bourbon, asked if he might like an "eye-opener" before breakfast. "I am sure the old Federal soldiers will agree this hospitable method of waking up a 'Yankee' soldier is much better than the way 'Morgan's Men,' had of doing during the war when they often woke us up by the crack of revolvers," Allen wrote good-humoredly in the GAR publication *National Tribune*. Speaking of Kentucky's distinctively divided past, Allen, a Covington resident, expressed thankfulness for living "on the border line," where he was glad of the "opportunity of saluting not only the men who wear the Grand Army button, but also frequently the veteran who wears the button of the Confederate Soldier."[5]

When Unionists and Confederates honored their respective dead only days apart at the end of May and beginning of June, they increasingly tempered their language with wishes for national peace. Members of the Kentucky GAR asked Unionists "not to forget the graves of these heroes who laid in tears and blood the basis of a united and happy nation, for all the future." Likewise at the Lexington centennial celebration of Robert E. Lee's birth, Captain R. H. Fitzhugh declared that Lee was "no longer a Virginian, no longer a Confederate," but the "heritage and glory of the nation, and in him are we, North and South, now made one." Maintaining harmonious feelings on such occasions seemed more about present concerns than about which army a soldier had fought for, forty years earlier. The man in charge of arranging the annual state Confederate reunion, though it was to feature some of the most prominent politicians in the state, remarked that they intended to have "friends of both political faiths present and Federal Soldiers as well as Confederates" and warned that any attempt "to discuss religion or politics" would be "promptly stopped."[6]

In this atmosphere of accord and mutual respect among white Kentuckians, however, white Confederates continued to be more successful in casting Kentucky's war memory as their own. One clear sign of this was the popularity of national Confederate veterans' and memorial associations. Groups like the Confederate Association of Kentucky, founded in Louisville in 1888, and the Confederate Veterans Association of Kentucky in Lexington, begun in 1890, served both a social and a benevolent function, providing funds or funeral expenses for aged and dying comrades. These organizations also became the public face of the Confederate cause, especially as they began to fold into the larger regionwide United

Confederate Veterans (UCV) following its formation in 1889. Kentucky males a generation removed from the fight found a home in the Sons of Confederate Veterans, an organization founded in 1896. Even with aging membership and natural attrition, the groups remained strong well into the twentieth century. These groups were so prominent that in Lexington they had their own "Confederate Room" in the Fayette County courthouse.[7]

The greatest testimony to the strength of the UCV in Kentucky came when the state leaders convinced the national organization to hold its annual reunion in Louisville in 1900. Delegates from Louisville's George B. Eastin Camp attempted to secure the event for two years at the Nashville and Atlanta reunions before finally achieving success at the 1899 gathering in Charleston. Serving as the delegation spokesman in Atlanta, Basil Duke offered a particularly impassioned plea for meeting on the banks of the Ohio: "Louisville is a Southern city. Your sons have helped build it up. Your trade has made it prosperous. . . . It is the greatest Commercial city in the South. . . . We come now to adjure you, not so much by what we have done, but by our love for your cause and our sacrifices for it, to come into our midst and let our people see the men with whom and for whom we fought." He assured them of the gracious hospitality and entertainment that Kentuckians would provide, declaring that the citizens of Louisville knew the "weaknesses of the old veterans." He promised: "We shall not only lead you beside the still waters, but, if you wish—beside the distilled waters also." In 1899, Bennett Young renewed his plea, again couching his appeal within Kentucky's southern identity and its sacrifice for the Confederacy. "Come to Louisville," he proclaimed, "and we will give you a reception that will thrill your gallant hearts, and will make you always love Louisville and Kentucky, who did not fight for their homes, but fought for you."[8]

Once Louisville finally procured the reunion in 1899, the city began preparing feverishly for the event. Citizens built a cavernous reunion hall, dubbed "Confederate Mecca," which stood on the banks of the Ohio River, only yards away from the former site of Fort Nelson, where Federal guns had kept vigil over the city during the war. By March 1900, Louisvillians had raised over $35,000 in private subscriptions and had received a $20,000 contribution from the city council, an amount that ex-Confederates noted with pride was greater than the contributions made by cities of Nashville, Atlanta, or Charleston.[9]

Although Confederate veterans and their families spearheaded the effort, mounting the reunion became a general civic undertaking for Louisville's white citizens. During the opening days of the event in late May, the *Courier-Journal* printed a special notice that the reunion committee was "extremely anxious" that every house and business along the parade route be decorated in Confederate-colored banners and bunting. The paper advised, "The work can be done appropriately at comparatively little expense, and the effect will add to the impressiveness [of the parade]." Many citizens, regardless of wartime sympathy, were willing to comply since they saw the reunion as a potential financial boon for the city's economy, since the thousands of visiting veterans would rent accommodations, patronize restaurants, and purchase merchandise from local businesses. Although Louisvillians were profit-minded, the city worked to make it possible for people of all financial means to come, by offering train fares and lodging at reduced rates.[10]

The extent of Unionist presence and participation made the Louisville reunion truly remarkable. During the opening night ceremonies, Federal veterans sat conspicuously on the platform in the front of the convention hall. Despite the fact that they were dressed in blue uniforms, they "joined no less enthusiastically than their brothers in gray in the applause which greeted the speakers and music." Union veterans also played an integral part in one of the most unusual events planned by the reunion committee, a reenactment of the battle of Perryville. The staged contest was to take place on the grounds of Churchill Downs and was to feature 1,000 local Union veterans against an equal number of Confederate veterans, each equipped with a rifle and several rounds of ammunition. Lest anyone confuse the reenactment with the original, however, the veterans were to shake hands upon its conclusion, "instead of as in the old time."[11]

Ex-Unionists exerted even greater influence behind the scenes. The Republican-controlled city council appropriated funds for the reunion and ex-Federals were involved with almost every facet of reunion planning. They held committee positions dealing with finance, accommodations, and the decoration and illumination of public buildings. "Half the committees," claimed the *Courier-Journal*, "are partially made up of Union men, and the sons of Union men, and as Southerners have worked more loyally . . . to welcome and entertain their old foes, now become brothers in a greater Southland." The paper continued: "This mingling of the Blue with the Gray will be the feature of the Louisville reunion."[12]

Louisvillians appeared universally to receive the veterans with goodwill. The *Commercial*, Louisville's Republican newspaper, described the sentiments of many Union sympathizers when it exclaimed, "And so we open our doors and our hearts to the followers of Jackson and Lee. They are among friends. They are entitled to the best we have. We welcome them as neighbors, friends, and fellow southerners, as Americans." The *Courier-Journal* echoed the spirit of sectional reconciliation, stating: "So let the flags of the Lost Cause float bravely to-day. Not one [citizen] will be less an American patriot because his heart throbs and his eyes fill at the memories of the camp and march and battle which they revive."[13]

Even though it was located in a border state and was, as one Virginia newspaper put it, "on the remote edge of the Confederacy," southerners treated Louisville as a full partner in the Confederate experience. At a time in which the Lost Cause movement embraced sectional reconciliation in the shadow of the Spanish-American War, some Louisvillians were actually able to use their city's location and its history of divided sentiment to claim an even greater sacrifice on their part. Prominent Confederate Bennett Young made a special case for the valor of border state men. "They had more to lose and less to gain than any others of the men who wore gray," he opined during the Louisville reunion, "and the thousands of nameless graves of these self-exiled heroes scattered among the valleys and along the hillsides of the southern land speak, as only the dead can speak, of chivalrous devotion and unselfish loyalty to the right." So successful was the hospitality of the self-professed "Gateway to the South" that the UCV selected Louisville to host the event again in 1904.[14]

Kentucky women were even more eager to participate in the counterpart organization, the United Daughters of the Confederacy (UDC). Upon the organization's founding in 1895, Kentucky women who had previously belonged to ladies' monument and aid societies formed local chapters of the UDC throughout the state. Between 1898 and 1920, over 5,300 Kentucky women joined the group in seventy towns. From Williamsburg in the southeastern corner to the northern towns along the Ohio River, from the large chapters in the cities of Lexington and Louisville to more modest chapters in dozens of western Kentucky towns, the UDC quickly became the civic activity of choice for women who had any connection, by way of father, brother, or husband, to the dead Confederacy.[15]

Due largely to the sheer scope of its activities, the UDC played a much larger role than the UCV in shaping Kentucky's Confederate memory in the late nineteenth and early twentieth centuries. The UCV primarily aided the financial, social, and memorial needs of veterans; the UDC undertook public projects that had more far-reaching effects in disseminating the conservative themes and values of the dead Confederacy and the Lost Cause. The women's monument campaigns between 1900 and 1920, which resulted in over twelve new stone shrines across the state, remain the most obvious fruits of their labor. In numerous other ways, thousands of Kentucky women, by putting Confederate history and ideals into public school classrooms, children's groups, and literature, helped shape the way future Kentuckians viewed the state's Civil War history.

The UDC in Kentucky and throughout the South wrapped potent historical and political messages in a cloak of upper-class femininity. In a time when women, especially those in the South, had few entrées into the public sphere, historical work was an acceptable and even expected task accorded them by men. As Karen Cox writes, they sought to "transform military defeat into a political and cultural victory, where states rights and white supremacy remained intact." Women in Kentucky often used UDC meetings to talk about their own wartime experiences, to present southern historical sketches, and to pay tribute to the sacrifices southern women made for the Confederacy.[16]

The UDC considered instilling veneration of the Confederacy into future generations one of its most important tasks. The group sponsored several chapters of the Children of the Confederacy, a national group designed to instill in young southerners patriotic and historical reverence. Largely confined to elite children, this organization offered its members a mixture of indoctrination of Confederate precepts and recreation. At one meeting of the James M. Graves chapter in Lexington, children learned of the daring deeds of John Hunt Morgan from one of his staff members, after which they answered roll call by mentioning a life incident or heroic deed of the celebrated general. Later, they enjoyed dainty treats, like ice cream forts and cakes colored with hues of the Confederacy, and played tetherball, ping pong, and croquet.[17]

The UDC's educational efforts were not limited to elite children, however. In 1901, the Lexington chapter installed pictures of Robert E. Lee in every public school in the city. Later that year, the UDC held a public ceremony in which the members presented the same schools with portraits of Jefferson Davis. In 1904, the Georgetown UDC chapter sponsored a contest for both pupils and teachers—the student with the best essay on Jefferson Davis received a medal, and teachers were honored for answering such questions as "What is the Doctrine of State's Rights?" "What is Rebellion? Is it ever Justifiable?" and "What is Secession?" By the 1905 state convention, the UDC professed to be "more interested in actual historical work in Kentucky than in any subject" and dedicated itself to introducing "nonpartisan" historical supplements to textbooks used in state public schools so that students could have "an impartial account of the conflict between the states."[18]

Confederate educational efforts appeared to have achieved their goals when, in one of the more celebrated conflicts over war memory in Kentucky public schools, thirteen-year-old Laura Galt, a pupil in Louisville's Eighth Ward school, refused to join her class in singing the old Union army standard "Marching through Georgia." Her teacher, Miss Sue Allen, noticed Galt's reticence and demanded she sing. Laura refused and placed her fingers in her ears so as not to hear the offending song. When Allen, in turn, lowered Galt's conduct grade (an action that purportedly could have imperiled her entrance into high school), her parents withdrew her from the school. Galt also leveled charges that her teacher refused to hear essays she wrote in which she praised Confederate soldiers for acts of bravery, leading her parents to lodge a formal complaint with the school superintendent and to retain the services of prominent Confederate attorney Bennett Young. Laura Galt earned applause from Confederates across the South, and her photograph appeared in an issue of the *Confederate Veteran*.[19]

The commonwealth was well represented within the national UDC. Local reporters at the 1901 national meeting in Wilmington, North Carolina, estimated that Kentucky had sent the largest delegation of any state. By that time, Kentucky boasted several well-known figures in the national Lost Cause movement, including Lexingtonian Nancy Lewis Green, who edited the UDC column in the *Confederate Veteran*, and Mrs. Dudley Reynolds, the national president of the Children of the Confederacy.[20]

The Kentucky UDC found the most unusual and powerful vehicle for their ideas in the form of the Louisville-based magazine, the *Lost Cause*. The magazine originally started in 1898 under Ben LeBree, a native Philadelphian who moved to Kentucky in 1878 and made a career of producing southern periodicals such as *The Illustrated Confederate War Journal* and books like *Campfires of the Confederacy*. Unlike the *Southern Bivouac*, the *Lost Cause* devoted as much of its coverage to accounts of southern memorial activity as it did to recounting the actual events of the war. In this regard, it was very similar to the more famous and longer-lived Nashville-based *Confederate Veteran*.[21]

The *Lost Cause* proved especially popular with women, and less than a year after founding it, LeBree sold the magazine to the young and unmarried Florence Barlow, who continued its publication under the auspices of Louisville's Albert Sidney Johnston chapter of the UDC. Unlike LeBree, Barlow had a solid Confederate pedigree. Her father, Captain Milton Barlow, had served with John Hunt Morgan during the war, and her mother, Anastasia, was nearly arrested and imprisoned for aiding Confederate soldiers and prisoners. In addition to her writing ability and business acumen, Barlow was a gifted public speaker. Before managing the *Lost Cause*, she served as a representative for Kentucky businesswomen at the 1893 Chicago World's Fair, where she spoke before the Congress of Women. With the help of Basil Duke's wife, Henrietta Morgan Duke, Barlow managed the *Lost Cause* and filled its pages with her own editorials while supporting herself and her mother with the profits.[22]

Under Barlow and Duke's guidance, the *Lost Cause* became the official organ of the Kentucky UDC. The editors also hoped that the magazine might serve the same function nationally. In the first years of its publication, the magazine's circulation widened and it received an increasing amount of material from other southern states. By 1902, firms from New York to Texas were placing ads in the periodical. Even as the journal's subscription base expanded and it began printing more and more material from other southern states, Kentuckians remained disproportionately represented within its pages, thus demonstrating that Kentucky citizens were heirs of the Confederate legacy and able keepers of the southern past. Furthermore, as the magazine gained a wider circulation, it transmitted this identity to thousands of people throughout the region. In the summer of 1903, Duke resigned her position, leaving Barlow to edit the *Lost Cause* alone, until an illness forced her to retire in April 1904. Thereafter, the magazine quickly faded out of existence.[23]

Like the *Southern Bivouac* before it, the *Lost Cause* provided an important touchstone for pro-Confederate Kentuckians. The periodical provided a place for remembering Kentucky's role in the Confederacy as well as a public forum in which to recount the efforts of Kentuckians to memorialize and celebrate that past, proving especially efficient at the latter. Before the 1899 UCV reunion, it exclaimed: "When the grizzled veterans of the Confederacy wheel through the streets of Charleston, S.C., that spot so dear to the memory of the Lost Cause, Kentucky and Louisville will be there." The *Lost Cause* sought to prove that Kentuckians were anxious to honor the efforts of the entire Confederate experience, beyond the role of their own state. Reporting on a Confederate monument erected in Harrodsburg, the magazine quoted an orator as stating, "There are here 97 graves; of these only two are Kentuckians, 13 are unknown; but it is Kentucky money that builds; and Kentucky love which prompts this memorial."[24]

The *Lost Cause* not only memorialized the dead but also called attention to the power of the Confederacy in the present. The journal asserted that the level of ex-Confederate influence within the state extended beyond the social realm to the political arena. The editors viewed the founding of a Kentucky Confederate veterans' home in 1902 as "new evidence of . . . unified action for the advancement of all matters affecting the Confederate interests in the state." The same year they reported that "more that half of the state offices in Kentucky have been filled by men who were either Confederate soldiers or who suffered by reason of their defense of Southern Rights."[25]

Barlow and Duke also infused the *Lost Cause* with racial politics. In 1900, for instance, they reported that several "old negroes" would attend the Louisville UCV reunion, adding, "There is no stranger sight in history than these faithful colored servants accompanying the master to the field, waiting on him, fighting with him, bearing home his letters and personal trinkets when dead." The faithful black slave enhanced romantic Lost Cause visions of wartime experience nicely. Another, less romantic, dispatch appeared in 1901. Tucked discreetly between an update on the Confederate Memorial Literary Society and an advertisement for Confederate sheet music, the editors announced that "for the first time since the civil war there is not a negro in the North Carolina Legislature."[26]

With these sentiments, Barlow and Duke joined thousands of other women throughout the South in an attempt to define the region's postwar racial order. As with the monuments they constructed and the organizations in which they participated, Kentucky Confederate women expressed opinions in the *Lost Cause* as a way to establish social order on many fronts. Upper-class women, as much as men, experienced the confusion of the New South's social, economic, and racial order. Much like the men in their community, Kentucky's elite white women joined their southern sisters as they "recoiled," as Fitzhugh Brundage has put it, "from the potential social chaos and committed themselves to reestablishing antebellum class and racial privileges." For white women across the South, "the commemoration of the Lost Cause celebrated the traditional privileges of race, gender and class while making them seem a natural and inviolable part of history."[27]

Many of the activities of Kentucky UDC chapters and members relegated African Americans to the subservient roles they had held before the war and quietly celebrated the return of white rule throughout the South. In 1902, Sophie Fox Sea, historian of Louisville's Albert Sidney Johnston chapter, delivered a paper at the annual state convention in Covington that she referred to as a "brief synoptical review of African Slavery in the United States." In it she compared slavery in early New England to that in the antebellum South and found that the latter form was "a benign and blessed institution in comparison." Sea also denounced the antebellum northern press and antislavery literature such as Harriet Beecher Stowe's *Uncle Tom's Cabin*, which had, in her opinion, "persistently exaggerated and misrepresented conditions" by painting a picture of slaveholders as "veritable monsters of oppression and cruelty."[28]

The means by which UDC chapters funded their memorial endeavors were often as racially loaded as the activities themselves. When chapters all over the South contributed items for a sale at a Richmond, Virginia, UDC bazaar to raise money for the Jefferson Davis Arch, the Kentucky delegation planned to sell dolls, both "home-spun Confederate" and "black mammies and pickaninnies." On another occasion, the Nicholasville UDC chapter sponsored a minstrel show that featured "buck and wing dancing" and a "pickinny [*sic*] dance by 40 children." The promotion promised that "the best home talent has been engaged, and all of the new coon songs will be on tap."[29]

Furthermore, in Kentucky, UDC members could rely on wartime opponents to aid them in sentimentalizing slavery. When the Paris UDC solicited contributions for a book they planned to publish, entitled "Our Southern Homes and Their Black Mammies," they engaged the help of outsiders. Alice Bruce Power wrote a Paris chapter member that although she had been "a red hot Unionist" during the war, the subject of their book "certainly appeal[ed] to [her.]" She gladly offered the UDC her happy recollections of slavery on the Flemingsburg farm where she grew up, remembering with pleasure the slave "husking bees" and the "clean white headrags and aprons" they wore. Recalling the slave children she played with, Power declared: "How we did boss them, making them carry the little white ones over the rough places!" Most vivid of all, however, were the memories of the frequent barn dances the black wards of her homestead hosted. "And the fun the darkies did have!" she declared. "Tell me the negroes of today are as happy as they were in those good old days! They, so free from the cares of the morrow, well knowing that 'old Marse and Missus' would provide? Ah, No! I cannot believe it." As this episode suggests, certainly one key to the UDC's popular appeal in Kentucky could be found in the fact that its racial politics resonated well beyond its Confederate base.[30]

Nothing is more revealing of this than the Lexington chapter's successful protest of a traveling production of *Uncle Tom's Cabin*. By the early twentieth century, traveling troupes performing Harriet Beecher Stowe's story were among America's most popular entertainments. Charles Scott, the manager of Lexington's Opera House, booked the show regularly, and it played to sold-out crowds of both white and African American theater-goers. In 1902, Lexington UDC officers drafted a petition requesting that Scott no longer book the play. Claiming that it was "injurious to the community," they asserted that both the production and the novel on which it was based "present[ed] a picture of slavery in the South that is essentially false—false because it presents what was rare and exceptional as normal and typical." Granting that there might have been some instances of cruelty under slavery, they believed that relations between master and slave were usually "kindly and mutually beneficial." The officers supported this contention by noting that when southern men left for war, leaving slaves as "protectors and breadwinners" for southern women, bondsmen were nothing but faithful and devoted to their "helpless charges."[31]

The rationale that the Confederate women gave for suppressing the production was another instance in which Confederate memorial activity was consumed not only with the memory of the war but also with the memory of southern life before it. The UDC wanted to vindicate the Lost Cause as well as the southern man's role as slaveholder. Lexington and its environs had been a "slaveholding community," they argued, and not necessarily by choice. Slavery, the UDC claimed, was "a most burdensome legacy," left to their fathers and grandfathers "by those of bygone days." "For a play to be brought every year to our town which represents the relation of master to slave as one of injustice and cruelty is a slur on the fair name of a generation of kindly and honorable gentlemen," they asserted. The Confederate women also showed concern over the play's influence upon children, noting a particular incident when the promotional parade for the show had passed by a local school during recess, leaving children to gaze upon "two immense bloodhounds, and a life size statue of a negro in chains." "We cannot but feel that the influence left on their plastic minds by such a spectacle as that passing unrebuked through our streets was injurious to them and unjust to the memories of their fathers."[32]

In addition to keeping memories of their fathers and husbands morally pure, the women presented an argument that white Kentuckians—not just former Confederates or slave owners—could embrace. They proposed that in a community like Lexington, "so largely composed of Negroes," it would be dangerous to give them "false conceptions of the lives of their fathers and grandfathers when they were slaves." Doing such, they asserted, would "inflame race prejudice among the large class of our Negro citizens." This argument carried particular appeal in Lexington, where both the white community and the black community boasted of "good" race relations and were ever aware of anything that might change the precarious stasis.[33]

Had the women of the UDC been as interested in extinguishing the "inflamed race prejudice" as they professed to be, they might have been more worried about what was happening on streets and in towns across the commonwealth than about what appeared on the stage of the opera house. African Americans in the state were still forced to ride in separate train coaches, and in Lexington, though they could ride unsegregated on Lexington streetcars, they had to wait for them in a separate room. Their children attended separate schools. In Lexington, and in Kentucky, as in the rest of the South, whites still relegated them to second-class status. An African American man, who would only sign his letter to the *Lexington Leader* as "Son of Ex-Slave," commented on the UDC's effort, pointing out that white people would not have to worry so much about the battles of the past should they "drop the color line and recognize ability and qualification even if the aspirant is the off-spring of the slave-pen and wears a dusky face." On the matter of cultural productions, he added that "a Negro minstrel, with its Negro dialect, and 'old plantation' melodies and 'memories of bye gone days,' are about as hurtful to the Negro as an Uncle Tom's show ever could be."[34]

Other dissenting opinions came from stranger quarters. One opponent of the UDC's action was Lexington native and Confederate veteran Milt Barlow. A famous Kentucky minstrel whom some considered the "greatest Negro character delineator" of the time, Barlow had himself played the role of Uncle Tom for years. He had made a handsome living as Uncle Tom, and he claimed that the play told the truth about prewar conditions in the South. Furthermore, although related to some members of the Lexington UDC, Barlow asserted that "as a Southerner and a man who stopped a chunk of shell and a Minnie ball in the service of the Confederacy," he believed the UDC to be "open to more criticism than 'Uncle Tom's Cabin,' for its members are doing their utmost to keep alive the sentiments which caused that terrible struggle." "We are one nation now," he announced in a conciliatory tone. "The stars and stripes are just as dear to the men in the South as to those in the North and I think that any organization formed for the purpose of keeping alive the remembrance of those times is to be condemned. It is the duty of every good American to forget."[35]

Opera house manager Charles Scott echoed Barlow's sentiments, replying to the UDC's petition by saying only: "The war has been over about 36 years." Scott's pithy remark struck straight at the organization's raison d'être of remembrance. When pressed, he later explained that he did not personally care for *Uncle Tom's Cabin* but noted: "White people patronize the show even more so than the colored people and fill the house every time it is given and send their children as well, and I do not see why I should not furnish such attractions when there seems to be a demand for them."[36]

Many people, however, applauded the effort of the Lexington chapter, which was, according to the *Lexington Leader*, "flooded with letters of encouragement and approval." In Louisville, the Albert Sidney Johnston chapter called *Uncle Tom's Cabin* "libel upon a Southern institution, a medium of incalculable perversion of history and tradition, thereby impressing as an object lesson upon the uninformed minds of children today and generations of children yet unborn a false conception of the institution of slavery as it really existed, and poisoning with distrust and resentment what should be amicable relations existing between the races." They pledged to join their Lexington sisters in "every feasible plan for the abolishment of the nuisance."[37]

Chapters throughout the South rallied around the Lexingtonians' effort. A Little Rock, Arkansas, chapter followed Lexington's example and requested that their local theater not show the play again. The members of the Cape Fear, North Carolina, branch lauded the Lexingtonians' "beautiful devotion and courageous loyalty to the old South" and resolved that "the Daughters of the border land of Kentucky [shall] not stand alone in their opinions." Attention and encouragement was not limited to southerners or even Confederate partisans. One man from Tacoma, Washington, who claimed to be a Republican and "always a Union man," wrote that though there was some use for the book, any use for the play had "passed away." "Now the play has deteriorated into a farcical and distressing reminder of days that are gone and would best be forgotten."[38]

Though they failed to achieve their objective in 1902, the Lexington Confederate community ultimately renewed its quest. In 1905, the UDC once again petitioned Charles Scott to not book Stowe's work. The local UCV chapter called a special meeting at which members drew up a resolution urging their comrades and their children to boycott the play that "misrepresented" their ancestors. Rather than wage another public relations battle as they had done in 1902, however, they took more direct action and sought to pass legislation that would ban the play in Kentucky. In January 1906, the UDC gathered the support of chapters across the state and began to pressure the state General Assembly to adopt the measure. Members from all corners of the state—from Fulton in the west, Flemingsburg in the east, and Covington in the north—pledged their support for banishing *Uncle Tom's Cabin* from the stages of the Bluegrass State. Together, they appealed to their local politicians to use, as Florence Ward of Grayson, Kentucky, put it, "their vote and influence in our behalf in the blotting out forever from Kentucky the disgraceful 'Uncle Tom's Cabin.'" Moreover, the women realized that by criminalizing the staging of Stowe's play by reason of the social danger it presented, they could prevent the showing of any similar productions in the future.[39]

Meanwhile, Lexington African Americans were using the UDC's argument against incendiary presentations for their own purposes. In January 1906, they protested the scheduled appearance of *The Clansman*, a play based upon Thomas Dixon's novel, which portrayed the purported misuses of "negro domination" in the Reconstruction era. Many saw Dixon's work as an ideological retort to *Uncle Tom's Cabin*, and within a short period of time these two works were vying for the attention of Lexington theatergoers. L. M. Hagood, a black minister from Lexington, complained that Dixon's "nefarious" play glorified the Klan and that his books were "a thousand times more baneful" than *Uncle Tom's Cabin*. "Are we not trying to forget the Civil War?" he demanded. "Are we not trying to mollify its wounds? Why force these old stories open for filthy lucre?" The play's object, he charged, was to "engender race hatred and fling disrepute into the face of the Goddess of Liberty," and he predicted that the production would "inflame the ignorant and dissolute blacks and whites and awaken the bitter memories of hatred days that ought to be forgotten." Although Hagood claimed to support the UDC effort, he equated prohibiting the performance of *Uncle Tom's Cabin* and allowing that of *The Clansman* to "strain[ing] at a gnat and swallow[ing] a camel."[40]

After seeing the play himself, J. E. Hunter, a black surgeon, seconded Hagood's opinion that the play was merely designed to create racial discord and expressed the fear that it might move white southerners to mob violence and lynching. Employing the UDC argument regarding *Uncle Tom's Cabin*, Hunter asserted that *The Clansman* contradicted the "true history" of southern blacks, specifically the notion that black men wanted nothing more than to force themselves upon white women, a theme that Dixon exploited effectively in his work. Hunter countered this by remarking that African Americans had made good Union soldiers as well as "faithful" Confederate servants. "With bleeding hearts," he stated, "the Negroes of this beautiful city most emphatically denounce ... [this] wicked play, as being the greatest curse that has ever been staged."[41]

Despite this protest, *The Clansman* appeared on the opera house stage as scheduled. After one performance, a white reviewer commented on the

divisive effect the production had on the audience as "called forth in varying dominations of the white man over the Negro and the Negro over the
white man." Referring to the segregated seating in the opera house, he remarked that "the momentary applause of the gallery is answered by hisses
from the pit and when the pit applauds the gallery hisses."[42]

Lexington's UDC women, meanwhile, successfully enlisted the support of several state legislators and sent several officers to meet with politicians in Frankfort in person. In March 1906, the state legislature passed
a statute known as the Uncle Tom's Cabin Law, which stated: "It shall be
unlawful for any person to present, or to participate in the presentation
of, or to permit to be presented in any opera house, theater, hall or any
other building under his control, any play that is based upon antagonism
alleged formerly to exist, between master and slave, or that excites race prejudice." Breaking this law was punishable by fines and imprisonment.[43]

Thus did Kentucky Confederates succeed in editing not only the history of Kentucky's role in the war but also the portrayal of the conditions
leading up to it. While affecting all the trappings of conservative southern womanhood, Lexington's UDC women wielded considerable political
power to censor historical interpretations that contradicted their own. As
a token of triumph, Governor Beckham gave the members of the chapter the pen with which he signed the bill and for posterity sent a copy of
the bill, framed with wood from a tree from John Hunt Morgan's family
home, to the Confederate Museum in Richmond.[44]

The Uncle Tom's Cabin Law ultimately became an effective tool for
censoring anything that might challenge the racial hierarchy. In 1910,
Lexington mayor John Skain employed it to bar the showing of the film
of the infamous boxing match between Jack Johnson and Jim Jeffries. He
feared that showing Jack Johnson, the epitome of black masculinity, defeating the "white hope" might disturb the peaceful and amicable relations between "our people" and the "colored race." Meanwhile, minstrel
shows replete with burnt cork faces, "coons," and "nigger talk" continued
to appear all over Kentucky unchallenged.[45]

The blatant white agenda did not, however, preclude Kentucky African
Americans from attempting to utilize the statute for their own purpose.
Although the bill came too late for Lexington's black community to stop
The Clansman, black leaders invoked the bill a decade later when the new-
est incarnation of the work, D. W. Griffith's film *Birth of a Nation*, was
slated to show in the city. The Colored Ministers Alliance and the Colored
Boosters Club, taking a cue from earlier national protests by the NAACP,
protested the proposed showing in Lexington. They were joined in their

sentiments by several white groups, including the Women's Clubs of central Kentucky and the Woman's Christian Temperance Union, as well as by then-mayor James C. Rogers. Despite the protests, the publicity and potential box office profits proved too much to keep *Birth of a Nation* away. City commissioners declared the Uncle Tom's Cabin Law inapplicable to the film or any other motion picture because the artistic medium was "in a nebulous and undeveloped state when these laws were enacted." In the six days it showed at the opera house, it became the best-attended theater attraction in the city's history, with an average of 1,400 viewers at each showing.[46]

As the passage of the Uncle Tom's Cabin Law indicated, one of the most remarkable aspects of Confederate memory in the twentieth century is the level of state sponsorship it received. The amount of power and money the state of Kentucky accorded to honoring Confederate causes was remarkable. The Confederate Home, built in Pewee Valley in 1902, serves as a potent example. When former Confederates decided that their destitute, disabled, and aging comrades needed a place to retire, the General Assembly passed a bill making the Confederate Home a state-supported institution and pledged $25,000 to the building effort. The governor took charge of appointing trustees of the home, and the state planned to set aside $125 yearly for each resident to help cover costs. Notably, the project also received the support of numerous prominent Unionists and Republicans who pledged to contribute to the project. After no fewer than eight towns across the state vied for the honor, the state legislature decided to locate the home in the Louisville suburb of Pewee Valley. The same month, the UDC, with the support of state commissioners, erected a monument to Confederate soldiers at the site of the battle of Perryville to mark a mass grave of unknown soldiers. The state legislature contributed $2,000 to the cost. Like the GAR and UCV reunions held in Kentucky, the unveiling ceremony boasted both Union and Confederate veterans and became an opportunity for symbolic reunion. A monument to the Union soldiers, who actually won the battle, was not erected until 1928, when the U.S. Congress approved funding for it.[47]

In another famous instance of the state providing funds to honor a wartime enemy, the legislature contributed money toward the building of the statue of John Hunt Morgan near the Lexington courthouse. A Lexington businessman and veteran of the Mexican War, Morgan was undoubtedly the state's most famous war figure. He gained the moniker "Thunderbolt of the Confederacy" for his destructive raids behind enemy lines. In an effort to divert Union forces from the front lines, Morgan and his men cut telegraph wires and burned railroad tunnels. His escape from the Ohio penitentiary in Columbus only enhanced his heroic reputation among Confederate sympathizers.[48]

During the war, Unionists had viewed him with a mixture of fear and disdain, as Morgan unleashed his slash-and-burn tactics on both loyal soldiers and citizens. Morgan conducted raids in Tennessee, Indiana, and Ohio but was especially devoted to the idea of rescuing Kentucky from what he saw as enemy occupation. His raiders robbed and looted trains, general stores, and banks in Mt. Sterling and Winchester. In Lexington, the men pilfered hats, boots, watches, money, and, most important, hundreds of valuable thoroughbreds to aid in their forays. In 1864, the raiders set several blocks of the town of Cynthiana ablaze. Basil Duke, Morgan's second in command, later wrote: "An avowal of 'belonging to Morgan' was thought, even in Kentucky, tantamount to a confession of murder and highway robbery." Indeed, the Confederate army itself was in the midst of investigating these "irregularities" in September 1864 when a Union man surprised and killed Morgan in Tennessee. After his death, the Confederate government buried Morgan in Richmond, Virginia, in Hollywood Cemetery. In 1868, Lexingtonians reinterred him in the city cemetery in an elaborate ceremony.[49]

By the early twentieth century, Morgan was a bona fide hero to many Kentucky whites. In 1906, the Lexington UDC embarked on an ambitious effort to gain both local and national financial support for a monument to Morgan. The women initially estimated the cost of the monument at $5,000, but once they decided upon an equestrian design by Italian-born sculptor Pompeo Coppini, the costs began to rise. Early fund-raising efforts included making and selling tea towels and auctioning gavels made from trees from Morgan's family home to UDC chapters around the South. UDC members held a "Dixie Carnival" in Louisville in 1906 and a bazaar the next year, to which urban UDC members donated handicrafts and historic dolls, while the members from rural areas offered hams and turkeys for sale. By far the most rarified fund-raising items, however, were the pieces of Viennese china, which included conserve trays, mayonnaise bowls, and almond dishes, each emblazoned with the likeness of Morgan, which the UDC planned to sell at Lexington retailer Smith & Chicks.[50]

But after years of effort, the UDC had only raised half of the $15,000 necessary to complete the project, at which time the Kentucky Senate voted to appropriate the other $7,500. With 10,000 people crowding the courthouse square and others standing on the rooftops and in the windows

Monument to Gen. John H. Morgan and his Men, and some of the members of the U.D.C. Committee that built it

United Daughters of the Confederacy members unveil the monument to
John Hunt Morgan in front of the Lexington courthouse in 1911.
Library of Congress, Prints and Photographs Division.

of surrounding buildings, the unveiling ceremony, in October 1911, was by any estimation a huge public event. Veterans of Morgan's cavalry paraded through downtown on horseback, while UCV men and UDC women walked and rode in over 100 carriages and cars. During the unveiling, as the shroud fell from horse and rider, the crowd erupted with applause and cheers.[51]

There was no outward sign of public objection to the man who had brought destruction to so many civilians during the war and no mention of the irony that the state on which he had inflicted so much damage and the state whose people he had robbed of thousands of dollars in species and horseflesh had spent many thousands of dollars more to honor him. The only aspect of the memorial that seemed to cause any controversy was its genitalia. Every Kentuckian knew that Morgan's favorite mount had been the legendary mare Black Bess, but the chauvinistic Coppini put accuracy aside, believing that such a manly human subject needed to sit astride a large stallion.[52]

In contrast to the abundant evidence of Confederate heritage, which by the turn of the century could be seen throughout the state, one had to look a little harder to find signs of white Unionism. Organizations for Union veterans, for instance, never achieved the public presence or the social cachet of their Confederate counterparts. Despite the fact that they had successfully attracted the national encampment to the state in 1895, the state's GAR chapters saw membership decline in the twentieth century. In 1895, the year of the Louisville encampment, the Union veterans' group had 219 state posts in the state with 5,703 members. A decade later, however, that number had dropped sharply. The numbers fluctuated, but a report by the state department commander in May 1909 listed only ninety-five posts.[53]

In comparison to the high profile of Kentucky Confederates and their organizations, GAR representation at national events was noticeably, and sometimes embarrassingly, sparse. The turnout of GAR men at the grand parade at the 1911 national encampment in Atlantic City was so low, according to state commander S. D. Van Pelt, that it attracted the attention of those who attended the parade, including representatives from *Collier's Weekly*, who published a photograph showing the whole Kentucky contingent and calling attention to their "thin ranks." Van Pelt wondered at the apathy in Kentucky indicated by the attendance but ultimately blamed the low turnout on high rail rates. Responsibility for the disparity in prominence rested in part with the state's newspapers, which afforded much more space to Confederate meetings and memorial activities than to Union ones. When the UDC and the GAR donated portraits of their respective heroes to Lexington public schools on the same day, even the Republican *Lexington Leader* covered the stories in two separate columns, according the UDC donation twice as much space as the GAR gift. The paper called the UDC ceremony "unique," "an impressive program," and "an important patriotic event." The GAR donation, by contrast, was relegated to the "social and personal" section of the paper, where it was deemed "very acceptable and much appreciated."[54]

The fact that the GAR was a marginal organization in Kentucky did not keep members from trying to exert influence over the interpretation of the Civil War past. In 1902, the historian of the state GAR protested the work by Confederate groups "to get a new and fictitious history of the war and its causes, incidents, and results," which sought to convince young generations of the glory and justness of their cause. Although he allowed that "a brave man may fight heroically for a bad cause, such fact does not make the cause a good one, and that cause which was the War of Rebellion was the cause of an Aristocracy against the Common People—the cause of Human Slavery and Barbarism." Despite such condemnations of slavery, however, the Kentucky GAR still struggled with racism in its own ranks in the late nineteenth and early twentieth centuries. In 1899, after a lengthy internal debate, one state post failed to pass a resolution against the practice of lynching; in 1908, Kentucky department commander Levant Dodge found he had to address the complaints of white members who "chafed at the presence of the colored soldiers in our department." In some places, black and white GAR chapters held separate Memorial Day ceremonies, laying flowers on soldiers' graves in segregated cemeteries. Clearly such divisiveness within its own ranks could only weaken the Kentucky GAR.[55]

Even more noticeable than the weakness of the GAR was the comparative dearth of Union monuments, which seemed to reflect the apathy of Union sentiment. Confederates placed nineteen monuments on Kentucky soil between 1895 and 1910. Unionists erected none. Even more telling was the fact that the greatest infusion of Unionist memory into the state, the restoration of Abraham Lincoln's birthplace, came from outside the commonwealth. Born in a small log cabin on Sinking Spring farm near Hodgenville in 1809, Lincoln lived there until his family moved to a different farm just over a year later. Over the next 100 years, various owners of the Lincoln land and cabin relocated the structure several times, and by 1909, no one was sure exactly where it had stood a century earlier. In 1895, New Yorker Alfred Dennett purchased Sinking Spring farm and the Lincoln cabin, which he dismantled and set up several times, alongside a cabin he claimed was the birthplace of Jefferson Davis, at expositions around the country.[56]

In 1904, Robert Collier, editor and publisher of *Collier's Weekly*, founded the Lincoln Farm Association with the purpose of making Lincoln's homestead a national shrine, to "perpetuate . . . as a birthplace of patriotism" and to attract visitors from all over the country. The New York–based association purchased the cabin for $1,000, shipped it back to the Lincoln farm in Kentucky, and commissioned architect John Russell Pope to design a marble building to house and protect it. The project would be dedicated in time to mark the centenary of Lincoln's birth. Rather than a political beacon of Unionist victory, however, the association intended the homestead to represent national reconciliation. The members hoped that since it lay upon "almost the centre of our population" it would become "the most accessible national shrine . . . the Nation's Commons, the meeting-place of North and South, of East and West, a great national school of peace and unity, where all sectional animosity will forever be buried."[57]

The effort to mark Lincoln's birthplace began and ended largely as a national effort rather than as a Kentucky one. Of the $100,000 the Lincoln Farm Association had raised by 1908, only $4,000 had come from the Kentucky legislature. The state did form a Lincoln Centenary Committee, headed by prominent Louisville Union veteran Andrew Cowan. In the spirit of sectional reconciliation, the committee included some of Kentucky's most esteemed citizens, former Unionists and former Confederates, including Supreme Court justice John Marshall Harlan and Joshua Speed, as well as former Confederates Henry Watterson, J. Stoddard Johnston, and Basil Duke.[58]

In a rare occasion of cooperative interracial memorialization, Kentucky African Americans, too, took part in the centennial remembrance. Governor Augustus Willson appointed a "Negro People's Centenary Committee," after deeming that "the negro people should have honored representatives present to bear witness to their love for Abraham Lincoln and their faithfulness to his memory and to be a part of the great scene just as they are a part of the great life of our country." The committee consisted of several of the most prominent African American leaders in the state, including Charles H. Parrish, head of a Louisville industrial school; physician Edward E. Underwood; and attorney Jordan Jackson.[59]

By including African Americans in the memorial effort, Governor Willson recognized the important place Abraham Lincoln occupied in black memory and sought to bring out in the memorialization "the ideal of blessed humanity which freed a race, and which is such a noble part of [his] life." As in other instances of Kentucky Unionist activity, however, including African Americans did not mean granting them equality. White organizers considered the black committee a separate entity and did not list its members on the state committee's letterhead or even in the official Lincoln Centenary Program. Once again, Kentucky whites relegated African Americans to the status of junior partners within their efforts to remember the Civil War.[60]

The national ceremony featured a Confederate Escort Committee, which stood alongside Union veterans in the ceremony. John Leathers, one of the Confederate veterans involved, considered the event a success and wrote Andrew Cowan afterward that "all passion and prejudice [had] gone with the flight of the years and we are now one reunited people with one flag and one country and common destiny and I think I can safely say that none among the great crowd present at the Lincoln Farm on the 12th were more sincere and honest in rendering tribute to the name and fame of the immortal Lincoln than the Ex-Confederates who were gathered there."[61]

Amid the reconciliationist overtones of the endeavor, the most radical Unionism came from President Theodore Roosevelt. In the keynote address he delivered at the cornerstone-laying ceremony, he celebrated Lincoln, the "homely backwoods idealist," for saving the nation when he freed the slaves. Roosevelt praised the native Kentuckian's "love for the Union," as well as his "abhorrence of slavery," calling him an "apostle of social revolution." In his remarks, Roosevelt brought up a part of Civil War legacy rarely heard in Kentucky, where what little white public memory of Union victory that existed concentrated on its military victory rather than on the social and racial revolution it brought. Roosevelt's mention of the "radical revolution," indeed his celebration of it, was an anomaly in white memory in the state. When completed in 1911, the monument's fifty-six steps, one for each year of the president's life, led up to the columned portico and heavy bronze doors. The end result was an impressive structure that seemed, according to one historian, "a little out of place in rural Kentucky." In 1916, the Lincoln Farm Association deeded the site to the United States, and it became Lincoln National Historical Park.[62]

With the relative absence of Union monumentalizing, conflicting interpretations of Kentucky Civil War history were more clearly and discursively illustrated in several reminiscences and histories published in the late nineteenth and early twentieth centuries. In particular, the work of Nathaniel Southgate Shaler and Thomas Speed illustrates different strands in the web of Unionist memory within Kentucky. Shaler, a Harvard-educated geologist and historian, was one of the most prolific early writers of Kentucky's wartime experience. In 1885, he published *Kentucky: A Pioneer Commonwealth* as part of the American Commonwealth series. In its treatment of the Civil War, the book provides insight into the conflicting impulses of Unionists. Shaler asserted that the "most important point in the history of Kentucky [was] the fact that she alone escaped the contagion of excitement that swept her sister states into hasty rebellion."[63]

Shaler also portrayed the postwar era as one in which wartime ruptures were quickly mended, blessing "the really quick restoration of the civil order in the State and the perfect reunion of the divided people." Mutual admiration and "the fact that both Federals and Confederates played a manly part in the struggle" meant the possibility that "they could wear their laurels and live their lives together without shame. What was left of

A group of African American and white Kentuckians examines what were believed
to be the original logs from the cabin in which Abraham Lincoln was born. The Lincoln
Farm Association briefly displayed the structure in Louisville's Central Park before
sending it on to Hodgenville, where it would become the centerpiece of Hodgenville
commemorative efforts. Matlack Collection, ULPA 1982.01.701.p.
Special Collections, University of Louisville.

the forty thousand who went away into the Southern service came back to
their place in the State sadder and wiser men, yet the better citizens for
their dearly bought experience." According to Shaler, these men occasionally relived "their battles over again in good-natured talk, but each dearer
to the other for the fearful parting of the war."[64]

Nearly a quarter of a century later, however, Shaler revealed in his autobiography that he had grown even more romantic in his opinions of
the Confederacy. Looking back to his wartime experience, he lamented
that in 1861 it had been "evident that the Confederacy was to have what
seemed to be—and indeed was—the flower of our youth and manhood;
nearly all the young men who by their qualities seemed to be the natural
leaders of their generation, cast their lot with the South. There remained
a strong body of the middle-aged and the old, the abler of the generations
that were passing and the youths of the plainer sort, more numerous than
we then judged them to be, whose reason discounted their sympathies;
for it is to be confessed that we all of us were in a sense sympathizers with
the South in our hearts—it was our heads that kept us in the Union."

By the end of his life, the sentimental esteem in which Shaler held the Confederacy had grown even more pronounced. In 1906, he composed a poem for *Atlantic Monthly* about the Orphan Brigade, Kentucky's legendary Confederate military unit. Even as he remembered the Union troops as victors, he praised the brigade for its bravery and dubbed the members the true conquerors: "That legion hath marched by the setting sun: Beaten? nay, victors: the realms they have won are the hearts of men who shall ever hear the throb of their far-off drums." In the course of his historical career, Shaler illustrated the tendencies of postbellum Kentucky Unionists to grow more forgiving and even sentimental toward their wartime enemies.[65]

Not all Unionists were ready to bestow such sentimental respect on the Confederacy. Thomas Speed, a Union veteran and Louisville attorney, was the preeminent apologist for Kentucky's Union war effort. In several forms, he endeavored to refute the "unjust" claims of historians like Shaler that the feats of the commonwealth's Confederates were somehow more valorous. His first effort came in 1897 with a 700-page tome entitled *The Union Regiments of Kentucky*, published by a group of Louisville Union veterans who hoped to sell the volume to raise money for a Union monument in the city. According to Speed, "the propriety of a monument, and the desire to have one erected, has been in the minds of the Union soldiers and their friends continuously." Though Louisville Unionists would not succeed in erecting a monument until 1914, the book stood as an exhaustive account of Union military achievement and one of the few written sources to focus exclusively on the merits of Kentucky's Federal war record.[66]

Complaining that Shaler took "small account" of Kentucky's "splendid contingent" of Union forces while "dwell[ing] with delight in the exploits of Morgan," Speed criticized other late nineteenth-century state histories for exhibiting "a manifest aversion to the Union Cause" or a "purely partisan view of the war period." The Union captain aimed to set the record straight but not to reargue the causes and justification for the war in general. Not desiring to "bring into view any of the asperities, and controversies of that period," this aging veteran simply wanted to correct the record as it related to Union military valor. Speed emphasized the prominent role Kentucky troops had played in the western campaigns and touted other details of Kentucky bravery evident in the U.S. government official war record but omitted from the state's Confederate-tinged homegrown history.[67]

Yet Speed's account intentionally distorted one key aspect of the Union war effort: black participation. The captain did not entirely ignore Kentucky's African American Union troops but instead shunted them to the back of the volume to the appendix. The fact that the state's 24,000 black soldiers do not appear in *Union Regiments* until page 701 is more telling than if Speed had not included them at all. Furthermore, Speed argued that the African American troops, which he underestimated to be only 14,000, had been omitted until the end of the volume because they served as U.S. troops rather than in the "state organization." "As they were never in or connected with the Kentucky regiments," he added, "an account of them in no way belongs to this work, which is a history of the Union state organizations." Speed's calculated effort to exclude the sacrifice of African Americans from the Kentucky Union war effort also signified that three decades after the end of the struggle the role African Americans played in the victory remained stigmatized. Many white Unionists continued to view the participation of black soldiers as a mark of shame.[68]

Speed did not stop at disowning Kentucky's African American Union troops but wrote at length about the Confederacy's use of black manpower to argue that any racial stigma should be shared with the southern military effort. "In regard to the use of negroes as soldiers," he argued, "the attitude of the Southern Confederacy was practically the same as that of the national government. This fact should not be forgotten whenever this subject is considered." He asserted that conscripted African Americans should be considered in the estimation of southern military strength and that the Confederacy went further by using them as army soldiers. "This policy has not been noticed in many histories of the war, but is none the less a fact," Speed stated resolutely. "The attitude of the Confederacy to the policy of using negroes as soldiers in the armies," he declared, "was the same as that of the national government." The fact that the premier white Union history of the war in Kentucky tried but failed to omit the role of and consequences for African Americans said everything about their ultimate vulnerability and the ineffectualness of white Unionist war memory and why it did not succeed in resonating with the public. Unlike the Lost Cause, the Union's victory could not be celebrated without disclaiming its racial implications.[69]

In 1907, Speed reiterated many of these points in the more widely published *The Union Cause in Kentucky*. Once again, however, Speed did not defend the Union cause so much as its army's military prowess, lamenting again that the most popular histories of the state seemed to "celebrate the services and exploits of those Kentuckians who went into the Confederacy, and miserably misrepresent Unionists." He further asserted that there existed "a demand for [his] work," because of the fact that "the

Southern side is already represented in the libraries, and the Union side is not."[70]

Speed's sentiment further emphasized that, in Kentucky, Confederates, even in the eyes of some former Unionists, had achieved what many people saw as the reigning interpretation of Civil War history. Yet, as in *Union Regiments*, although Speed was clearly troubled by what he saw as historical inaccuracies, he showed little concern for the postwar interpretation of Kentucky's Civil War experience outside the military realm. Clearly what was most important to him was establishing the military valor and strength of his fellow Federal soldiers, not the larger significance of a shift toward a pro-Confederate interpretation. His work attempted only partially to correct the state's lapse in historical memory, limiting his challenges to Confederate estimations of wartime performance rather than what the Confederacy had come to represent in the postwar period.[71]

Thus the Confederate effort, uncompromised by excuses and with the benefit of Kentucky's preferred racial politics on its side, came to dominate the state's public memory. Perhaps the greatest example of this was the 351-foot-tall obelisk, which Robert Penn Warren later referred to as "an immobile thrust of concrete," that jutted into the Todd County sky as a monument to the only president of the Confederacy. Several months after the Lincoln Farm Association laid the cornerstone of the Lincoln shrine, members of the Jefferson Davis Memorial Association dedicated seventeen acres of land twelve miles east of the southern Kentucky town of Hopkinsville, near the site of the Confederate president's birth. The idea for a shrine to Davis originally materialized at a 1907 reunion of the Orphan Brigade in Glasgow. There, the aging veterans resolved to make the Davis homestead as "memorable to the South as Lincoln's [was to] the entire nation."[72]

S. B. Buckner, Bennett Young, and S. A. Cunningham, the editor of the *Confederate Veteran*, quickly organized the memorial association and began soliciting contributions for the land and the monument from all over the South. After wartime delays, construction began in 1917 on the obelisk of poured concrete designed to resemble the Washington monument. Rising costs further hampered the building effort, and builders could only complete the project with help from the UDC, which contributed $20,000 to the project, and the Kentucky legislature, which appropriated another $15,000. Confederates dedicated the monument in June 1924 and pronounced that the town of Fairview, as the place of Davis's birth, had become a "Southern Shrine, a spot forever dear to the heart of Dixie."[73]

Noting that most people in Todd County (which was part of Christian County at the time of Davis's birth in 1808) had sided with the Union during the war, journalist Tony Horwitz has described the monument as an example of "'recovered memory,'" in which locals "reclaimed a past of their own creation in which Todd County was staunch rebel territory, a pastoral land of Southern belles and brave Confederates." The key to such creation had been a long time developing. The secret to the monument's appeal, and that of so many other Confederate endeavors in the commonwealth, could be found in a single sentence within the Jefferson Davis Monument souvenir booklet, which claimed that many of the "warmest advocates of the Memorial were sons of Union soldiers and in some instances Union Veterans themselves." In the end, Kentucky appeared Confederate because Davis's monument and the other Confederate memorials in the state represented the sort of history that spoke to grand possibilities lost in the name of defending a beautiful world of the past. This past was more compelling than white Kentuckians' complicated historical choices, replete with too many disclaimers, contingencies, and ambiguities to be inspirational.[74]

On July 4, 1924, less than a month after the dedication of Davis's monument, another Civil War monument was dedicated in the Green Hill Cemetery, in Frankfort, Kentucky. The work of the black Woman's Relief Corps No. 8 of the GAR, it honored African American Union soldiers of central Kentucky. This one was also an obelisk, bearing on one side the seal of the GAR and on the other three sides the names of 142 black soldiers. The modest fourteen-foot limestone shaft would have been dwarfed in the shadow of Jefferson Davis's monument. According to a newspaper report, the monument cost "several hundreds of dollars," which "patriotic citizens of both races" helped raise, and today it stands as one of only four monuments in the nation to honor black Union troops. The black GAR women probably expected few tourists and printed no souvenir booklets. Despite its modesty, however, it provided a potent reminder that long after their state seemed to have joined the Confederacy, Kentuckians continued to write other Civil War histories.[75]

Afterword

In 1980, Robert Penn Warren recalled his childhood growing up in Guthrie, Kentucky, and the "ever-present history" of the Civil War, which continued to hang like a miasma there in the early twentieth century. He reminisced: "I had picked up a vaguely soaked-in popular notion of the Civil War, the wickedness of Yankees, the justice of the Southern cause (whatever it was; I didn't know), the slave question, with Lincoln somehow a great man but misguided. The impression of the Civil War certainly did not come from my own household, where the war was rarely mentioned." He added, "No, I didn't get my impression of the Civil War from home. I got it from the air around me (with the ambiguous Lincoln bit probably from a schoolroom)." This is why it came as a shock when his grandfather, the patriarch of the family, a veteran "who *was* history" to Warren, claimed to have been a reluctant secessionist. "One afternoon," he recalled, "I almost jumped out of my skin when he musingly remarked that he had been a Union man . . . against secession." For Warren, as for many other Kentuckians who grew up under the cloud of a Confederate-tinged history, reminders that their ancestors had conflicted loyalties, and had perhaps even sided with the North, often came as a surprise.[1]

By the mid-twentieth century, however, Confederate identity surfaced within Kentucky only intermittently. Nearly all of Kentucky's Civil War memorials were in place by 1935, and with more soldiers "mustering out" each year, reminders of the Civil War faded in number and intensity. In the Bluegrass State, as in the rest of the South, the Lost Cause movement lost much of its potency. According to Gaines Foster, "Defused and diminished by so many diverse meanings and uses, the Confederate tradition lost much if not all of its cultural power." Yet it continued to exist in the Bluegrass State as a reservoir that white Kentuckians could draw upon whenever they needed to. And when they did, the meaning was clear. In 1966, for instance, at the historic NCAA basketball championship game against an all–African American Texas Western team, University of

Kentucky fans cheered for Adolph Rupp's all-white squad by waving Confederate flags. Once again, Confederate symbols served as a message of the state's racial conservatism.[2]

Another contest over Confederate symbols and their meanings came to a head infamously and tragically in 1995, when two African American teenagers were convicted of shooting and killing a white Todd County man because he had displayed the rebel flag on his pick-up truck. When journalist Tony Horwitz arrived in the town of Guthrie to cover the incident for his book *Confederates in the Attic*, he was surprised to find that in Kentucky the old conflict was "still a shooting war." Perhaps he should not have been surprised, given Robert Penn Warren's assertion that for many of the Guthrie residents he knew in his youth, "the Civil War seemed to have been fought for the right to lynch without legal interference." Although the 1995 incident is the only known modern case in which the contest over Civil War interpretation has turned deadly, it is clear that there is much at stake and that like contested memory in the nineteenth century, much of the debate openly centers around the racial implications of venerating a Confederate past.[3]

In the twenty-first century, Civil War history remains a contested subject within the state. Although school textbooks emphasize the state's neutrality and loyalty to the Union, the Kentucky State Park Service continues to host an annual "Miss Confederacy" pageant on the grounds of Jefferson Davis's birthplace and monument. Contestants are judged on "authentic period clothing, styles and accessories, interviews, and overall appeal," as well as on their answers to questions about how they intend to defend southern heritage. The gift shop sells T-shirts made by the Dixie Outfitters company and other Confederate-themed items. Kentucky newspapers still carry combative letters-to-the-editor, some suggesting that Kentuckians celebrate Confederate Memorial Day, others writing that they "resent this continuing attempt to rewrite history and turn Kentucky into a Confederate state," and still others responding that "Kentuckians should proudly fly the Confederate flag whenever they can and think of that 13th star in the center as being the one representing Kentucky."[4]

In recent years, however, Kentuckians have chosen to recall their state's Civil War memory in more varied and nuanced ways. African American citizens have begun to challenge the symbolism of the past more directly than ever. In 2003, civil rights activists requested that a bronze statue of Jefferson Davis be removed from its place in the state capitol rotunda. The University of Louisville, on whose campus the city's towering Confederate monument now stands, has begun plans to make the space around the statue more broadly interpretive of Kentucky's Civil War experience. When promoting the project to the school's Board of Trustees, Blaine Hudson, head of the university's Pan-African Department, noted what Henry Watterson forgot a century earlier: that thousands of white and African American troops had been stationed in Louisville during the war and that "they were not [t]here as an army of occupation" but as "Union soldiers in a Union city in a Union state." The proposed Freedom Park will include a monument and other exhibits portraying the African American struggle for freedom before, during, and after the war. Hudson expressed the desire to "put all of the historical information on the table and develop an interpretation on the table that reflects as accurately as possible the totality of the Civil War and the late antebellum experience in this area." And in an effort to show that the role of African Americans in the Civil War transcended their status as slaves, a group of African American reenactors who portray members of the 12th U.S. Colored Heavy Artillery Regiment have established their base at the Camp Nelson Civil War Heritage Site, near Nicholasville. In 1864, Camp Nelson became the state's largest recruitment center for African American troops, as well as a destination for the wives and children of black enlistees who sought freedom and protection. Modern efforts to preserve and interpret Camp Nelson tell a complicated story of the Union army as both a beacon of freedom and an instrument of racial cruelty. Although exhibits highlight the bravery of the thirteen U.S. Colored Troops regiments based there, they also portray the horrific incident in which over 100 women and children refugees died from exposure after the camp's commander, Brigadier General Speed S. Fry, forced them out of the camp into freezing temperatures, in November 1864.[5]

The preservation efforts at Perryville, site of Kentucky's largest Civil War battle, are similarly rich and multifaceted. Despite the decisive Federal victory there in 1862, which ended Confederate hopes for rallying thousands of Kentuckians to their cause, Confederate monumentalizing dominated the landscape until 1931. In 1991, the Perryville Battlefield Preservation Association formed and, using a combination of public and private funds and local resources, developed a plan for conservation that has become a model for interpreting not only the battlefield experience but the social and racial context of the community as well. A recent expansion of the grounds includes the site of the former African American community of Sleettown, founded by former slaves and Union veterans.[6]

There is, however, no better evidence of the broadening historical memory than Kentucky's efforts to reclaim Abraham Lincoln on the 200th anniversary of his birth. On one level, it is not surprising that in the

A monument to African American refugees at the Camp Nelson Cemetery in Jessamine County testifies to a broadened Civil War memory in Kentucky at the end of the twentieth century. Photograph by the author.

twenty-first century state officials and citizens alike might be swept up in the national excitement surrounding Lincoln's birthday. But such positive public outpouring does mark a sea change in regard for the sixteenth president—one that even he would recognize if he were to come back to see it. As a presidential candidate in 1860, Lincoln briefly considered making a campaign stop in Kentucky. Though he knew he had no chance of winning the state, he told a friend: "A visit to the place of my nativity might be pleasant," but he followed up this wistful sentiment with a dose of humorous realism when he pondered: "Would not the people lynch me?" A few months later, after winning the presidency and losing Kentucky, Lincoln once again considered returning to his natal state, this time on his trip from Illinois to Washington, D.C. Though he ultimately got only as close as Cincinnati, he had written an address in the event of a stop in the Bluegrass State in which he appealed to Kentuckians to call upon their "Kentucky virtues of consistency, loyalty, and honor" and to remain peaceful and steadfast to the Union. "What Kentuckian, worthy of his birthplace, would not do this," he planned to ask his audience, before asserting his own birthright by proclaiming: "Gentlemen, I, too am a Kentuckian."[7]

In the years and decades following, however, many white Kentuckians bitterly denied any such connection with the heroic president. He may have saved the Union, but he had trampled over their property rights and betrayed their loyalty, and they did not want much to do with him. Memory of Lincoln was, of course, never nonexistent in his home state. But although his Hodgenville birthplace and later his wife's home in Lexington became national historic sites and Kentuckians honored him with a couple of sizable statues (one in the state capitol rotunda and one in front of the Louisville Public library) and made him the namesake of several segregated African American schools, Lincoln mostly remained underappreciated within the commonwealth. Indeed, the Kentucky state legislature waited until 1976 to ratify the Thirteenth Amendment. All of this began to change, however, in the early twenty-first century as the State of Kentucky started plans for celebrating the 200th anniversary of Lincoln's birth. Like official historical organizations around the nation, various entities in the Bluegrass State developed plans for a two-year-long tribute to the revered president. Under the auspices of the Kentucky Abraham Lincoln Bicentennial Commission, historical societies, public libraries, tourist sites, and other civic groups developed dozens of programs, events, and exhibits to mark Kentucky's connection to Lincoln.

The state also developed the Kentucky Lincoln Heritage Trail, which included nearly twenty sites around the state linked (some more closely than others) to Lincoln's life and his Civil War legacy. Aside from obvious sites such as the Mary Todd Lincoln House and Lincoln's Boyhood Home, these include locations such as the Lincoln Marriage Temple, which shelters the log cabin in which historians believe Nancy Hanks and Thomas Lincoln married; the home of Lincoln's uncle Mordecai; and a replica of a cabin similar to the one once inhabited by his stepmother, Sarah Bush Johnston Lincoln. It seemed that even though (and perhaps because) Lincoln resided for such a brief period of his young life in Kentucky, no connection to the president was too small to include. A number of other sites made their way onto the trail due to their connection to the Civil War: the Camp Nelson Civil War Heritage Park, which marks the third-largest African American recruitment camp in the nation, and the Perryville Battlefield Historical Site. Even Jefferson Davis's monument and birthplace won a spot on the map. In both style and substance, the events and places highlighted in the commonwealth stressed Lincoln's humble roots, his unlikely rise to the highest office in the land, and his lasting legacy in keeping the Union intact during the Civil War. Not surprisingly, the bicentennial effort highlighted his role in emancipating enslaved African Americans, the very act that had made him so unpopular in his home state almost a century and a half before. In the post–civil rights era, it seemed that Kentuckians were ready to embrace Lincoln for the same reasons they had once maligned him. Meanwhile, Jefferson Davis, who was also born in Kentucky in 1809, went largely unobserved. Vestiges of Confederate partisanship remained, however. In 2007, the state division of the Sons of Confederate Veterans protested that the Kentucky Lincoln Bicentennial Commission had not followed proper procedures to have the Transportation Cabinet approve a Lincoln bicentennial license plate bearing the official Kentucky Lincoln Bicentennial emblem. The Kentucky United Confederate Veterans, which was also seeking approval for its own specialty plate, denied that the tag's honoree had anything to do with their outrage, but the group used the opportunity to call for the resignation of the co-chairs of the bicentennial celebration and the executive director of the Kentucky Historical Society.[8]

As the Lincoln celebration reveals, there are more voices than ever joining in the chorus of Kentucky Civil War memory. The stories that they tell, their motivations, and their impact in defining the state's past and present identity—both for themselves and for others—are growing ever more varied and complicated. However present and future generations of Kentuckians choose to remember the narrative of their state's experience in the Civil War, there is no doubt that it will continue to be a subject of debate and contention for a long time to come because so many people invest so much importance and emotion in those four years of epic struggle. Robert Penn Warren, who managed to capture the relationship between memories of the past and their uses in the present better than most historians of his time, understood this well. He recalled driving himself in the family car when he was only eleven (a pillow behind his back so he could reach the pedals) to see the Jefferson Davis Monument under construction just outside of his hometown. Even as an adolescent boy, he pondered the complicated ramifications of that cold piece of granite: "Was the blank shaft that was rising there trying to say something about that war of long ago when young men had ridden away from the same countryside to die for whatever they had died for?" he remembered asking. "Was the tall shaft, now stubbed at the top, what history was?" Perhaps more aware of his own personal motives than many of his fellow Kentuckians, Warren reflected: "It seems that in facing the blank-topped monument I was trying to focus some meaning, however hard to define, on the relation of the past and present, old pain and glory and new pain and glory."[9]

ABBREVIATIONS

GAR	Grand Army of the Republic
HL-BC	Hutchins Library, Berea College, Berea, Kentucky
KHC	Kentucky Heritage Council, Frankfort
KHS	Martin F. Schmidt Archives and Research Library, Kentucky Historical Society, Frankfort
SC-FHS	Special Collections, Filson Historical Society, Louisville
SC-KSU	Paul G. Blazer Library, Special Collections, Kentucky State University, Frankfort
SC-UK	Margaret I. King Library, Special Collections, University of Kentucky, Lexington
SHC-UNC	Southern Historical Collection, University of North Carolina, Chapel Hill
UDC	United Daughters of the Confederacy

INTRODUCTION

1. Henry Watterson, "Address of Welcome to Be Delivered to the Grand Army of the Republic on Behalf of the City of Louisville," Henry Watterson Papers, SC-FHS.

2. Military figures from Harrison and Klotter, *New History of Kentucky*, 195, 265. Deriving accurate enlistment numbers for white Kentuckians is difficult, given that many left the state to enlist in the northern and the southern armies during the period in which the state remained officially neutral.

3. Ibid. See information on governors Preston Leslie, James B. McCreary, Luke Blackburn, and Simon Bolivar Buckner, in ibid., 241, 245–46, 257, 260, 262–63, 447–48.

4. Coulter, *Civil War and Readjustment in Kentucky*, 439; Webb, "Kentucky: Pariah among the Elect," 105, 110–11, 145; Webb, *Kentucky in the Reconstruction Era*, 92–93.

5. Connelly, "Neo-Confederatism or Power Vacuum," 268–69.

6. Ibid., 258; Flannery, "Kentucky History Revisited," 27; Coulter, *Civil War and Readjustment in Kentucky*, 410.

7. My thinking about "political culture" is informed by Lynn Hunt, who breaks down distinctions between politics and culture in her study of the French Revolution, arguing that cultural practices such as symbols, rituals, rhetoric, and festivals did not merely reflect politics but constituted politics. She defines political culture as "the values, expectations, and implicit rules that expressed and shaped collective intentions and actions." Hunt, *Politics, Culture*, 10–11.

8. Warren, *Legacy of the Civil War*, 60.

9. Brundage, *Where These Memories Grow*, 5.

10. Blight, *Race and Reunion*, 4.

CHAPTER ONE

1. Maria Southgate Hawes Reminiscences, 26, SHC-UNC.

2. Casualty figures in Harrison and Klotter, *New History of Kentucky*, 215; and Duke, *Civil War Reminiscences*, 400.

3. McPherson, *Abraham Lincoln and the Second American Revolution*, 29–37.

4. Harrison and Klotter, *New History of Kentucky*, 168–69; Aron, *How the West Was Lost*, 89–95.

5. For a full discussion of the debate over slavery in early Kentucky, see Aron, *How the West Was Lost*, 93–101.

6. Dunaway, "Put in Master's Pocket," 116–30.

7. Harrison and Klotter, *New History of Kentucky*, 135; Edward Conrad Smith, *Borderland*, 28–29. See a cogent refutation of this notion in Tallant, *Evil Necessity*, 62–64.

8. Harrison and Klotter, *New History of Kentucky*, 168; U.S. Bureau of the Census, *Eighth Census of Agriculture, 1860*, 228–29; Coulter, *Civil War and Readjustment in Kentucky*, 7–8; Jewett and Allen, *Slavery in the South*, 99, 104.

9. T. D. Clark, "Slave Trade between Kentucky and the Cotton Kingdom," 331–32; Coleman, "Lexington's Slave Dealers," 1–2.

10. T. D. Clark, "Slave Trade between Kentucky and the Cotton Kingdom," 337, 341–42; Freehling, *The South vs. the South*, 20, 27; Jewett and Allen, *Slavery in the South*, 113.

11. Turner, "Abolitionism in Kentucky," 334, 338.

12. Breckinridge quoted in Howard, "Robert J. Breckinridge," 332; *Lexington Observer and Reporter*, December 16, 1848; *Free South* quoted in Turner, "Abolitionism in Kentucky," 338.

13. Tallant, *Evil Necessity*, 4–7; Marion B. Lucas, *From Slavery to Segregation*, 108; Jewett and Allen, *Slavery in the South*, 98; Coulter, *Civil War and Readjustment in Kentucky*, 197.

14. Tapp, "Slavery Controversy," 162, 165; Tallant, *Evil Necessity*, 12.

15. Blight, *Race and Reunion*, 235; Coleman, "Mrs. Stowe, Kentucky, and Uncle Tom's Cabin," 4–5.

16. Stowe elaborated on this notion when she wrote: "The general prevalence of agricultural pursuits of a quiet and gradual nature, not requiring those periodic seasons of hurry and pressure that are called for in the business of more southern districts, makes the task of the Negro a more healthful and reasonable one; while the master, content with a more gradual style of acquisition, has not those temptations to hardheartedness which always overcome frail human nature when the prospect of sudden and rapid gain is weighed in the balance, with no heavier counterpoise than the interests of the helpless and unprotected." Stowe, *Uncle Tom's Cabin*, 8–9.

17. Saunders and Root, "My Old Kentucky Home," 235–39.

18. Edward Conrad Smith, *Borderland*, 64–65.

19. For a more detailed account of Kentucky's legislative sectional struggle and division within the state on the question of secession, see Harrison and Klotter, *New History of Kentucky*, 185–94; Coulter, *Civil War and Readjustment in Kentucky*, 18–124; and Freehling, *The South vs. the South*, 53–54.

20. Harrison and Klotter, *New History of Kentucky*, 185–94. For a comprehensive treatment of pro-Confederate sentiment in western Kentucky, see Hoskins, "The Old First Is with the South."

21. Coulter, *Civil War and Readjustment in Kentucky*, 18–21.

22. Letter from E. F. Drake to Salmon P. Chase, in "Letters to Secretary Chase from the South, 1861," 343–44; Speed quoted in Coulter, *Civil War and Readjustment in Kentucky*, 119–20.

23. Berry, *Voices from the Century Before*, 282.

24. Christopher Clay to Brutus Clay, April 23, 1861, May 5, 1861, Clay Family Papers, SC-UK. For an excellent account on family divisions in Civil War Kentucky, see Amy Murrell Taylor, *Divided Family*.

25. Breckinridge, "The Civil War: Its Nature and End," 645–46.

26. Holt, *Letter from the Honorable Joseph Holt*, 18.

27. Cassius Clay quoted in Berry, *Voices from the Century Before*, 270; Harrison, "Kentucky-Born Generals in the Civil War," 130. To arrive at the number of white Union recruits, I have subtracted the estimated 24,000 African American Kentuckians who fought in the Union army from the state's total Federal manpower estimates of 90,000 to 100,000. Coulter, *Civil War and Readjustment in Kentucky*, 190–91; Howard, *Black Liberation in Kentucky*, 63; Freehling, *The South vs. the South*, 131.

28. Journal of Ellen Kenton McGaughey Wallace, August 5, 1862, Wallace-Starling Diaries and Papers, KHS. For more examples of Wallace's experience with irregular warfare, see entries August 7–8, 1862, and September 1 and 25, 1862, ibid. Hiram Hogg to Henry C. Hogg, March 1, 1863, Hiram Hogg Papers, KHS; J. R. Thornton to Maggie Harris, April 11, 1865, Raynor Purchase, KHS. Valuable treatments of irregular warfare in Kentucky include Cooling, "A People's War"; Crane, "The Rebels Are Bold"; Scott J. Lucas, "Indignities, Wrongs, and Outrages"; Martin, "Black Flag over the Bluegrass"; Rhyne, "Rehearsal for Redemption"; Rhyne, "We Are Mobed & Beat"; Astor, "Belated Confederates"; and McKnight, *Contested Borderland*.

29. Coulter, *Civil War and Readjustment in Kentucky*, 148, 152.

30. Ibid. George Smith quoted in Yonkers, "Civil War Transformation of George W. Smith," 678.

31. Lincoln quoted in Freehling, *The South vs. the South*, 82.

32. Coulter, *Civil War and Readjustment in Kentucky*, 153.

33. Myers, "Union General Stephen Gano Burbridge," 144.

34. Green Clay to Brutus Clay, August 16, 1852, Clay Family Papers, SC-UK; Garrett Davis to Salmon P. Chase, September 3, 1861, in "Letters to Secretary Chase from the South, 1861," 347; Coulter, *Civil War and Readjustment in Kentucky*, 111–12, 156.

35. Coulter, *Civil War and Readjustment in Kentucky*, 158–59; Harrison and Klotter, *New History of Kentucky*, 179.

36. Benjamin Buckner to Helen Martin, May 5, 1862, June 5, 1862, Benjamin F. Buckner Collection, SC-UK.

37. Ibid., November 5, 1862, November 22, 1862, December 2, 1862.

38. Diary of John F. Jefferson, January 2, 1863, John F. Jefferson Diaries, SC-FHS; letter from Alfred Pirtle to Henry Pirtle, May 31, 1862, Alfred Pirtle Papers, SC-FHS; John Harrington to Jennie Swift, January 19, 1863, John T. Harrington Letters, KHS; Robert H. Earnest to James H. Earnest, April 2, 1863, Robert H. Earnest Papers, KHS.

39. Diary of Ellen Kenton McGaughey Wallace, April 29, 1861, September 29, 1862, December 13, 1862, Wallace-Starling Diaries and Papers, KHS.

40. Ibid. For examples of Wallace's comments regarding troublesome slaves, see entries dated February 20, 1864, January 28, 1864, December 23 and 25, 1863, March 22 and 24, 1864, September 29, 1862, December 13, 1862, and December 23, 1862.

41. Collins and Collins, *Collins' Historical Sketches*, 159; Howard, *Black Liberation in Kentucky*, 79–80.

42. Rawick, *American Slave*, vol. 6, *Alabama and Indiana Narratives*, 79–80; Rawick, *American Slave*, vol. 16, *Kansas, Kentucky, Maryland, Ohio, Virginia, and Tennessee Narratives*, 85; "Message of the President of the United States, Communicating, in Compliance with a Resolution of the Senate of December 20, 1864, Information in Relation to the Arrest of Colonel Richard T. Jacobs, Lieutenant Governor of the State of Kentucky, and Colonel Frank Wolford, One of the Presidential Electors of That State"; Marion B. Lucas, *From Slavery to Segregation*, 149–52, 177; Howard, *Black Liberation in Kentucky*, 45–54; Freehling, *The South vs. the South*, 131.

43. *Tri-weekly Commonwealth*, September 2, 1863; Coulter, *Civil War and Readjustment in Kentucky*, 199; Pamphlet, "Message of the President of the United States, Communicating, in Compliance with a Resolution of the Senate of December 20, 1864, Information in Relation to the Arrest of Colonel Richard T. Jacobs, Lieutenant Governor of the State of Kentucky, and Colonel Frank Wolford, One of the Presidential Electors of That State," 4, 10, 11, KHS; Sidney Clay in Berry, *Voices from the Century Before*, 390–91; Rawick, *American Slave*, vol. 16, *Kansas, Kentucky, Maryland, Ohio, Virginia, and Tennessee Narratives*, 116; Benjamin Buckner to Helen Martin, February 5, 1863, Benjamin F. Buckner Collection, SC-UK.

44. Diary of Ellen Kenton McGaughey Wallace, June 7, 1864, November 12, 1863, December 25, 1863, January 28, 1864, Wallace-Starling Diaries and Papers, KHS.

45. Berry, *Voices from the Century Before*, 358, 371, 408–9.

46. Diary, Edward O. Guerrant Papers, June 10, 1864, SHC-UNC.

47. Andrew Phillips Letter, October 19, 1863, KHS; Diary of Ellen Kenton McGaughey Wallace, December 12, 1864, Wallace-Starling Diaries and Papers, KHS; Micah Saufley to Sallie Rowan Saufley, September 6, 1865, Sallie Rowan Saufley Papers, SHC-UNC.

48. Letter, April 30, 1865, Charles B. Simrall Papers, SHC-UNC; letter from Micah Saufley to Sallie Rowan Saufley, October 18, 1865, Sallie Rowan Saufley Papers, SHC-UNC.

49. Sue Bullitt Dixon to Thomas Bullitt, January 22, 1865, Bullitt Family Papers, SC-FHS; Micah Saufley to Sallie Rowan Saufley, October 18, 1865, Sallie Rowan Saufley Papers, SHC-UNC.

50. Reprint, "Speech of Hon. Brutus J. Clay, of Kentucky, On the Subject of Amending the Constitution So as to Abolish and Prohibit Slavery," 4, Clay Family Papers, SC-UK; Martha Davenport to Brutus Clay, March 31, 1862, Clay Family Papers, SC-UK.

CHAPTER TWO

1. Hardin, *Private War*, 280.

2. Ibid., 287–89.

3. *Lexington Observer and Reporter*, October 5, 1866.

4. Woodward, *Origins of the New South*, 6.

5. *Lexington Observer and Reporter*, May 22, 1867.

6. Harrison and Klotter, *New History of Kentucky*, 234–35; Reid, *After the War*, 294.

7. Hardin, *Private War*, 284.

8. Ibid., 286.

9. Collins and Collins, *Collins' Historical Sketches*, 163–64.

10. *Cincinnati Gazette*, January 12, 1865, July 28, 1865.

11. Ibid., July 28, 1865; *New York Times*, August 27, 1868; D. C. Phillips to W. K. White, July 25, 1865, D. C. Phillips Letter, KHS; *Lexington Observer and Reporter*, semiweekly edition, October 5, 1867.

12. Eric Foner succinctly explains the difference between Kentucky and other border states: "The elements that would transform Kentucky's neighbors were either weak or absent. Although loyal to the Union, the state's mountain region was politically inactive; there was no major city (like Baltimore or St. Louis) with an antislavery cadre ready to lead in reconstructing the state; and the traditional leadership retained sufficient unity to fend off challenges of authority." Foner, *Reconstruction*, 38. For a more detailed account of Reconstruction-era politics in the southern border states, see Hancock, "Reconstruction in Delaware"; Parrish, "Reconstruction Politics in Missouri"; and Wagandt, "Redemption or Reaction."

13. For a detailed account of the complicated shifts among political factions in postwar Kentucky, see Harrison and Klotter, *New History of Kentucky*, 239–44; Webb, *Kentucky in the Reconstruction Era*, 12–35; and Webb, "Kentucky: Pariah among the Elect," 107–45.

14. *Cincinnati Gazette*, November 4, 1865.

15. The state legislature had first rejected the Thirteenth Amendment in February 1865, by a vote of 56 to 18 in the house and 23 to 10 in the senate. Coulter, *Civil War and Readjustment in Kentucky*, 261, 281–82; Harrison and Klotter, *New History of Kentucky*, 240; Webb, *Kentucky in the Reconstruction Era*, 15; Collins and Collins, *Collins' Historical Sketches*, 176; *Lexington Observer and Reporter*, January 10, 1866; *New York Times*, February 15, 1866.

16. James Speed, *James Speed: A Personality*, 77–78.

17. *Cincinnati Gazette*, June 23, 1865, November 4, 1865. For examples of blended Democratic and Confederate rhetoric, see *Cincinnati Gazette*, July 29, 1865, July 4, 1866.

18. Webb, *Kentucky in the Reconstruction Era*, 21; *Daily Kentucky Yeoman* (Frankfort), July 26, 1866, quoted in Webb, "Kentucky: Pariah among the Elect," 121; Prentice and Haldeman quoted in Webb, *Kentucky in the Reconstruction Era*, 22; *Cincinnati Gazette*, June 22, 1866, July 29, 1866.

19. Webb, *Kentucky in the Reconstruction Era*, 22; *Cincinnati Gazette*, July 29, 1866, June 29, 1866.

20. *Tri-weekly Commonwealth* quoted in Harrison and Klotter, *New History of Kentucky*, 241.

21. *Cincinnati Gazette*, August 10, 1866.

22. *Tri-weekly Commonwealth*, January 8, 1867.

23. *Cincinnati Commercial*, May 13, 1867.

24. Harrison and Klotter, *New History of Kentucky*, 241–42; *Daily Kentucky Statesman*, semiweekly edition, August 9, 1867.

25. *Tri-weekly Yeoman*, May 30, 1867; *Lexington Observer and Reporter*, May 22, 1867.

26. The list of rebel officeholders originated in the *Tri-weekly Commonwealth*, August 9, 1867, and was reprinted by the *New York Times*, August 18, 1867. For information on governors John Stevenson, James B. McCreary, Luke Blackburn, John Knott, and Simon Bolivar Buckner, see Harrison and Klotter, *New History of Kentucky*, 243–48, 257–63, 447–48.

27. *New York Times*, December 25, 1866; Tapp and Klotter, *Kentucky: Decades of Discord*, 14; *Louisville Courier-Journal*, April 9, 1995; *Cincinnati Gazette*, April 21, 1866.

28. *New York Times*, December 25, 1866; *Chicago Tribune*, January 11, 1867, quoted in Russ, "Role Of Kentucky in 1867," 107; *New York Times*, March 15, 1874.

29. J. Stoddard Johnston, *Kentucky Confederate Military History*, 198–99.

30. Wolford quoted in Astor, "Belated Confederates," 274. One other explanation for Confederate political ascendance after the war may lie in the phenomenon of prominent Union military leaders emigrating from Kentucky after the war just as their Confederate counterparts were allowed to return. For an interesting, if impressionistic, testimony to this effect, see Lowell Harrison's biographical sketches of Kentucky-born Confederate and Union leaders, "Kentucky-Born Generals in the Civil War."

31. *Cincinnati Gazette*, February 2, 1866, March 13, 1866, August 16, 1866, August 21, 1866.

32. Miller, *Dear Wife*, 120, 125, 127.

33. Letter from Jesse W. Kinchloe to Joseph Holt, September 18, 1866, in Russ, "Role of Kentucky in 1867," 107; *New York Times*, August 27, 1868.

34. *Cincinnati Commercial*, January 3, 1866; Coulter, *Civil War and Readjustment in Kentucky*, 350. For other examples of African American political meetings in Kentucky, see *Cincinnati Commercial*, May 13, 1867, September 20, 1867; and *New York Times*, August 18, 1867.

35. *Cincinnati Commercial*, January 2, 1867; Howard, *Black Liberation in Kentucky*, 146.

36. *Cincinnati Commercial*, September 20, 1867; *Lexington Observer and Reporter*, semiweekly edition, October 5, 1867; Coulter, *Civil War and Readjustment in Kentucky*, 350–51.

37. *Kentucky's Black Heritage*, 45; *Lexington Observer and Reporter*, semiweekly edition, October 5, 1867.

38. *Kentucky Statesman*, August 16, 1867, August 23, 1867.

39. Ibid., August 30, 1867.

40. Locke, *Ekkoes from Kentucky*.

41. Ibid., 96, 273, 14–15.

42. Ibid., 23, 166, 251–52; Austin, *Petroleum V. Nasby*, 77–79.

43. Coulter, *Civil War and Readjustment in Kentucky*, 414; *New York Times*, August 27, 1868.

44. Coulter, *Civil War and Readjustment in Kentucky*, 414; Watterson, *Compromises of Life*, 101.

45. Watterson, *Editorials*, 20–22.

46. Watterson, *Marse Henry*, 240, 176, 241. Kentucky Bourbon Democrats shared several key convictions with their southern counterparts: unequivocal opposition to ratification of the Reconstruction amendments, support for retrenchment, and their intention that ex-Confederates dominate state politics. They differed, however, in their contempt for industry and railroads and in their commitment to an agricultural economy and way of life. The Bluegrass region, with its large farms and stately manors, provided both the geographical and the metaphorical center of Bourbon Democracy. Until the populist insurgency of the 1880s and 1890s, western Kentucky also proved a Bourbon stronghold. See Tapp and Klotter, *Kentucky: Decades of Discord*, 33–36.

47. Watterson, *Marse Henry*, 240–41.

48. Ibid., 240–41, 173, 240.

49. Margolies, *Henry Watterson*, 28–30.

50. Ibid., 23, 43–44.

51. Pringle, "Kentucky Bourbon," 221; Krock, *Myself When I Was Young*, 109–10; Wall, *Henry Watterson*, 215–16. Other informative treatments of Henry Watterson's life and career include Margolies, "God's Promise Redeemed"; Osthaus, *Partisans of the Southern Press*; and Wharton, "Henry Watterson."

52. *Cincinnati Gazette*, March 13, 1867.

53. *Tri-weekly Commonwealth*, August 9, 1867. For more about Kentuckians and the Liberal Republican Party in 1872, see Tapp and Klotter, *Kentucky: Decades of Discord*, 118–23; and *New York Times*, September 10, 1874.

CHAPTER THREE

1. *Cincinnati Gazette*, January 12, 1865.

2. Hardin, *Private War*, 254; Coulter, *Civil War and Readjustment in Kentucky*, 358, 363.

3. For more on postwar violence in Missouri, see Stiles, *Jesse James*; and Fellman, *Inside War*. For a very useful comparison of violence in postwar Kentucky and postwar Missouri, see Astor, "Belated Confederates," 218–82.

4. Coulter, *Civil War and Readjustment in Kentucky*, 231, 257–58, quote from 286; Tuttle, *The Union, the Civil War*, 232–33.

5. Letter from Susan Bullitt Dixon to Tom Bullitt, July 15, 1864, Bullitt Family Papers, SC-FHS; letter from J. R. Thornton to Maggie Harris, April 11, 1865, Raynor Purchase, KHS.

6. Collins and Collins, *Collins' Historical Sketches*, 174; Coulter, *Civil War and Readjustment in Kentucky*, 358–59; Tuttle, *The Union, the Civil War*, 232–33.

7. Coulter, *Civil War and Readjustment in Kentucky*, 359; Tapp and Klotter, *Kentucky: Decades of Discord*, 380. Numerous scholars have conducted thorough studies of violence in Reconstruction-era Kentucky, including George Wright, *Racial Violence in Kentucky*; Tapp and Klotter, *Kentucky: Decades of Discord*, 377–409; Trelease, *White Terror*, 90; Astor, "Belated Confederates"; and Rhyne, "Rehearsal for Redemption."

8. Trelease, *White Terror*, 89; Apple, Johnston, and Evans, *Scott County Kentucky*, 222; *New York Times*, December 16, 1874.

9. Howard, *Black Liberation in Kentucky*, 98, 101; Collins and Collins, *Collins' Historical Sketches*, 174; Tapp and Klotter, *Kentucky: Decades of Discord*, 378–79.

10. Wright, *Racial Violence in Kentucky*, 38–39; Collins and Collins, *Collins' Historical Sketches*, 215.

11. Low, "Freedman's Bureau in the Border States," 265; Howard, *Black Liberation in Kentucky*, 101, 103.

12. Williamson, *Crucible of Race*, 183–89; Wright, *Racial Violence in Kentucky*, 7–8.

13. Collins and Collins, *Collins' Historical Sketches*, 173; Trelease, *White Terror*, 90, 280; Tuttle, *The Union, the Civil War*, 274.

14. Wright, *Racial Violence in Kentucky*, 77; Collins and Collins, *Collins' Historical Sketches*, 170–72, 181, 199; Williamson, *Crucible of Race*, 183–84.

15. *New York Times*, August 12, 1877.

16. *Lexington Gazette*, reprinted in *New York Times*, January 28, 1878.

17. *Kentucky's Black Heritage*, 51; Webb, *Kentucky in the Reconstruction Era*, 48.

18. *New York Times*, December 4, 1868.

19. Low, "Freedman's Bureau in the Border States," 254, 251.

20. Ibid.; Webb, *Kentucky in the Reconstruction Era*, 47.

21. *Louisville Daily Courier* quoted in Wright, *Racial Violence in Kentucky*, 43–44.

22. Ibid., 26, 34, 48.

23. Ibid., 49–51.

24. Ibid., 59, 29, 58; Trelease, *White Terror*, 125; *New York Times*, August 29, 1874.

25. Joanne Grant, *Black Protest*, 154–56; *Kentucky's Black Heritage*, 53.

26. Burton, *What Experience Has Taught Me*, 29–30.

27. Rawick, *American Slave*, vol. 16, *Kansas, Kentucky, Maryland, Ohio, Virginia, and Tennessee Narratives*, 31, 61–62; Rawick, *American Slave*, vol. 6, *Alabama and Indiana Narratives*, 171–72.

28. Coulter, *Civil War and Readjustment in Kentucky*, 327; *New York Times*, January 3, 1871; Trelease, *White Terror*, 90; *New York Times*, September 10, 1874.

29. *Cincinnati Commercial*, July 22, 1867; *New York Times*, November 23, 1868; Coulter, *Civil War and Readjustment in Kentucky*, 359. For more on James Bridgewater, see Rhyne, "Rehearsal for Redemption," especially 162–89.

30. Apple, Johnston, and Evans, *Scott County Kentucky*, 209; second quote from Trelease, *White Terror*, 281.

31. *New York Times*, October 3, 1871.

32. Ibid., July 14, 1876.

33. Ibid.

34. *New York Times*, August 12, 1874, February 23, 1870, December 4, 1868.

35. *Kentucky's Black Heritage*, 52.

36. *Louisville Courier-Journal*, March 22, 1871; *New York Times*, April 26, 1871.

37. *Kentucky's Black Heritage*, 52; Wright, *Racial Violence in Kentucky*, 27.

38. Coulter, *Civil War and Readjustment in Kentucky*, 364. For more on Kentucky's county structure, see Ireland, *Little Kingdoms*; *Louisville Courier-Journal*, September 17, 1873; and *New York Times*, December 16, 1874, November 11, 1877.

39. *Louisville Courier-Journal*, September 10, 1873, August 25, 1873; *New York Times*, January 3, 1871.

40. *New York Times*, March 25, 1871; Webb, *Kentucky in the Reconstruction Era*, 77.

41. John Hawes to Thomas Young, November 2, 1866, Young/Wooten Collection, SC-UK. By the 1880s, the most memorable journalistic coverage of violence in Kentucky centered on the feuding that had "emerged" in eastern Kentucky. Appalachian violence will be the subject of chap. 5. For examples of heavy coverage of violence in Kentucky on a monthly basis, see *New York Times*, November 5, 1872, February 10, 1874, June 12, 1874, and September 6, 1877.

42. *Louisville Courier-Journal*, September 15, 1873.

43. *Pittsburgh Commercial* reprinted in *Louisville Courier-Journal*, September 9, 1873; *New York Times*, December 16, 1874, December 26, 1878.

44. *Louisville Courier-Journal*, August 13, 1870, September 10, 1873, September 9, 1873.

45. Ibid., January 8, 1877.

46. Woodward, *Reunion and Reaction*, 110–11, 120; Pringle, "Kentucky Bourbon," 222.

47. Wall, *Henry Watterson*, 151.

48. Redfield, *Homicide, North and South*, 40, 42, 37; Tapp and Klotter, *Kentucky: Decades of Discord*, 400.

49. Wyatt-Brown, *Southern Honor*; Klotter, *Kentucky Justice*, 42. For a fuller discussion of Kentucky's reputation for violence, see ibid., 42–48; Ireland, "Law and Disorder," 281–304; Ireland, "Violence"; Singal, *War Within*, 13; and Aron, *How the West Was Lost*, 127.

50. Ireland, "Violence," 161.

51. William Taylor, *Cavalier and Yankee*, 93; Singal, *War Within*, 17–18.

52. Bederman, *Manliness and Civilization*, 11–12.

53. Klotter, *Kentucky Manhood*, 43, 52.

54. Woodward, *Origins of the New South*, 160; *New York Times*, December 26, 1878.

55. Ibid., August 12, 1874, December 16, 1874.

56. *Princeton (Ky.) Banner* and *Lafayette (Ind.) Courier* quoted in *Louisville Courier-Journal*, September 9, 1873; *New York Times*, August 12, 1877, November 11, 1874; Redfield, *Homicide, North and South*, 57–58.

57. *New York Times*, September 6, 1877; *Louisville Courier-Journal*, August 25, 1873.

58. *New York Times*, September 10, 1874, October 16, 1877; Watterson, *Marse Henry*, 178.

59. *Cincinnati Commercial*, July 24, 1869; Field, *Blood Is Thicker Than Water*, 146.

60. *New York Times*, December 16, 1874; *Louisville Courier-Journal*, August 13, 1870, September 9, 1873.

61. James C. Hawes to Thomas R. Young, November 2, 1866, Young/Wooten Collection, SC-UK; *New York Times*, August 12, 1877, October 15, 1874.

62. Ibid., September 21, 1874.

CHAPTER FOUR

1. Hardin, *Private War*, 280–82; Rawick, *American Slave*, vol. 16, *Kansas, Kentucky, Maryland, Ohio, Virginia, and Tennessee Narratives*, 94.

2. Coulter, *Civil War and Readjustment in Kentucky*, 275.

3. *Cincinnati Commercial*, April 27, 1867; Collins and Collins, *Collins' Historical Sketches*, 229, 246d, 246g, 199, 189; E. Kirby Smith to William Preston, January 23, 1872, Wickliffe-Preston Papers, SC-UK. Kentuckians began commemorating dead Confederates in April shortly after the end of the Civil War. By the early twentieth century, they had moved their Confederate observances to the beginning of June.

4. *Lexington Observer and Reporter*, May 22, 1867, November 21, 1866; undated clipping, box 57, folder 1, Wickliffe-Preston Papers, SC-UK; J. Stoddard Johnston, *Kentucky Confederate Military History*, 198–99.

5. General studies on the Lost Cause include Osterweis, *Myth of the Lost Cause*; Charles Reagan Wilson, *Baptized in Blood*; Connelly and Bellows, *God and General Longstreet*; and Foster, *Ghosts of the Confederacy*; quote from ibid., 37.

6. Collins and Collins, *Collins' Historical Sketches*, 182; *Historic Southern Monuments*, 135–37. Complete listings and detailed descriptions of Civil War monuments in Kentucky can be found in the Civil War Monument Files, KHC.

7. *Lexington Observer and Reporter*, May 22, 1869, June 5, 1869; *Frank Leslie's* article reprinted in *Louisville Courier-Journal*, July 16, 1880.

8. There is a growing body of literature about women and the Lost Cause. See Brundage, "White Women and the Politics of Historical Memory"; Cox, *Dixie's Daughters*; Brundage, *Southern Past*; and Bishir, "Landmarks of Power." Quote from Brundage, "White Women and the Politics of Historical Memory," 115. For more on the political cover that women's memorial activity provided in the Reconstruction-era South, see Janney, *Burying the Dead*. For arguments about southern women rehabilitating southern men, see Faust, *Mothers of Invention*, 234–47, 252; and Whites, *Civil War as a Crisis in Gender*, 160–224.

9. S. Bassett French to William Preston, undated, box 64, folder November–December 1878, Wickliffe-Preston Papers, SC-UK; James Klotter, "John Cabell Breckinridge," in Kleber, *Kentucky Encyclopedia*, 117–18.

10. Ibid.; Collins and Collins, *Collins' Historical Sketches*, 195; *Lexington Observer and Reporter*, March 17, 1869.

11. *New York Times*, March 10, 1878; *Lexington Daily Transcript*, June 27, 1881, September 20, 1887, November 13, 1887.

12. Kentucky Historic Resources Individual Survey Form, Thompson & Powell Martyrs Monument, Civil War Monuments Files, folder 1, KHC; Kentucky Historic Resources Individual Survey Form, Eminence Martyrs Monument, Civil War Monuments Files, folder 2, KHC; Kentucky Historic Resources Individual Survey Form, Midway Martyrs Monument, Civil War Monuments Files, folder 3, KHC.

13. Harrison, "Basil Duke," in Kleber, *Kentucky Encyclopedia*, 273.

14. Blight, *Race and Reunion*, 147; Humphrey Marshall to Edward Guerrant, June 20, 1867, Edward O. Guerrant Papers, SC-FHS. For more background on veterans' remembrances, see Blair, *Cities of the Dead*; and McConnell, *Glorious Contentment*.

15. *Southern Historical Society Papers* 7 (January–December 1879): 159–60.

16. *Southern Historical Society Papers* 8 (January–December 1880): 324; J. William Jones to William Preston, May 13, 1880, Wickliffe-Preston Papers, SC-UK; Durrant, "Gently Furled Banner," 46.

17. Foster, *Ghosts of the Confederacy*, 60–62; *Southern Bivouac* 3, no. 7 (March 1885): 88 (advertisement); *Southern Bivouac* 2, no. 1 (August 1883), "The Editor's Table"; *Southern Bivouac* New Series 2, no. 10 (June 1885); *Southern Bivouac* 2, no. 2 (October 1883): 94–95.

18. *Southern Bivouac* New Series 4, no. 1 (June 1885): 62.

19. *Southern Bivouac* New Series 2, no. 11 (April 1887): 710–12. For examples of stories glorifying slavery in the Old South, see Louis Pendleton, "The Story of Black Dan," *Southern Bivouac* New Series 1, no. 8 (January, 1886): 525–28; and "The Runaways," *Southern Bivouac* New Series 1, no. 4 (September 1885): 318.

20. Moore, *Southern Literary Journal* 2, no. 2 (Spring 1970): 63; *Southern Bivouac* New Series 2, no. 12 (May 1887): 773.

21. *Proceedings of the First to Tenth Meetings 1866–1876 of the National Encampment of the Grand Army of the Republic*, 117–21.

22. *Louisville Post*, September 1895, clipping, GAR Scrapbook, 200, Grand Army of the Republic, 1895 encampment, SC-FHS; *Proceedings of the First to Tenth Meetings 1866–1876 of the National Encampment of the Grand Army of the Republic*, 169, 291, 385; *Louisville Times*, September 9, 1895, GAR Scrapbook, 214–15, Grand Army of the Republic, 1895 encampment, SC-FHS.

23. Clipping, *Louisville Times*, September 9, 1895, GAR Scrapbook, 214–15, Grand Army of the Republic, 1895 encampment, SC-FHS. Contrary to the example provided by Kentucky chapters, Barbara Gannon argues that within many integrated northern chapters the GAR served as an important force for remembering and celebrating African American contributions to the Civil War. Gannon, "The Won Cause."

24. Bontemps, "Autobiography of James L. Smith," 227.

25. For more on African Americans' symbolism and ordering of parades and memorial activity, see Kathleen Clark, "Celebrating Freedom," 119–23; Kathleen Clark, "Making History," 46–63; Kathleen Clark, *Defining Moments*; Kachun, *Festivals of Freedom*; Wiggins, *O Freedom*; and Brown and Kimball, "Mapping the Terrain of Black Richmond."

26. Howard, *Black Liberation in Kentucky*, 131, 148, 139, 153–54, 142–43; Collins and Collins, *Collins' Historical Sketches*, 204.

27. *Cincinnati Commercial*, September 20, 1867, January 2, 1867; Collins and Collins, *Collins' Historical Sketches*, 246b.

28. Blight, *Race and Reunion*, 3–4.

29. Coulter, *Civil War and Readjustment in Kentucky*, 199–200; *Indianapolis Freeman*, February 21, 1891, May 2, 1891.

30. Collins and Collins, *Collins' Historical Sketches*, 184.

31. "Robert E. Lee: In Memoriam," 5, 6, 34–35, 22–23.

32. Coulter, *Civil War and Readjustment in Kentucky*, 439; *Louisville Courier-Journal*, September 11, 1872; Collins and Collins, *Collins' Historical Sketches*, 231; *Southern Bivouac* New Series 1, no. 4 (September 1885): 255; *Southern Bivouac* New Series 1, no. 3 (August 1885): 189; George L. Kilmer, "A Note of Peace," *Century Illustrated Monthly Magazine*, July 1888, 440–42; *Lexington Leader*, April 16, 1905.

33. *Louisville Courier-Journal*, May 2, 1877.

34. Ibid.

35. Weaver, "Louisville's Labor Disturbance," 177–86.

36. Pinkerton, *Strikers, Communists, Tramps, and Detectives*, 386–87.

37. Caleb Ross, "The Destruction of Louisville," *Southern Bivouac* New Series 2, no. 1 (June 1886): 49–58.

38. Ibid., "The Editor's Table," 68–69.

39. Wall, *Henry Watterson*, 175–77; Watterson, *Compromises of Life*, 97.

40. Watterson, *Compromises of Life*, 97, 100. Watterson's line of racial reunion reflected the redeemer's strategy laid out by Edward Pollard, who asserted of the South, "Now, when she asserts the ultimate supremacy of the white man, she has not lost her cause, but merely developed its higher significance, and in the new contest she stands, with a firm political alliance in the North, with the binding instincts of race in her favour." Pollard, *Lost Cause Regained*, 155.

41. Watterson, *Compromises of Life*, 277; Wharton, "Henry Watterson," 114.

42. Watterson, *Compromises of Life*, 289; Wharton, "Henry Watterson," 141–46.

43. Blight, *Race and Reunion*, 307; *Louisville Courier-Journal*, September 8, 1883; Blassingame and McKivigan, *Frederick Douglass Papers*, 92, 94, 96, 99, 92, 94, 101–3, 107–8.

44. *Louisville Courier-Journal*, September 8, 1883.

45. Blassingame and McKivigan, *Frederick Douglass Papers*, 100–101.

46. Ibid.

47. *Louisville Courier-Journal*, September 25, 1883.

48. Ibid., September 27, 1883.

49. *Southern Bivouac* 2, no. 2 (October 1882): 91–92.

50. S. E. Smith, *History of the Anti–Separate Coach Movement*, 31, 32, 33.

51. Ibid., 25, 43.

52. *Louisville Post*, November 9, 1895, GAR Scrapbook, 200, Grand Army of the Republic, 1895 encampment, SC-FHS; Davies, *Patriotism on Parade*, 272–74.

53. Davies, *Patriotism on Parade*, 272–74.

54. Clipping, *Camden (N.J.) Review*, April 25, 1895, GAR Scrapbook, 28; clipping, *Louisville Commercial*, March 31, 1895, GAR Scrapbook, 15; clipping, unknown origin, GAR Scrapbook, 86; all in Grand Army of the Republic, 1895 encampment, SC-FHS.

55. Clipping, *Louisville Commercial*, April 14, 1895, GAR Scrapbook, 19; clipping, *Louisville Courier-Journal*, March 14, 1895, GAR Scrapbook, 86; clipping, *Louisville Commercial*, July 21, 1895, GAR Scrapbook, 70; all in Grand Army of the Republic, 1895 encampment, SC-FHS.

56. Clipping, *Camden (N.J.) Review*, April 27, 1895, GAR Scrapbook, 28, Grand Army of the Republic, 1895 encampment, SC-FHS.

57. Clipping, *Hopkinsville Kentuckian*, March 24, 1895, GAR Scrapbook, 11; unidentified clipping, March 24, 1895, GAR Scrapbook, 11; unidentified clipping, GAR Scrapbook, 103; all in Grand Army of the Republic, 1895 encampment, SC-FHS.

58. *Louisville Commercial*, July 19, 1895.

59. Abraham Levering to Local Arrangements Committee, July 17, 1895, box 1, folder 10, GAR Scrapbook; letter from T. H. Apple to Chairman of the GAR, July 17, 1895, box 1, folder 7, GAR Scrapbook; both in Grand Army of the Republic, 1895 encampment, SC-FHS.

60. Clipping, *Cleveland Gazette*, undated, GAR Scrapbook, 85; clipping, *Chicago Record*, July 27, 1895, GAR Scrapbook; clipping, *Boston Standard*, July 16, 1895, GAR Scrapbook, 75; unidentified clipping, GAR Scrapbook, 102; all in Grand Army of the Republic, 1895 encampment, SC-FHS.

61. Clipping, *Louisville Commercial*, September 10, 1895, GAR Scrapbook, 222–23, Grand Army of the Republic, 1895 encampment, SC-FHS.

62. Clipping, *Louisville Courier-Journal*, September 9, 1895, GAR Scrapbook, 229–30, Grand Army of the Republic, 1895 encampment, SC-FHS. In 1895, there were thirteen Ladies of the GAR circles, four of which were in Louisville. Kentucky reportedly had twenty-seven chapters of the Woman's Relief Corps containing 595 members in 1895. The Warner Post was the city's only African American Woman's Relief Corps post, and it was also the city's largest. Figures from *Louisville Commercial*, September 10, 1895, GAR Scrapbook, 221, Grand Army of the Republic, 1895 encampment, SC-FHS.

63. Davies, "Problem of Race Segregation," 367–68. For a good account of the internal debate within the Woman's Relief Corps, see O'Leary, *To Die For*, 82–90.

64. Clipping, *Louisville Post*, September 9, 1895, GAR Scrapbook, 199; clipping, *Louisville Post*, September 9, 1895, GAR Scrapbook, 199; clipping, *Louisville Commercial*, September 12, 1895, GAR Scrapbook, 298; clipping, *Louisville Post*, September 9, 1895, GAR Scrapbook, 201; all in Grand Army of the Republic, 1895 encampment, SC-FHS; Silber, *Romance of Reunion*, 78–79.

65. *Louisville Post*, September 9, 1895, GAR Scrapbook, 201, Grand Army of the Republic, 1895 encampment, SC-FHS.

66. Clipping, *Louisville Courier-Journal*, GAR Scrapbook, 324; clipping, unidentified newspaper, GAR Scrapbook, 258; clipping, *Louisville Commercial*, September 12, 1895, GAR Scrapbook, 298; all in Grand Army of the Republic, 1895 encampment, SC-FHS; *New York Times*, September 12, 1895.

67. Clipping, *Louisville Courier-Journal*, September 10, 1895, GAR Scrapbook, 263, Grand Army of the Republic, 1895 encampment, SC-FHS; *Confederate Veteran* 3, no. 10 (October 1895): 289.

68. *New York Times*, September 9, 1895; clipping, *Louisville Courier-Journal*, September 13, 1895, GAR Scrapbook, 324, Grand Army of the Republic, 1895 encampment, SC-FHS.

CHAPTER FIVE

1. Henry D. Shapiro coined the phrase "two Kentuckys" in relation to Allen's writing, in *Appalachia on Our Mind*, 27. See James Lane Allen, "Through the Cumberland Mountains on Horseback," 50; and James Lane Allen, "Mountain Passes of the Cumberland," 561, 576.

2. For a description of the process of the "discovery" of Appalachia, see Shapiro, *Appalachia on Our Mind*, 3–31.

3. Ibid., 15; Harkins, *Hillbilly*, 29–33.

4. James Lane Allen, "Through the Cumberland Gap on Horseback"; James Lane Allen, "Mountain Passes of the Cumberland"; Warner, "Comments on Kentucky," 255.

5. Warner, "Comments on Kentucky," 256; Woodward, *Origins of the New South*, 160.

6. Semple, "Anglo-Saxons of the Kentucky Mountains," 592.

7. Ibid., 592–93.

8. Ibid., 611.

9. James Lane Allen, "Mountain Passes of the Cumberland," 562–63.

10. Barton, *Hero in Homespun*, viii–xi, 24.

11. Semple, "Anglo-Saxons of the Kentucky Mountains," 594, 612.

12. Drake, "Slavery and Anti-Slavery in Appalachia," 17–18; Dunaway, "Put in Master's Pocket," 118–30.

13. Drake, *A History of Appalachia*; John Alexander Williams, *Appalachia: A History*, 154.

14. Preston, *Civil War in the Big Sandy Valley*, 81–82, copy at SC-UK; John Alexander Williams, *Appalachia: A History*, 163; McKinney, *Southern Mountain Republicans*, 20.

15. McKinney, *Southern Mountain Republicans*, 50, 27; Preston, *Civil War in the Big Sandy Valley*, 86–89.

16. McKinney, *Southern Mountain Republicans*, 58; McKinney, "Southern Mountain Republicans and the Negro," 202.

17. Kentucky Historic Resources Individual Survey Form, Union Monument, Lewis County Courthouse, Civil War Monuments Files, folder 3, KHC.

18. My ideas about the importance of Berea College in the formation of a Unionist Appalachian war narrative are greatly informed by Shannon Wilson's article "Lincoln's Sons and Daughters," 246.

19. Ibid.; Pamphlet, ca. 1888, Office of Information, Record Group 5.23 7-1, HL-BC.

20. Pamphlet, ca. 1888, Office of Information, Record Group 5.23 7-1, HL-BC; Shannon Wilson, "Lincoln's Sons and Daughters," 246.

21. Batteau, *Invention of Appalachia*, 74. Works that discuss Frost's role in defining Appalachia include ibid., 74–85; Klotter, "Black South in White Appalachia," 843–48; Shapiro, *Appalachia on Our Mind*, 113–32; and Shannon Wilson, "Lincoln's Sons and Daughters." Berea's efforts to educate African Americans faltered in 1904 when, in a direct effort to undermine Berea's original mission, the Kentucky legislature passed the Day Law, which barred interracial education.

22. Frost, "Our Contemporary Ancestors," 319, 311; *New York Times*, December 12, 1898.

23. Frost, "Our Contemporary Ancestors," 318; Frost, "An Educational Program for Appalachian America," *Berea Quarterly* 4 (May 1896): 12. Frost's appeals came at a time of changing northern public opinion regarding race and sectional reunion. A combination of reconciliationist impulse and their own racism and xenophobia led northerners to replace black southerners with mountain residents as the most worthy recipients of their benevolence. As Nina Silber has explained, "Once the racial wholesomeness of southern mountaineers had been established, northern whites could embrace them, no longer excluding them as strange and alien, but instead bringing them into their national heritage at precisely the same moment when northern culture had begun to cast southern black people aside." Silber, "What Does America Need So Much as Americans?" 250.

24. Frost, "Our Contemporary Ancestors," 313–14; *Berea Quarterly* 2 (February 1897): 13–14.

25. *Berea Quarterly* 1 (February 1896): 19; *Berea Quarterly* 1 (May 1896): 16–17.

26. Shannon Wilson, "Lincoln's Sons and Daughters," 252; *Berea Quarterly* 1 (November 1895): 3–8; *Berea Quarterly* 1 (February 1896): 20–25. See also "Anti-Slavery in Kentucky," 3–13, in ibid.

27. Barton, "The Cumberland Mountains and the Struggle for Freedom," *Berea Quarterly* 2 (May 1897): 14–20.

28. Pamphlet, 1888, Berea College, Archives Office of Information Records, RG 5.23 7-1; Shannon Wilson, "Lincoln's Sons and Daughters," 256–57; *Berea Quarterly* 2 (February 1897): 3.

29. Frost, "Our Contemporary Ancestors," 318; Frost, "Southern Mountaineer," 303–11; Barton, "Abraham Lincoln, Kentucky Mountaineer," 2, 4, 13.

30. "Lincoln's Birthday, 1911, the Berea Association of New York at Carnegie Hall," *Berea Quarterly* 15 (April 1911): 14.

31. Minutes and Records of Captain James C. West Post #171, GAR, Department of Kentucky, 1890–1904, entries: April 6, 1891, June 23, 1892, May 27, 1894, May 20, 1895, November 18, 1905, April 17, 1915, box 1, folder 6, HL-BC; Decoration Day Banner, 1898, Minutes and Records of James C. West Post #171, GAR, Department of Kentucky, 1890–1904, box 1, folder 6, HL-BC.

32. Letters from John Fox Jr. to Micajah Fible, June 30, 1887, May 13, 1887, June 2, 1886, transcript, John Fox Jr. Letters, 1883–1889, SHC-UNC.

33. York, *John Fox Jr.*, 104.

34. Fox, "The Kentucky Mountaineer," in *Bluegrass and Rhododendron*, 6–7.

35. Fox, *Little Shepherd of Kingdom Come*, 42, 24.

36. Ibid., 149, 87, 309, 104.

37. Ibid., 170–71.

38. Ibid., 188.

39. Ibid., 192, 188–89.

40. Ibid., 188–91.

41. Ibid., 195–203, 273.

42. Ibid., 206, 309, 292.

43. Ibid., 310–11, 319. For another treatment of *Little Shepherd of Kingdom Come* in the context of reunion, see Silber, *Romance of Reunion*, 147–50.

44. York, *John Fox Jr.*, 175, 126, 176, 207, 212.

45. Batteau, *Invention of Appalachia*, 57; Harkins, *Hillbilly*, 34; Klotter, "Feuds in Appalachia," 291.

46. *New York Times*, September 23, 1888, July 12, 1888; Fox, "Through the Cumberland Gap on Horseback," 60.

47. Fox, "Kentucky Mountaineer," in *Bluegrass and Rhododendron*, 38–40.

48. Ibid., 41; Semple, "Anglo-Saxons of the Kentucky Mountains," 616.

49. Altina Waller, "Feuding in Appalachia," 361.

50. Fox, *The Kentuckians*, 11–12.

51. John Gilmer Speed, "The Kentuckian," 947.

52. Altina Waller, "Feuding in Appalachia," 351–53, 358–60; *New York Times*, September 20, 1887; James Lane Allen, "Mountain Passes of the Cumberland," 300–301.

53. Warner, "Comments on Kentucky," 270–71; Drake, *A History of Appalachia*, 104.

54. Elijah Dizney, "Mountain Feuds," *Berea Quarterly* 8 (April 1909): 10, 12; Frost, "Our Contemporary Ancestors," 316; Fox, "Civilizing the Cumberland," in *Bluegrass and Rhododendron*, 209.

55. Altina Waller, "Feuding in Appalachia," 353, 367; *New York Times*, June 23, 1887; McKinney, "Industrialization and Violence in Appalachia," 131–44.

CHAPTER SIX

1. Annie Fellows Johnston, *Little Colonel*, 9, 15, 30, 163.

2. McGuire, "Little Colonel: A Phenomenon in Popular Literary Culture," 121; Blight, *Race and Reunion*, 211. See Nina Silber's treatment of sentimental reunion literature, *Romance of Reunion*, 105–23.

3. *Collier's Weekly* quoted in *Lexington Leader*, May 27, 1906.

4. Klotter, *Kentucky: Portrait in Paradox*, 57–65. For more detailed studies of the Black Patch tobacco wars, see Campbell, *Politics of Despair*; Marshall, *Violence in the Black Patch of Kentucky and Tennessee*; Waldrep, *Night Riders*; and Millichap, "Tobacco Wars," 906.

5. Robert Penn Warren quoted in Singal, *War Within*, 346; *Lexington Herald*, September 6, 1908.

6. *Philadelphia Inquirer* quoted in *Lexington Leader*, January 12, 1908; *Washington Times* quoted in *Lexington Leader*, December 29, 1907.

7. Klotter, *Kentucky: Portrait in Paradox*, 51; *Chicago Tribune* reprinted in *Lexington Leader*, March 1, 1908.

8. Woodward, *Origins of the New South*, 168; *Lexington Leader*, November 18, 1906, July 7, 1908.

9. For more information on James Lane Allen, see Bottorff, *James Lane Allen*; and Knight, *James Lane Allen*.

10. "Two Gentlemen of Kentucky," in James Lane Allen, *Flute and Violin*, 101, 99, 109–12.

11. Ibid., 100, 101, 108, 118.

12. Ibid., 119, 132.

13. Ibid., 6; "Magnetism of Pewee Valley," 20; "Annie Fellows Johnston," *Dictionary of American Biography* 10:137–38.

14. Annie Fellows Johnston, *Land of the Little Colonel*, 95, 3–4.

15. Ibid., 3–5; *Louisville Courier-Journal*, August 7, 1969. For a historical treatment of another popular children's book and its relation to historical memory, see Ozouf and Ozouf, "Le Tour de France"; and <<http://www.littlecolonel.com/MomBeck>>, accessed January 10, 2010.

16. Annie Fellows Johnston, *Little Colonel*, 10, 15.

17. Annie Fellows Johnston, *Little Colonel: Maid of Honor*, 56–57; Annie Fellows Johnston, *Little Colonel*, 15; Ward, "Anni Mirabiles," 40.

18. Silber, *Romance of Reunion*, 39–65.

19. Annie Fellows Johnston, *Little Colonel*, 41–42; Annie Fellows Johnston, *Little Colonel: Maid of Honor*, 242.

20. Annie Fellows Johnston, *Little Colonel*, 41–42; Annie Fellows Johnston, *Little Colonel: Maid of Honor*, 253.

21. Annie Fellows Johnston, *Little Colonel*, 41–43; Annie Fellows Johnston, *Little Colonel's Hero*, 187.

22. Annie Fellows Johnston, *Little Colonel in Arizona*, 89, 312; Scott, *Making the Invisible Woman Visible*, 243.

23. Annie Fellows Johnston, *Little Colonel, Maid of Honor*, 45, 53–54; Annie Fellows Johnston, *Little Colonel in Arizona*, 313; Annie Fellows Johnston, *Little Colonel's Knight Comes Riding*, 101, 254; Annie Fellows Johnston, *Little Colonel's Holidays*, 175; Foster, *Ghosts of the Confederacy*, chap. 11; Silber, *Romance of Reunion*, 178–85. For more information on the Confederate Veterans' Home in Pewee Valley, see Rusty Williams, *My Old Confederate Home*.

24. Gaston, *New South Creed*, 170.

25. Mann, "Author of the Little Colonel Series," 1925–27; Klotter, *Kentucky: Portrait in Paradox*, 5; Janet Lowell Walker, "The Beeches Takes New Roots," *Louisville Courier-Journal*, August 7, 1969; Vanderhook, "Annie Fellows Johnston: The Beloved Writer of Books for Young Folk," 130.

26. *Louisville Courier-Journal*, February 23, 1935; *Louisville Times*, February 23, 1935.

27. *Louisville Courier-Journal*, August 7, 1969.

28. *Louisville Courier-Journal*, February 23, 1935; *Louisville Times*, February 23, 1935.

29. Krock, *Myself When I Was Young*, 194–200; Durrant, "Gently Furled Banner," 65–66; *Lexington Leader*, October 5, 1905.

30. Irvin S. Cobb, *Back Home*, vii–ix.

31. Ibid., vii–ix; quoted from Lieb, "Irvin S. Cobb," 85; and Louis D. Rubin Jr., *History of Southern Literature*, 250.

32. "The County Trot," in Irvin S. Cobb, *Back Home*, 46–47.

33. Lloyd, *Stringtown-on-the-Pike*, 176; *New York Times*, November 3, 1900.

34. *New York Times*, November 3, 1900, December 14, 1901.

35. The five stories include "The Ordeal at Mt. Hope," "The Trial Sermons on Bullskin," "A Family Feud," "Nelse Hatton's Vengeance," and "The Deliberation of Mr. Duncan," all in Dunbar, *Folks from Dixie*.

36. "After a Visit," first and fourth stanzas, in Dunbar, *Lyrics of Lowly Life*, 91–92.

37. "A Family Feud," in Dunbar, *Folks from Dixie*, 137–38.

38. "Nelse Hatton's Vengeance," in ibid., 190–91.

39. Ibid., 201.

40. Ibid.; "The Finish of Patsy Barnes," in Dunbar, *Strength of Gideon*, 117.

41. "The Tragedy at Three Forks," in Dunbar, *Strength of Gideon*, 273, 280.

42. Dunbar, *Lyrics of Lowly Life*, introduction, xvi–xvii. For a brief overview of the scholarly controversy over Dunbar's work, see Braxton, "Paul Laurence Dunbar," 119–20.

43. *Lexington Leader*, May 31, 1906.

44. Annie Fellows Johnston, *Land of the Little Colonel*, 3.

45. Billy Reed, "Premier Comes Home to Pewee Valley," *Louisville Courier-Journal*, October 27, 1974; *Louisville Courier-Journal*, August 7, 1969.

46. Annie Fellows Johnston, *Land of the Little Colonel*, 6.

CHAPTER SEVEN

1. *Louisville Courier-Journal*, February 8, 1890.

2. Kentucky Historic Resources Individual Survey Form, Nicholasville/Jessamine County Confederate Monument, Civil War Monuments Files, folder 2, KHC.

3. Between 1895 and 1930 Kentuckians built Confederate monuments in Augusta (1903); Bardstown (1903); Bowling Green (1901); Cadiz (1913); Danville (1910); Fairview

(1924); Fulton (1902); Glasgow (1905); Harrodsburg (1902); Hickman (1913); Jeffersontown (1904); Lexington (1911); Louisville (1895, 1913); Madisonville (1907); Mayfield (1917); Morgantown (a Confederate and Union monument; 1907); Murray (1917); Nancy (1910); Nicholasville (1896); Owensboro (1900); Owingsville (1907); Paducah (1909); Pewee Valley (1904); Perryville (1902); Princeton (1912); Russellville (1910); and Water Valley (1909). In the same period, white Kentuckians built three Unionist monuments: Covington (1929); Louisville (1914); and Perryville (1928). Frankfort African Americans dedicated their own Unionist monument in 1924. All information and dates regarding the above monuments can be found in the Civil War Monument Files, KHC. Historian Thomas Clark claims that as of 1994 Kentucky had seventy-two Confederate monuments and only two Union monuments. In Loewen, *Lies across America*, 106, 109n.

4. *Lexington Leader*, May 30, 1899, September 18, 1901, September 1, 1898; Diary of Edward O. Guerrant, September 6, 1898, Edward O. Guerrant Papers, SHC-UNC. For more on the Spanish-American War and sectional reconciliation, see Silber, *Romance of Reunion*, 178–86; and Foster, *Ghosts of the Confederacy*, chap. 11.

5. *National Tribune* reprinted in the *Lexington Leader*, August 11, 1907.

6. *Lexington Leader*, May 29, 1905, January 22, 1907, September 15, 1903.

7. Ibid., January 10, 1902, February 13, 1903, May 28, 1907.

8. *Minutes of the Eighth Annual Meeting and Reunion*, 90–95; *Minutes of the Ninth Annual Meeting and Reunion*, 176–77.

9. *Louisville Commercial*, May 31, 1900; *Lost Cause* 3, no. 8 (March 1900): 135.

10. *Louisville Courier-Journal*, May 30, 1900.

11. Ibid., May 29, 1900, May 31, 1900.

12. Ibid., May 30, 1900.

13. *Louisville Commercial*, May 30, 1900; *Louisville Courier-Journal*, May 30, 1900.

14. *Minutes of the Tenth Annual Meeting and Reunion*, 17. According to Gaines Foster and other historians, southern participation in the Spanish-American War produced a feeling of patriotism among southerners and a level of respect for southern military valor among northerners, which helped bridge sectional differences. See Foster, *Ghosts of the Confederacy*, chap. 11.

15. UDC, Kentucky Division, membership index [ca. 1898–1920], United Daughters of the Confederacy Collection, KHS.

16. Cox, *Dixie's Daughters*, 2; *Lost Cause* 4, no. 10 (May 1901): 153; *Lexington Leader*, May 13, 1902. I borrow the term "Confederate culture" from Karen Cox.

17. *Lexington Leader*, October 25, 1902, June 17, 1906. For more on the UDC's educational impetus, see Cox, *Dixie's Daughters*, 118–40.

18. *Lexington Leader*, June 14, 1901, November 13, 1901; Cox, *Dixie's Daughters*, 129; *Lexington Leader*, November 17, 1901.

19. *Lexington Leader*, June 12, 1902. This article incorrectly identifies Galt as Laura Ross Talbot; see Cox, *Dixie's Daughters*, 118–19.

20. *Lexington Leader*, November 17, 1901.

21. Biographical information, Benjamin LeBree Papers, SC-FHS.

22. *Lost Cause* 5, no. 5 (December 1901): 71; *Lost Cause* 3, no. 3 (October 1899): 44; Durrant, "Gently Furled Banner," 175.

23. *Lost Cause* 3, no. 3 (October 1899): 42; *Lost Cause* 3, no. 8 (March 1900): 129. For an example of geographically diverse advertisers, see *Lost Cause* 4, no. 4 (May 1902): 160; *Lost Cause* 10, no. 2 (September 1903): 28; and *Lost Cause* 10, no. 9 (April 1904): 134.

24. *Lost Cause* 2, no. 5 (May 1899): 74; *Lost Cause* 7, no. 1 (August 1902): 4; *Lost Cause* 7, no. 2 (September 1902): 20.

25. *Lost Cause* 7, no. 3 (October 1902): 44; *Lost Cause* 7, no. 1 (August 1902): 12.

26. *Lost Cause* 3, no. 1 (March 1900): 135; *Lost Cause* 4 (April 1901): 136.

27. Brundage, "White Women and the Politics of Historical Memory," 163–64.

28. Sophie Fox Sea, "Slavery," pamphlet, Lucy Stuart Fitzhugh Scrapbook, SC-FHS.

29. *Lexington Leader*, April 10, 1903, April 14, 1902.

30. Alice Bruce Power, memoir of slavery on the Bruce homestead, February 17, 1914, 1, 4–5, 9, Dudley Family Papers, SC-FHS.

31. *Lexington Leader*, January 10, 1902; Gregory A. Waller, *Main Street Amusements*, 33.

32. *Lexington Leader*, January 10, 1902.

33. Ibid.

34. Wright, *In Pursuit of Equality*, 54–62; *Lexington Leader*, February 14, 1902, February 9, 1902.

35. *Lexington Leader*, February 14, 1902.

36. Ibid., January 12, 1902.

37. Ibid., January 25, 1902, January 16, 1902.

38. *Lexington Leader*, February 16, 1902, February 15, 1902, January 25, 1902. For other local arguments given in favor of banning the play, see *Lexington Leader*, February 2, 1902.

39. Minute book, 121, Confederate Veteran Association of Kentucky, Records, 1890–1915, SC-UK; *Lexington Leader*, November 5, 1905. For examples of correspondence, see Georgia Blackburn Pierce to Mrs. W. M. Bateman, January 22, 1906; Mrs. M. M. Teager to Mrs. W. M. Bateman, January 12, 1906; and Mrs. Benjamin Ashbrook to Mrs. W. M. Bateman, February 9, 1906; all in United Daughters of the Confederacy Collection, series 4, box 28, folder 6, KHS. Quote from Mrs. Florence Ward, in Mrs. Florence Ward to Mrs. Bateman, January 25, 1906, United Daughters of the Confederacy Collection, series 4, box 28, folder 6, KHS.

40. *Lexington Leader*, January 18, 1906.

41. Ibid., January 26, 1906.

42. Ibid., January 24, 1906.

43. Text of statute appears in Gregory A. Waller, *Main Street Amusements*, 273.

44. *Lexington Leader*, April 13, 1906, December 14, 1906, May 23, 1905, April 17, 1906.

45. Skain quoted in Gregory A. Waller, *Main Street Amusements*, 138.

46. Ibid., 151–60.

47. *Lexington Leader*, February 26, 1902, April 1, 1902, April 6, 1902, April 8, 1902, April 30, 1902, February 6, 1902, October 7, 1902; Kentucky Historic Resources Individual Survey Form, Perryville Battlefield State Historic Site/Boyle County Union Monument, Civil War Monument Files, folder 1, KHC; *Lexington Leader*, August 24, 1902. For more on commemorative and preservation efforts at Perryville, see Noe, *Perryville*, 358–67.

48. Ramage, *Rebel Raider*, 166.

49. Ibid., 218–23; Duke quote on 223.

50. *Lexington Leader*, October 20, 1906, May 1, 1907, July 23, 1908.

51. *Lexington Herald*, March 5, 1910. By one account, the UDC was only able to raise $1,500 of the $15,000, with the state providing the remainder. *Lexington Herald*, January 9, 1955.

52. Ramage, *Rebel Raider*, 256–58; *Lexington Herald*, March 5, 1910; *Lexington Herald-Leader*, April 30, 1989. For an interesting treatment of historical memory and the Morgan

statue, see Bishir, "Memorial Observances." Of all the public memory surrounding the Civil War, this seems to be one of the few aspects the state's population has not forgotten over time, as generations of University of Kentucky students have, in the dark of night, taken paintbrushes and cans of Rustoleum to the horse's ahistorical anatomy.

53. J. Stoddard Johnston, *Memorial History of Louisville*, 2:5–19; *Louisville Post*, September 9, 1895, GAR Scrapbook, 200, Grand Army of the Republic, 1895 encampment, SC-FHS; *Kentucky GAR Yearbook, 1910–1911*, 36–37, Minutes and Records of Captain James C. West Post #171, GAR, Department of Kentucky, 1890–1904, HL-BC.

54. *Kentucky GAR Yearbook, 1910–1911*, 53, Minutes and Records of Captain James C. West Post #171, GAR, Department of Kentucky, 1890–1904, HL-BC; *Lexington Leader*, November 13, 1901.

55. Quotes from Gannon, "The Won Cause," 218–19, 259, 267–68, 272; and *Kentucky Leader*, May 30, 1890.

56. Loewen, *Lies across America*, 167–68.

57. According to some accounts, when the Lincoln and Davis cabins were traveling together by train to Coney Island, the logs got mixed together, and the cabin that resulted was dubbed the "Lincoln and Davis Cabin." For this reason, along with the uncertain origins of the logs of the Lincoln cabin in the first place, it is questionable whether any of the logs under the Lincoln shrine ever housed the future president. See Loewen, *Lies across America*, 167–70; and Richard Lloyd Jones, "The Lincoln Birthplace Farm," *Collier's*, February 10, 1906, 13.

58. Richard Lloyd Jones, "The Lincoln Birthplace Farm," *Collier's*, February 10, 1906, 13. Committee members are listed on letterhead from correspondence in folder 1, Andrew Cowan Papers, SC-FHS.

59. Letterhead, folder 1, Andrew Cowan Papers, SC-FHS; Wright, *In Pursuit of Equality*, 111–13, 66, 70.

60. Folder 1, Andrew Cowan Papers, SC-FHS.

61. John H. Leathers to Andrew Cowan, February 15, 1909, Andrew Cowan Papers, SC-FHS.

62. Braden, *Building the Myth*, 165–67, 159–60.

63. Shaler, *Kentucky: A Pioneer Commonwealth*, 380.

64. Ibid., 386–87.

65. Shaler, *Autobiography*, 173; Shaler, "Orphan Brigade," 570–71.

66. "Thomas Speed," in J. Stoddard Johnston, *Memorial History of Louisville*, 1:460–62; Thomas Speed, *Union Regiments of Kentucky*, 6.

67. Thomas Speed, *Union Regiments of Kentucky*, 1–2.

68. Ibid., 701–2.

69. Ibid.

70. Thomas Speed, *Union Cause in Kentucky*, xii.

71. Ibid.

72. Horwitz, *Confederates in the Attic*, 101; *Lexington Leader*, June 3, 1909.

73. "Cradle of the Lost Cause: Birthplace of Jefferson Davis," 3.

74. Horwitz, *Confederates in the Attic*, 101; "Cradle of the Lost Cause: Birthplace of Jefferson Davis," 11.

75. *Frankfort State Journal*, July 3, 1924, quoted in pamphlet "Green Hill Cemetery, Frankfort Kentucky" (Frankfort: Kentucky Historical Society, 1998), Kentucky State University; Kentucky Historic Resources Individual Survey Form, Green Hill Cemetery/ Franklin County Union Monument, Civil War Monument Files, folder 2, KHC.

1. Warren, "Jefferson Davis Gets His Citizenship Back," 45–46.

2. Foster, *Ghosts of the Confederacy*, 197; Fitzpatrick, *And the Walls Came Tumbling Down*, 24.

3. *Louisville Courier-Journal*, April 10, 1998; Horwitz, *Confederates in the Attic*, 89–124; Warren, "Jefferson Davis Gets His Citizenship Back," 48.

4. *United Daughters of the Confederacy Magazine* 62, no. 5 (May 1999): 33; Horwitz, *Confederates in the Attic*, 101; *Lexington Herald-Leader*, July 10, 2001, September 11, 2001.

5. *Louisville Courier-Journal*, May 31, 2003, December 1, 2002; *Lexington Herald-Leader*, April 27, 2002.

6. Noe, *Perryville*, 363–67; Sanders, "Perryville"; *Lexington Herald-Leader*, September 30, 2001, June 5, 2007.

7. *Louisville Courier-Journal*, February 3, 2008.

8. This was actually the second Lincoln Heritage Trail to run through Kentucky. The first iteration came in the 1960s in the midst of the Civil War centennial celebration and was created by the marketing forces at the American Petroleum Institute in an effort to encourage Americans to take to the road and buy more gasoline. The 1960s version was less historically and more tourist-oriented, including sites such as Churchill Downs and the Lake Cumberland Resort golf course, places which did not exist in Lincoln's lifetime. See Ferguson, *Land of Lincoln*, 201–2; and <<http://johnhuntmorgan.scv.org/articles/lincolnplate.htm>>, accessed July 26, 2009.

9. Warren, "Jefferson Davis Gets His Citizenship Back," 49.

Bibliography

MANUSCRIPT COLLECTIONS

Berea, Kentucky
  Berea College, Hutchins Library
    Appalachian Feuds Collection
    William Goodell Frost Collection
    Gibson-Humphrey Family Papers
    Guerrant Family Papers
    Joseph Horace Lewis Papers
    Abraham Lincoln Collection
    Minutes and Records of Captain James C. West Post #171, GAR,
      Department of Kentucky, 1890–1904
Chapel Hill, North Carolina
  University of North Carolina, Chapel Hill, Southern Historical Collection
    John Fox Jr. Letters
    Edward O. Guerrant Papers
    Leeland Hathaway Recollections
    Maria Southgate Hawes Reminiscences
    Sallie Rowan Saufley Papers
    Charles B. Simrall Papers
    Nannie Haskins Williams Diary
Frankfort, Kentucky
  Kentucky Heritage Council, State Historic Preservation Office
    Civil War Monument Files
  Kentucky Historical Society, Martin F. Schmidt Archives and Research Library
    Simon Bolivar Buckner Papers Collection
    Robert H. Earnest Papers
    Andrew Harding Letters
    John T. Harrington Letters
    Hiram Hawkins Papers
    Hiram Hogg Papers
    Kentucky Confederate Home Records
    Thomas Leech Letters
    Andrew Phillips Letter
    D. C. Phillips Letter
    Raynor Purchase

Scroggin/Haviland Collection
D. Howard Smith Papers
Stone Family Papers
J. R. Thornton Letter
United Daughters of the Confederacy Collection
Wallace-Starling Diaries and Papers
Alfred West Papers
Kentucky State University, Paul G. Blazer Library, Special Collections
Green Hill Cemetery Records
History of the Anti–Separate Coach Movement of Kentucky (published under the
auspices of the State and Central Executive Committees of Kentucky)
Lexington, Kentucky
University of Kentucky, Margaret I. King Library, Special Collections and Archives
Benjamin Helm Bristow Collection
Benjamin F. Buckner Collection
Clay Family Papers
J. Winston Coleman Collection
Confederate Soldiers Home and Widows and Orphans Asylum, Scott County
Record Book
Confederate Veteran Association of Kentucky, Records, 1890–1915
Sprague Family Papers
Ward Family Papers
Wickliffe-Preston Papers
Young/Wooten Collection
Louisville, Kentucky
Filson Historical Society, Special Collections
Bullitt Family Papers
Andrew Cowan Papers
Dudley Family Papers
Lucy Stuart Fitzhugh Scrapbook
Grand Army of the Republic, 1895 encampment
Edward O. Guerrant Papers
Haldeman Family Papers
John F. Jefferson Diaries
Kentucky Colonels Records
Benjamin LeBree Papers
Alfred Pirtle Papers
Henry Watterson Papers
Enid Yandell Papers
Bennett Young Papers

NEWSPAPERS AND PERIODICALS

American Review of Reviews
Atlantic Monthly
Berea Quarterly
Century Illustrated Monthly Magazine
Cincinnati Commercial

Cincinnati Gazette
Confederate Veteran
Daily Kentucky Statesman
Harper's New Monthly Magazine
Indianapolis Freeman

Kentucky Leader
Kentucky Review
Kentucky Statesman
Lexington Herald
Lexington Herald-Leader
Lexington Leader
Lexington Observer and Reporter
Lexington Transcript
Lost Cause

Louisville Commercial
Louisville Courier-Journal
Louisville Post
Louisville Times
New York Times
Southern Bivouac
Southern Living
Tri-weekly Commonwealth (Frankfort, Ky.)
Tri-weekly Yeoman (Frankfort, Ky.)

PUBLISHED DOCUMENTS

"The Cradle of the Lost Cause: Birthplace of Jefferson Davis, Only President of the Confederacy, Fairview, Kentucky; Monument Souvenir" (Mrs. T. C. Underwood copyright 1928).

Louisville Blue Book of Selected Names of Louisville and Suburban Towns . . . for the Year Ending 1904. 1904.

"Message of the President of the United States, Communicating, in Compliance with a Resolution of the Senate of December 20, 1864, Information in Relation to the Arrest of Colonel Richard T. Jacobs, Lieutenant Governor of the State of Kentucky, and Colonel Frank Wolford, One of the Presidential Electors of that State." Washington, D.C., 1865.

The Minutes of the Third Annual Meeting and Reunion of the United Confederate Veterans, New Orleans, 1892. New Orleans: Hopkins Printing Office, 1892.

The Minutes of the Seventh Annual Meeting and Reunion of the United Confederate Veterans, Nashville, 1897. New Orleans: Hopkins Printing Office, 1897.

The Minutes of the Eighth Annual Meeting and Reunion of the United Confederate Veterans, Atlanta, 1898. New Orleans: Hopkins Printing Office, 1898.

The Minutes of the Ninth Annual Meeting and Reunion of the United Confederate Veterans, Charleston, S.C., 1899. New Orleans: Hopkins Printing Office, 1900.

The Minutes of the Tenth Annual Meeting and Reunion of the United Confederate Veterans, Louisville, 1900. New Orleans: Hopkins Printing Office, 1901.

Proceedings of the First to Tenth Meetings 1866–1876 of the National Encampment of the Grand Army of the Republic. Philadelphia: Samuel P. Town, 1877.

"Robert E. Lee: In Memoriam, a Tribute of Respect Offered by the Citizens of Louisville." Louisville: John P. Morton, 1870.

Southern Historical Society Papers.

U.S. Bureau of the Census. *Eighth Census of Agriculture: 1860*. Washington, D.C.: Government Printing Office, 1860.

WEBSITES

www.culbertsonmansion.us
www.littlecolonel.com

Allen, James Lane. *The Flute and Violin and Other Kentucky Tales and Romances*. New York: Harper, 1899.

———. "Mountain Passes of the Cumberland." *Harper's New Monthly Magazine*, September 1890, 561–76.

———. "Through the Cumberland Mountains on Horseback." *Harper's New Monthly Magazine*, June 1886, 50–66.

Barton, William E. "Abraham Lincoln, Kentucky Mountaineer." An address delivered before the faculty and students of Berea College, Berea, Ky., Thursday, March 8, 1923. Berea: Berea College Press, 1923.

———. *A Hero in Homespun: A Tale of the Loyal South*. Boston: Lamson, Wolfe, 1897.

Blassingame, John W., and John R. McKivigan, eds. *The Frederick Douglass Papers, Series One: Speeches, Debates, and Interviews, Volume 5: 1881–95*. New Haven: Yale University Press, 1992.

Breckinridge, Robert J. "The Civil War: Its Nature and End." (Reprinted from *Danville Quarterly Review*, December 1861.) Louisville: Lost Cause Press, 1869.

Bruner, Peter. *A Slave's Adventures toward Freedom: Not Fiction, but the True Story of a Struggle*. [1918.] Chapel Hill: University of North Carolina Press, 2000.

Burton, Thomas William. *What Experience Has Taught Me: An Autobiography of Thomas William Burton*. Cincinnati: Press of Jennings and Graham, 1910.

Castleman, John B. *Active Service*. Louisville: Courier-Journal Job Printing Co., 1917.

Cobb, Irvin S. *Back Home: Being the Narrative of Judge Priest and His People*. New York: Grosset & Dunlap, 1911.

Coleman, J. Winston, Jr. "Mrs. Stowe, Kentucky, and Uncle Tom's Cabin." Harrogate Department of Lincolnia, Lincoln Memorial University, 1946.

Collins, Lewis, and Richard Collins. *Collins' Historical Sketches of Kentucky*. Rev. ed., Vol. 1. Covington, Ky., 1882.

Duke, Basil. *The Civil War Reminiscences of Basil W. Duke, C.S.A.* Garden City, N.Y.: Doubleday, Page, 1911.

Dunbar, Paul Laurence. *Folks from Dixie*. New York: Dodd, Mead, 1898.

———. *Lyrics of Lowly Life*. New York: Dodd, Mead, 1906.

———. *Strength of Gideon and Other Stories*. New York: Dodd, Mead, 1900.

Field, Henry M. *Blood Is Thicker Than Water: A Few Days among Our Southern Brethren*. New York: George Munro, 1886.

Fox, John, Jr. *Bluegrass and Rhododendron*. New York: Charles Scribner's, 1901.

———. "Comments on Kentucky." *Harper's New Monthly Magazine*, January 1889, 255–71.

———. *The Kentuckians*. New York: Harper, 1897.

———. *The Little Shepherd of Kingdom Come*. Lexington: University Press of Kentucky, 1987.

———. "Mountain Passes of the Cumberlands." *Harper's New Monthly Magazine*, September 1890, 561–76.

———. "Through the Cumberland Gap on Horseback." *Harper's New Monthly Magazine*, June 1886, 50–66.

Frost, William Goodell. "Our Contemporary Ancestors in the Southern Mountains." *Atlantic Monthly*, March 1899, 311–19.

———. "The Southern Mountaineer: Our Kindred of the Boone and Lincoln Type." *American Review of Reviews*, March 1900, 303–11.

Hardin, Elizabeth. *The Private War of Lizzie Hardin: A Kentucky Confederate Girl's Diary of the Civil War in Kentucky, Virginia, Tennessee, Alabama, and Georgia.* Edited by G. Glenn Clift. Frankfort: Kentucky Historical Society, 1963.

Historic Southern Monuments: Representative Memorials of the Heroic Dead of the Southern Confederacy. Compiled by Mrs. B. A. C. Emerson. New York: Neale, 1911.

Holt, Joseph. *Letter from the Honorable Joseph Holt upon the Policy of the General Government, the Pending Revolution, Its Objects, Its Probable Results If Successful, and the Duty of Kentucky in the Crisis.* Washington, D.C.: Henry Polkinhorn, 1861.

Johnston, Annie Fellows. *The Little Colonel.* Boston: L. C. Page, 1895.

———. *The Little Colonel Stories.* Boston: L. C. Page, 1899.

———. *The Little Colonel's House Party.* Boston: L. C. Page, 1900.

———. *The Little Colonel at Boarding School.* Boston: L. C. Page, 1903.

———. *The Little Colonel's Hero.* Boston: L. C. Page, 1903.

———. *The Little Colonel's Holidays.* Boston: L. C. Page, 1903.

———. *The Little Colonel in Arizona.* Boston: L. C. Page, 1905.

———. *The Little Colonel's Christmas Vacation.* Boston: L. C. Page, 1905.

———. *The Little Colonel: Maid of Honor.* Boston: L. C. Page, 1906.

———. *The Little Colonel's Knight Comes Riding.* Boston: L. C. Page, 1907.

———. *The Land of the Little Colonel: Reminiscence and Autobiography.* Boston: L. C. Page, 1929.

Johnston, J. Stoddard. *The Commercial History of the Southern States Covering the Post-Bellum Period, Kentucky.* Edited by A. B. Lipscomb. Louisville: John Morton, 1903.

———. *Kentucky Confederate Military History.* Vol. 9. Atlanta: Confederate Publishing Company, 1899.

———. *A Memorial History of Louisville from Its First Settlement to the Year 1896.* Vols. 1 and 2. Chicago: American Biographical Publishing Company, 1896.

Krock, Arthur. *Myself When I Was Young: Growing Up in the 1890's.* Boston: Little, Brown, 1973.

"Letters to Secretary Chase from the South, 1861." *American Historical Review* 4 (January 1899): 331–47.

Lloyd, John Uri. *Stringtown-on-the-Pike: A Tale of Northernmost Kentucky.* New York: Dodd, Mead, 1900.

Locke, David Ross. *Ekkoes from Kentucky, by Petroleum V. Nasby, P.M. at Confedrit X Roads (Which Is in the State uv Kentucky), and Perfesser uv Biblikle Polity in the Southern Military and Classikle Institoot: Bein a Perfect Record uv the Ups and Downs and Experiences uv the Democricy, doorin the Eventful Year 1867, ez Seen by a Naturalized Kentuckian.* Boston: Lee and Shepard, 1868.

Miller, Maude Barnes. *Dear Wife: Letters from a Union Colonel.* Irvine, Ky.: Estill County Historical and Genealogical Society, 2001.

Pinkerton, Alan. *Strikers, Communists, Tramps, and Detectives.* New York: G. W. Carleton, 1883.

Rawick, George P., ed. *The American Slave: A Composite Autobiography.* 19 vols. Westport, Conn.: Greenwood Press, 1972.

Redfield, H. V. *Homicide, North and South.* Philadelphia: J. B. Lippincott, 1880.

Reid, Whitelaw. *After the War: A Tour of the Southern States, 1865–1866.* New York: Harper Torch Books, 1866.

Semple, Ellen Churchill. "The Anglo-Saxons of the Kentucky Mountains: A Study in Anthropogeography." *Geographic Journal* 17 (June 1901): 588–623.

Shaler, Nathaniel Southgate. *The Autobiography of Nathaniel Southgate Shaler*. Boston: Houghton Mifflin, 1909.

———. *Kentucky: A Pioneer Commonwealth*. Boston: Houghton Mifflin, 1893.

———. "The Orphan Brigade." *Atlantic Monthly*, October 1906, 570–71.

Smith, James L. "Autobiography of James L. Smith." In *Five Black Lives*, edited by Arna Bontemps. Middletown, Conn.: Wesleyan University Press, 1971.

Smith, S. E., ed. *History of the Anti–Separate Coach Movement of Kentucky*. Evansville, Ind., n.d. [ca. 1895].

Speed, James. *James Speed: A Personality*. Louisville: John P. Morton, 1914.

Speed, John Gilmer. "The Kentuckian." *Century Magazine*, April 1900, 946–52.

Speed, Thomas, *The Union Cause in Kentucky, 1860–1865*. New York: G. P. Putnam's, 1907.

———. *The Union Regiments of Kentucky: Published under the Auspices of the Union Soldiers and Sailors Monument Association*. Louisville: Courier Journal Job Printing Co., 1897.

Stowe, Harriet Beecher. *Uncle Tom's Cabin, or, Life among the Lowly*. New York: Viking, 1982.

Tuttle, John. *The Union, the Civil War, and John W. Tuttle: A Kentucky Captain's Account*. Edited by Hambleton Tapp and James C. Klotter. Frankfort: Kentucky Historical Society, 1980.

Underwood, Josie. *Josie Underwood's Civil War Diary*. Edited by Nancy Disher Baird. Lexington: University Press of Kentucky, 2009.

Warner, Charles Dudley. "Comments on Kentucky." *Harper's New Monthly Magazine*, January 1889, 255–71.

Watterson, Henry. *The Compromises of Life and Other Lectures and Addresses, Including Some Observations on the Downward Tendencies of Modern Society*. New York: Fox, Duffield, 1903.

———. *The Editorials of Henry Watterson*. Edited by Arthur Krock. Louisville: Louisville Courier-Journal Co., 1923.

———. *"Marse Henry," An Autobiography*. Vol. 1. New York: George H. Doran, 1919.

Young, Cale Rice. "Annie Fellows Johnston." *Library of Southern Literature*. Vol. 17. Edited by John Calvin Metcalf, 325–27. Atlanta: Martin and Hoyt, 1923.

SECONDARY SOURCES

Anderson, Benedict. *Imagined Communities: Reflections on the Origin and Spread of Nationalism*. London: Verso, 1983.

"Annie Fellows Johnston." *Dictionary of American Biography* 10, edited by Dumas Malone, 137–38. New York: Charles Scribner's, 1933.

Apple, Lindsey, Frederick A. Johnston, and Anne Bolton Evans, eds. *Scott County Kentucky: A History*. Georgetown, Ky.: Scott County Historical Society, 1993.

Aron, Stephen. *How the West Was Lost: The Transformation of Kentucky from Daniel Boone to Henry Clay*. Baltimore: Johns Hopkins University Press, 1996.

Austin, James C. *Petroleum V. Nasby (David Ross Locke)*. New York: Twayne, 1965.

Ayers, Edward L. *Vengeance and Justice: Crime and Punishment in the 19th Century American South*. New York: Oxford University Press, 1984.

Batteau, Allen. *The Invention of Appalachia*. Tucson: University of Arizona Press, 1990.

Bederman, Gail. *Manliness and Civilization: A Cultural History of Gender and Race in the United States, 1880–1917*. Chicago: University of Chicago Press, 1995.

Berry, Mary Clay. *Voices from the Century Before: The Odyssey of a 19th-Century Kentucky Family*. New York: Arcade, 1997.

Bigham, Darrel. *On Jordan's Banks: Emancipation and Its Aftermath in the Ohio River Valley*. Lexington: University Press of Kentucky, 2005.

Bishir, Catherine. "Building a Southern Past, 1855–1915." In *Where These Memories Grow: History, Memory, and Southern Identity*, edited by W. Fitzhugh Brundage, 139–68. Chapel Hill: University of North Carolina Press, 2000.

"Landmarks of Power: Building a Southern Past, 1855–1915." *Southern Cultures* 1 (1993): 5–45.

———. "Memorial Observances." *Southern Cultures* 15 (Summer 2009): 61–85.

Blair, William. *Cities of the Dead: Contesting the Memory of the Civil War in the South, 1865–1914*. Chapel Hill: University of North Carolina Press, 2003.

Blight, David W. *Race and Reunion: The Civil War in American Memory*. Cambridge: Belknap Press of Harvard University Press, 2001.

Bodnar, John. *Remaking America: Public Memory, Commemoration, and Patriotism in the Twentieth Century*. Princeton, N.J.: Princeton University Press, 1992.

Bolin, James Duane. *Bossism and Reform in a Southern City: Lexington, Kentucky, 1880–1940*. Lexington: University Press of Kentucky, 2000.

Botkin, B. A. *Treasures of Southern Folklore: Stories, Ballads, Traditions, and Folkways of People of the South*. New York: Crown, 1949.

Bottorff, William K. *James Lane Allen*. New York: Twayne, 1964.

Braden, Waldo A. *Building the Myth: Selected Speeches Memorializing Abraham Lincoln*. Urbana: University of Illinois Press, 1990.

Braxton, Joanne. "Paul Laurence Dunbar." In *The Concise Oxford Companion to African American Literature*, edited by William Andrews, Frances Smith Foster, and Trudier Harris, 119–20. New York: Oxford University Press, 2001.

Brown, Elsa Barkley, and Gregg D. Kimball. "Mapping the Terrain of Black Richmond." In *The New African American Urban History*, edited by Kenneth W. Goings and Raymond A. Mohl, 66–115. Thousand Oaks, Calif.: Sage, 1996.

Brown, Kent Masterson. "A Tribute to the Orphan Brigade of Kentucky." In *The Civil War in Kentucky: Battle for the Bluegrass State*, edited by Kent Masterson Brown, 271–305. Mason City, Iowa: Savas, 2000.

Brundage, W. Fitzhugh. *The Southern Past: A Clash between Race and Memory*. Cambridge: Belknap Press of Harvard University Press, 2005.

———. *Where These Memories Grow: History, Memory, and Southern Identity*. Chapel Hill: University of North Carolina Press, 2001.

———. "White Women and the Politics of Historical Memory in the New South, 1880–1920." In *Jumpin' Jim Crow: Southern Politics from Civil War to Civil Rights*, edited by Jane Dailey, Glenda Gilmore, and Bryant Simon, 115–39. Princeton, N.J.: Princeton University Press, 2000.

———. "'Woman's Hand and Heart and Deathless Love': White Women and the Commemorative Impulse in the New South." In *Monuments to the Lost Cause: Women, Art, and the Landscapes of Southern Memory*, edited by Cynthia Mills and Pamela H. Simpson, 64–82. Knoxville: University of Tennessee Press, 2003.

Campbell, Tracy. *The Politics of Despair: Power and Resistance in the Tobacco Wars*. Lexington: University Press of Kentucky, 1993.

Cobb, James C. *Away Down South: A History of Southern Identity*. New York: Oxford University Press, 2005.

Connelly, Thomas L., and Barbara G. Bellows. *God and General Longstreet: The Lost Cause and the Southern Mind*. Baton Rouge: Louisiana State University Press, 1982.

Coulter, E. Merton. *The Civil War and Readjustment in Kentucky*. Chapel Hill: University of North Carolina Press, 1926.

Cox, Karen. *Dixie's Daughters: The United Daughters of the Confederacy and the Preservation of Confederate Culture*. Gainesville: University Press of Florida, 2003.

Clark, Kathleen. "Celebrating Freedom: Emancipation Day Celebrations and African American Memory in the Early Reconstruction South." In *Where These Memories Grow: History, Memory, and Southern Identity*, edited by Fitzhugh Brundage, 107–32. Chapel Hill: University of North Carolina Press, 2001.

———. *Defining Moments: African American Commemoration and Political Culture in the South, 1863–1913*. Chapel Hill: University of North Carolina Press, 2005.

———. "Making History: African American Commemorative Celebrations in Augusta, Georgia, 1865." In *Monuments to the Lost Cause: Women, Art, and the Landscapes of Southern Memory*, edited by Cynthia Mills and Pamela H. Simpson, 46–63. Knoxville: University of Tennessee Press, 2003.

Clark, T. D. "The Slave Trade between Kentucky and the Cotton Kingdom." *Mississippi Valley Historical Review* 21 (December 1934): 331–42.

Coleman, J. Winston, Jr. "Lexington's Slave Dealers and Their Southern Trade." *Filson Club History Quarterly* 12 (1938): 1–23.

Connelly, Thomas. "Neo-Confederatism or Power Vacuum? Post-War Kentucky Politics Reappraised." *Register of the Kentucky Historical Society* 64 (October 1966): 257–69.

Cooling, B. Franklin. "A People's War: Partisan Conflict in Tennessee and Kentucky." In *Guerrillas, Unionists, and Violence on the Confederate Home Front*, edited by Daniel E. Sutherland, 112–32. Fayetteville: University of Arkansas Press, 1999.

Copeland, James E. "Where Were the Kentucky Unionists and Secessionists?" *Register of the Kentucky Historical Society* 71 (October 1973): 344–63.

Crane, Michael. "'The Rebels Are Bold, Defiant, and Unscrupulous in Their Dementions of All Men': Social Violence in Daviess County, Kentucky, 1861–1868." *Ohio Valley History* 2 (Spring 2002): 17–29.

Davies, Wallace Evan. *Patriotism on Parade: The Story of Veterans' and Hereditary Organizations in America, 1783–1900*. Cambridge: Harvard University Press, 1955.

———. "The Problem of Race Segregation in the Grand Army of the Republic." *Journal of Southern History* 13 (August 1947): 354–72.

Doyle, Don H. *New Men, New Cities, New South: Atlanta, Nashville, Charleston, Mobile, 1860–1910*. Chapel Hill: University of North Carolina Press, 1990.

Drake, Richard. *A History of Appalachia*. Lexington: University Press of Kentucky, 2001.

———. "Slavery and Anti-Slavery in Appalachia." In *Appalachians and Race: The Mountain South from Slavery to Segregation*, edited by John C. Inscoe, 16–26. Lexington: University Press of Kentucky, 2001.

Dunaway, Wilma. "Put in Master's Pocket: Cotton Expansion and Interstate Slave Trading in the Mountain South." In *Appalachians and Race: The Mountain South from Slavery to Segregation*, edited by John C. Inscoe, 116–33. Lexington: University Press of Kentucky, 2001.

Ellis, William, H. E. Everman, and Richard Sears. *Madison County: 100 Years in Retrospect*. Richmond, Ky.: Madison County Historical Society, 1985.

Faust, Drew Gilpin. *Mothers of Invention: Women of the Slaveholding South in the American Civil War*. Chapel Hill: University of North Carolina Press, 1996.

Fellman, Michael. *Inside War: The Guerrilla Conflict in Missouri during the Civil War*. New York: Oxford University Press, 1989.

Ferguson, Andrew. *Land of Lincoln: Adventures in Abe's America*. New York: Atlantic Monthly Press, 2007.

Fink, Leon. *Workingmen's Democracy: The Knights of Labor and American Politics*. Urbana: University of Illinois Press, 1983.

Flannery, Michael A. "Kentucky History Revisited: The Role of the Civil War in Shaping Kentucky's Collective Consciousness." *Filson Club History Quarterly* 71 (January 1997): 27–51.

Foner, Eric. *Reconstruction: America's Unfinished Revolution, 1863–1877*. New York: Harper and Row, 1988.

Foster, Gaines. *Ghosts of the Confederacy: Defeat, the Lost Cause, and the Emergence of the New South*. New York: Oxford University Press, 1987.

Freehling, William. *The South vs. the South: How Anti-Confederate Southerners Shaped the Course of the Civil War*. New York: Oxford University Press, 2001.

Gallagher, Gary W., and Alan T. Nolan, eds. *The Myth of the Lost Cause and Civil War History*. Bloomington: Indiana University Press, 2000.

Gaston, Paul M. *The New South Creed: A Study in Southern Mythmaking*. New York: Vintage, 1970.

Gilliam, Will D. "Robert J. Breckinridge: Kentucky Unionist." *Register of the Kentucky Historical Society* 69 (October 1971): 362–84.

Grant, Joanne. *Black Protest: History, Documents, and Analyses, 1619 to the Present*. Greenwich, Conn.: Fawcett, 1968.

Grant, Susan-Mary. *North over South: Northern Nationalism and American Identity in the Antebellum Era*. Lawrence: University Press of Kansas, 2000.

Halbwachs, Maurice. *On Collective Memory*. Translated by Lewis A. Coser. Chicago: University of Chicago Press, 1992.

Hale, Grace Elizabeth. *Making Whiteness: The Culture of Segregation in the South, 1890–1940*. New York: Pantheon, 1998.

Hancock, Harold B. "Reconstruction in Delaware." In *Radicalism, Racism, and Party Realignment: The Border States during Reconstruction*, edited by Richard O. Curry, 188–219. Baltimore: Johns Hopkins University Press, 1969.

Harkins, Anthony. *Hillbilly: A Cultural History of an American Icon*. New York: Oxford University Press, 2004.

Harrison, Lowell H. "Kentucky-Born Generals in the Civil War." *Register of the Kentucky Historical Society* 64 (April 1966): 129–60.

Harrison, Lowell, and James Klotter. *A New History of Kentucky*. Lexington: University Press of Kentucky, 1997.

Hobsbawm, Eric, and Terrence Ranger, eds. *The Invention of Tradition*. London: Cambridge University Press, 1983.

Horwitz, Tony. *Confederates in the Attic: Dispatches from the Unfinished Civil War*. New York: Vintage, 1999.

Howard. Victor. *Black Liberation in Kentucky: Emancipation and Freedom, 1862–1884*. Lexington: University Press of Kentucky, 1983.

———. "Robert J. Breckinridge and the Slavery Controversy in Kentucky in 1849." *Filson Club History Quarterly* 53 (1979): 328–43.

Hunt, Lynn. *Politics, Culture, and Class in the French Revolution*. Berkeley: University of California Press, 1984.

Ireland, Robert M. "Law and Disorder in Nineteenth Century Kentucky." *Vanderbilt Law Review* 32 (1979): 281–304.

———. *Little Kingdoms: The Counties of Kentucky, 1850–1891*. Lexington: University Press of Kentucky, 1977.

———. "Violence." In *Our Kentucky: A Study of the Bluegrass State*, edited by James C. Klotter, 156–71. Lexington: University Press of Kentucky, 2000.

Jewett, Clayton E., and John O. Allen. *Slavery in the South: A State-by-State History*. Westport, Conn.: Greenwood, 2004.

Kachun, Mitch. *Festivals of Freedom: Memory and Meaning in African American Emancipation Celebrations, 1808–1915*. Amherst: University of Massachusetts Press, 2003.

Kaye, Marilyn. "Annie Fellows Johnston." In *American Writers for Children before 1900*. Vol. 42 of *Dictionary of Literary Biography*, edited by Glenn Estes, 251–77. Detroit: Gale, 1985.

Kentucky's Black Heritage: The Role of Black People in the History of Kentucky from the Pioneer Days to the Present. Frankfort: Kentucky Commission on Human Rights, 1971.

Kirby, Jack Temple. *Media-Made Dixie: The South in the American Imagination*. Rev. ed. Athens: University of Georgia Press, 1986.

Kleber, John, ed. *The Kentucky Encyclopedia*. Lexington: University Press of Kentucky, 1992.

Klotter, James. "The Black South in White Appalachia." *Journal of American History* 66 (March 1980): 832–49.

———. "Feuds in Appalachia: An Overview." *Filson Club History Quarterly* 56 (1982): 290–317.

———. *Kentucky: Portrait in Paradox, 1900–1950*. Frankfort: Kentucky Historical Society, 1996.

———. *Kentucky Justice, Southern Honor, and American Manhood: Understanding the Life and Death of Richard Reid*. Lexington: University Press of Kentucky, 2003.

Klotter, James C., and Hambleton Tapp. *Kentucky: Decades of Discord*. Frankfort: Kentucky Historical Society, 1974.

Knight, Grant C. *James Lane Allen and the Genteel Tradition*. Chapel Hill: University of North Carolina Press, 1935.

Krock, Arthur. *Myself When I Was Young: Growing Up in the 1890's*. Boston: Little, Brown, 1973.

Kunitz, Stanley, and Howard Haycraft, eds. "Annie Fellows Johnston." In *The Junior Book of Authors*. New York: H. W. Wilson, 1934.

Leighton, George R. *Five Cities: The Story of Their Youth and Old Age*. New York: Harper, 1939.

Lieb, Sandra. "Irvin S. Cobb." In *American Humorists, 1800–1950*. Vol. 11 of *Dictionary of Literary Biography*, edited by Stanley Trachtenberg, 8288. Detroit: Gale, 1982.

Loewen, James. *Lies across America: What Our Historic Sites Get Wrong*. New York: W. W. Norton, 1999.

Low, W. A. "The Freedman's Bureau in the Border States." In *Radicalism, Racism, and Party Realignment: The Border States during Reconstruction*, edited by Richard O. Curry, 245–64. Baltimore: Johns Hopkins University Press, 1969.

Lowenthal, David. *The Past Is a Foreign Country*. Cambridge: Cambridge University Press, 1985.

Lucas, Marion B. *From Slavery to Segregation, 1760–1891*. Vol. 1 of *A History of Blacks in Kentucky*. Frankfort: Kentucky Historical Society, 1992.

Lucas, Scott J. "'Indignities, Wrongs, and Outrages': Military and Guerrilla Incursions on Kentucky's Civil War Home Front." *Filson History Quarterly* 73 (October 1999): 355–76.

Mackey, Robert Russell. *The Uncivil War: Irregular Warfare in the Upper South, 1861–1865*. Norman: University of Oklahoma Press, 2004.

"The Magnetism of Pewee Valley." *Southern Living*, October 1970, 20.

Mann, Dorothea. "The Author of the Little Colonel Series." *Publishers Weekly*, October 24, 1931, 1925–27.

Margolies, Daniel S. *Henry Watterson and the New South: The Politics of Empire, Free Trade, and Globalization*. Lexington: University Press of Kentucky, 2006.

Marshall, Suzanne. *Violence in the Black Patch of Kentucky and Tennessee*. Columbia: University of Missouri Press, 1994.

Martin, James B. "Black Flag over the Bluegrass: Guerrilla Warfare in Kentucky, 1863–1865." *Register of the Kentucky Historical Society* 86 (Autumn 1988): 352–75.

Martinez, J. Michael, William D. Richardson, and Ron McNinch-Su. *Confederate Symbols in the Contemporary South*. Gainesville: University Press of Florida, 2000.

McConnell, Stuart. *Glorious Contentment: The Grand Army of the Republic, 1865–1900*. Chapel Hill: University of North Carolina Press, 1997.

McDowell, Richard E. *City of Conflict: Louisville during the Civil War, 1861–1864*. Louisville: Louisville Civil War Round Table, 1962.

McGuire, Sue Lynn. "The Little Colonel: A Phenomenon in Popular Literary Culture." *Register of the Kentucky Historical Society* 89, no. 2 (1991): 121–46.

McKinney, Gordon. "Industrialization and Violence in Appalachia in the 1890's." In *An Appalachian Symposium: Essays in Honor of Crastis D. Williams*, edited by J. W. Williamson, 131–46. Boone, N.C.: Appalachian State University Press, 1977.

———. "Southern Mountain Republicans and the Negro, 1865–1900." In *Appalachians and Race: The Mountain South from Slavery to Segregation*, edited by John C. Inscoe, 199–219. Lexington: University Press of Kentucky, 2001.

———. *Southern Mountain Republicans, 1865–1900: Politics and the Appalachian Community*. Chapel Hill: University of North Carolina Press, 1978.

McKnight, Brian. *Contested Borderland: The Civil War in Appalachian Kentucky and Virginia*. Lexington: University Press of Kentucky, 2006.

McPherson, James M. *Abraham Lincoln and the Second American Revolution*. New York: Oxford University Press, 1991.

Messmer, Charles K. "The End of an Era: Louisville in 1865." *Filson Club History Quarterly* 53 (July 1980): 239–71.

Millichap, Joseph. "Tobacco Wars." In *The Companion to Southern Literature: Themes, Genres, Places, People, Movements, and Motifs*, edited by Joseph M. Flora and Lucinda H. Mackethan, 906–7. Baton Rouge: Louisiana State University Press, 2002.

Mills, Cynthia, and Pamela H. Simpson. *Monuments to the Lost Cause: Women, Art, and the Landscapes of Southern Memory*. Knoxville: University of Tennessee Press, 2003.

Mott, Frank Luther. *Golden Multitudes: The Story of Best Sellers in the United States*. New York: Macmillan, 1947.

Myers, Marshall. "Union General Stephen Gano Burbridge: The Most Hated Man in Kentucky." In *Kentucky's Civil War, 1861–1865*, edited by Jerlene Rose, 144. Clay City, Ky.: Back Home Again in Kentucky, 2005.

Noe, Kenneth W. *Perryville: This Grand Havoc of Battle*. Lexington: University Press of Kentucky, 2001.

O'Leary, Cecilia Elizabeth. *To Die For: The Paradox of American Patriotism*. Princeton, N.J.: Princeton University Press, 1999.

Osterweis, Rollin. *The Myth of the Lost Cause, 1865–1900*. New York: Archon Books, 1973.

Osthaus, Carl. *Partisans of the Southern Press: Editorial Spokesmen of the Nineteenth Century*. Lexington: University Press of Kentucky, 1994.

Ozouf, Jacques, and Mona Ozouf. "Le Tour de France par deux enfants: The Little Red Book of the Republic." In *Traditions*, vol. 2 of *Realms of Memory: The Construction of the French Past*, edited by Pierre Nora, 124–48. New York: Columbia University Press, 1997.

Parrish, William E. "Reconstruction Politics in Missouri, 1865–1870." In *Radicalism, Racism, and Party Realignment: The Border States during Reconstruction*, edited by Richard O. Curry, 1–36. Baltimore: Johns Hopkins University Press, 1969.

Peterson, Gloria. *An Administrative History of Abraham Lincoln Birthplace National Historic Sites, Hodgenville, Kentucky*. Washington, D.C.: National Park Service, U.S. Department of Interior, September 20, 1968.

Phillips, Christopher. "The Chrysalis State: Slavery, Confederate Identity, and the Creation of the Border South." In *Inside the Confederate Nation: Essays in Honor of Emory Thomas*, edited by Lesley J. Gordon and John C. Inscoe, 147–64. Baton Rouge: Louisiana State University Press, 2005.

Pollard, Edward. *The Lost Cause Regained*. New York: G. W. Carleton, 1868.

Preston, John David. *The Civil War in the Big Sandy Valley of Kentucky*. Baltimore: Gateway, 1984.

Pringle, Henry. "Kentucky Bourbon: Henry Watterson." In *Highlights in the History of the American Press: A Book of Readings*, edited by Edwin H. Ford and Edwin Emery, 211–28. Minneapolis: University of Minnesota Press, 1954.

Ramage, James A. *Rebel Raider: The Life of General John Hunt Morgan*. Lexington: University Press of Kentucky, 1986.

Rhyne, J. Michael. "'We Are Mobed & Beat': Regulator Violence against Free Black Households in Kentucky's Bluegrass Region, 1865–1867." *Ohio Valley History* 2 (Spring 2002): 30–42.

Roach, Abby Meguire. "The Authors Club of Louisville: An Inside Story—I Remember." *Filson Club History Quarterly* 31 (1957): 29–37.

Rubin, Anne Sarah. *A Shattered Nation: The Rise and Fall of the Confederacy, 1861–1868*. Chapel Hill: University of North Carolina Press, 2007.

Rubin, Louis D., Jr., ed. *The History of Southern Literature*. Baton Rouge: Louisiana State University Press, 1982.

Russ, William A., Jr. "The Role Of Kentucky in 1867." *Susquehanna University Studies* 1 (January 1938): 106–14.

Sanders, Stuart W. "Perryville: The Bloody Tide–Turning Battle, the Aftermath, and Modern Preservation." In *Kentucky's Civil War, 1861–1865*, edited by Jerlene Rose, 94–97. Clay City, Ky.: Back Home Again in Kentucky, 2005.

Saunders, Steven, and Deane L. Root. "My Old Kentucky Home." In *The Music of Stephen C. Foster*, prepared by Steven Saunders and Deane L. Root, vol. 1, *1844–1855*, 235–39. Washington, D.C.: Smithsonian Institution Press, 1990.

Savage, Kirk. *Standing Soldiers, Kneeling Slaves: Race, War, and Monument in Nineteenth-Century America*. Princeton, N.J.: Princeton University Press, 1997.

Scott, Anne Firor. *Making the Invisible Woman Visible*. Urbana: University of Illinois Press, 1984.

Sears, Richard. *Camp Nelson, Kentucky: A Civil War History*. Lexington: University Press of Kentucky, 2007.

Shackel, Paul A., ed. *Myth, Memory, and the Making of the American Landscape*. Gainesville: University Press of Florida, 2001.

Shapiro, Henry D. *Appalachia on Our Mind: The Southern Mountains and Mountaineers in the American Consciousness, 1870–1920*. Chapel Hill: University of North Carolina Press, 1978.

Silber, Nina. *The Romance of Reunion: Northerners and the South, 1865–1900*. Chapel Hill: University of North Carolina Press, 1993.

———. "What Does America Need So Much as Americans?" In *Appalachians and Race: The Mountain South from Slavery to Segregation*, edited by John C. Inscoe, 245–58. Lexington: University Press of Kentucky, 2001.

Simon, Bryant. "The Novel as Social History: Erskine Caldwell's *God's Little Acre* and Class Relations in the New South." *Southern Cultures* (December 1996): 375–92.

Singal, Daniel. *The War Within: From Victorian to Modernist Thought in the South, 1919–1945*. Chapel Hill: University of North Carolina Press, 1982.

Smith, Edward Conrad. *The Borderland in the Civil War*. New York: Macmillan, 1927.

Soderberg, Susan Cooke. *"Lest We Forget": A Guide to Civil War Monuments in Maryland*. Shippensberg, Pa.: White Mane, 1995.

Steele, Elizabeth. "Mrs. Johnston's Little Colonel." In *Challenges in American Culture*, edited by Ray B. Brown et al., 217–23. Bowling Green, Ohio: Bowling Green Popular Press, 1970.

Stiles, T. J. *Jesse James: Last Rebel of the Civil War*. New York: Alfred A. Knopf, 2002.

Tallant, Harold. *Evil Necessity: Slavery and Political Culture in Antebellum Kentucky*. Lexington: University Press of Kentucky, 2003.

Tapp, Hamilton. "The Slavery Controversy between Robert Wickliffe and Robert J. Breckinridge Prior to the Civil War." *Filson Club History Quarterly* 19 (July 1945): 120–44.

Tapp, Hamilton, and James C. Klotter. *Kentucky: Decades of Discord, 1865–1900*. Frankfort: Kentucky Historical Society, 1978.

Taylor, Amy Murrell. *The Divided Family in Civil War America*. Chapel Hill: University of North Carolina Press, 2005.

Taylor, William. *Cavalier and Yankee: The Old South and American National Character*. New York: Harper and Row, 1961.

Thelen, David. "Memory and American History." *Journal of American History* 75 (March 1989): 1117–29.

Thomas, Samuel W., and William Morgan. *Old Louisville: The Victorian Era*. Louisville: Courier-Journal/Louisville Times/Data Courier, 1975.

Townsend, John Wilson, ed. "Mrs. Annie Fellows Johnston." In *Kentucky in American Letters*, vol. 2, 165–67. Cedar Rapids, Iowa: Torch Press, 1913.

Trelease, Alan. *White Terror: The Ku Klux Klan Conspiracy and Southern Reconstruction*. Baton Rouge: Louisiana State University Press, 1971.

Trouillot, Michel-Rolph. *Silencing the Past: Power and the Production of History*. Boston: Beacon, 1995.

Turner, Wallace B. "Abolitionism in Kentucky." *Register of the Kentucky Historical Society* 69 (October 1971): 319–38.

Vandercook, Margaret. "Annie Fellows Johnston: The Beloved Writer of Books for Young Folk." *St. Nicholas, an Illustrated Magazine for Young Folks*, December 1913, 127–30.

Wagandt, Charles L. "Redemption or Reaction?—Maryland in the Post–Civil War Years." In *Radicalism, Racism, and Party Realignment: The Border States during Reconstruction*, edited by Richard O. Curry, 146–87. Baltimore: Johns Hopkins University Press, 1969.

Waldrep, Christopher. *Night Riders: Defending Community in the Black Patch, 1890–1915.* Durham: Duke University Press, 1993.

Wall, Joseph. *Henry Watterson: Reconstructed Rebel.* New York: Oxford University Press, 1956.

Waller, Altina. *Feud: Hatfields, McCoys, and Social Change in Appalachia, 1860–1900.* Chapel Hill: University of North Carolina Press, 1988.

———. "Feuding in Appalachia: The Evolution of a Cultural Stereotype." In *Appalachia in the Making: The Mountain South in the Nineteenth Century*, edited by Mary Beth Pudup, Dwight Billings, and Altina Waller, 347–76. Chapel Hill: University of North Carolina Press, 1995.

Waller, Gregory A. *Main Street Amusements: Movies and Commercial Entertainment in a Southern City, 1896–1930.* Washington, D.C.: Smithsonian Institution Press, 1995.

Ward, William. "Anni Mirabiles: Kentucky Literature at the Turn of the Century." *Kentucky Review* 5 (1985): 32–45.

Warren, Robert Penn. "Jefferson Davis Gets His Citizenship Back." *New Yorker*, February 25, 1980, 44–99.

———. *The Legacy of the Civil War: Meditations on the Centennial.* New York: Random House, 1961.

Weaver, Bill. "Louisville's Labor Disturbance, July 1877." *Filson Club History Quarterly* 48 (July 1974): 177–86.

Webb, Ross A. "Kentucky: Pariah among the Elect." In *Radicalism, Racism, and Party Realignment: The Border States during Reconstruction*, edited by Richard O. Curry, 105–45. Baltimore: Johns Hopkins University Press, 1969.

———. *Kentucky in the Reconstruction Era.* Lexington: University Press of Kentucky, 1979.

Whites, LeeAnn. *The Civil War as a Crisis in Gender, Augusta, Georgia, 1860–1890.* Athens: University of Georgia Press, 1995.

———. *Gender Matters: Civil War, Reconstruction, and the Making of the New South.* New York: Palgrave Macmillan, 2005.

Wiggins, William H., Jr. *O! Freedom: Afro-American Emancipation Celebrations.* Knoxville: University of Tennessee Press, 1987.

Will, Thomas E. "Bradley T. Johnson's Lost Cause: Maryland's Confederate Identity in the New South." *Maryland Historical Magazine* 94 (Spring 1999): 5–30.

Williams, John Alexander. *Appalachia: A History.* Chapel Hill: University of North Carolina Press, 2002.

Williams, Rusty. *My Old Confederate Home: A Respectable Place for Veterans.* Lexington: University Press of Kentucky, 2010.

Williamson, Joel. *The Crucible of Race: Black-White Relations in the American South since Emancipation.* New York: Oxford University Press, 1984.

Wilson, Charles Reagan. *Baptized in Blood: The Religion of the Lost Cause, 1895–1920.* Athens: University of Georgia Press, 1980.

Wilson, Shannon. "Lincoln's Sons and Daughters: Berea College, Lincoln Memorial University, and the Myth of Unionist Appalachia, 1866–1910." In *The Civil War in Appalachia: Collected Essays*, edited by Kenneth W. Noe and Shannon B. Wilson, 242–64. Knoxville: University of Tennessee Press, 1997.

Woodward, C. Vann. *Origins of the New South, 1877–1913*. Baton Rouge: Louisiana State University Press, 1951.

———. *Reunion and Reaction: The Compromise of 1877 and the End of Reconstruction*. New York: Oxford University Press, 1991.

Wright, George. *Life behind a Veil: Blacks in Louisville, Kentucky, 1865–1930*. Baton Rouge: Louisiana State University Press, 1985.

———. *In Pursuit of Equality, 1890–1980*. Vol. 2 of *A History of Blacks in Kentucky*. Frankfort: Kentucky Historical Society, 1992.

———. *Racial Violence in Kentucky, 1865–1940: Lynchings, Mob Rule, and "Legal Lynchings."* Baton Rouge: Louisiana State University Press, 1990.

Wyatt-Brown, Bertram. *Southern Honor: Ethics and Behavior in the Old South*. New York: Oxford University Press, 2007.

Yater, George H. *Two Hundred Years at the Falls of the Ohio: A History of Louisville and Jefferson County*. Louisville: Heritage Corporation of Louisville and Jefferson County, 1979.

Yonkers, Charles E. "The Civil War Transformation of George W. Smith: How a Western Kentucky Farmer Evolved from a Unionist Whig to Pro-Southern Democrat." *Register of the Kentucky Historical Society* 103 (Autumn 2005): 661–90.

York, Bill. *John Fox Jr., Appalachian Author*. Jefferson, N.C.: McFarland, 2003.

THESES AND DISSERTATIONS

Astor, Aaron. "Belated Confederates: Black Politics, Guerrilla Violence, and the Collapse of Conservative Unionism in Kentucky and Missouri, 1860–1872." Ph.D. diss., Northwestern University, 2006.

Durrant, Susan Speare. "The Gently Furled Banner: The Development of the Myth of the Lost Cause, 1865–1900." Ph.D. diss., University of North Carolina–Chapel Hill, 1972.

Finch, Herbert. "Organized Labor in Kentucky, 1880–1914." Ph.D. diss., University of Kentucky, 1965.

Gannon, Barbara A., "The Won Cause: Black and White Comradeship in the Grand Army of the Republic." Ph.D. diss., Pennsylvania State University, 2005.

Harlow, Luke. "From Border South to Solid South: Religion, Race, and the Making of Confederate Kentucky, 1830–1880." Ph.D. diss., Rice University, 2009.

Hoskins, Patricia. "'The Old First Is with the South': The Civil War, Reconstruction, and Memory in the Jackson Purchase Region of Kentucky." Ph.D. diss., Auburn University, 2009.

Margolies, Daniel Stuart. "God's Promise Redeemed: Marse Henry and the Compromises of American Empire." Ph.D. diss., University of Wisconsin–Madison, 1999.

Morelock, Kolan. "Literary Societies, Dramatic Clubs, and Community Culture: A Study of Lexington Intellectual Life during the Gilded Age and Progressive Era." Ph.D. diss., University of Kentucky, 1999.

Rhyne, J. Michael. "Rehearsal for Redemption: The Politics of Post-Emancipation Violence in Kentucky's Bluegrass Region, 1865–1867." Ph.D. diss., University of Cincinnati, 2006.

Rockenbach, Stephen I. "'War upon Our Border': War and Society in Two Ohio Valley Communities, 1861–1865." Ph.D. diss., University of Cincinnati, 2005.

Streater, Kristen Lenore. "She-Rebels on the Border: Gender and Politics in Civil War Kentucky." Ph.D. diss., University of Kentucky, 2001.

Sullivan, James P. "Louisville and Her Southern Alliance, 1865–1890." Ph.D. diss., University of Kentucky, 1965.

Wharton, George Christopher. "Henry Watterson—A Study of Selected Speeches on Reconciliation in the Post-Bellum Period." Ph.D. diss., Louisiana State University, 1974.

Index

African Americans: and memory of Civil War, 4, 5, 167–71; and postwar politics, 5, 46–48, 62–64; as federal soldiers, 20, 21, 26–29; enlistment of, as cause of white disloyalty, 26–30; enlistment of, and historical memory, 29, 44, 91–93, 99–103, 179–80, 182; and Republican Party, 46–48; and memorial celebrations, 47, 81, 92–93; gain suffrage, 54; violence against, 58–70; lynching of, 60–65; and self-defense against violence, 63; violence against, and historical memory, 64; and Civil War monuments, 94, 182, 184–86; and 1883 national convention in Louisville, 99–102; and Jim Crow laws, 102–3; participation in 1895 GAR encampment, 105–8; objectification of, in historical memory, 107–8, 164–71; presence of, in Appalachian Kentucky, 115–16, 118–20, 122, 126, 201 (n. 23); participation of, in Lincoln birthplace dedication, 176–77. *See also* Slavery
Allen, James Lane, 111, 112, 114, 123, 128, 134, 137
Allen, Sue, 162
Allen, Theodore, 157
Allen County, Ky., 57
American Review of Reviews, 119
"The Anglo-Saxons of the Kentucky Mountains" (Semple), 113–14
Appalachia, 111–14. *See also* Appalachian Kentucky
Appalachian Kentucky, 11, 16; literature on, 111, 148; unionism in, 111–12, 114, 116, 118–21, 127, 132; and Kentucky's

post–Civil War identity, 111–32 passim; perceived whiteness of, 113–14, 119, 122, 124, 129, 131, 201 (n. 23); feuding and violence in, 127–32
Aron, Stephen, 75
Atlanta Constitution, 53
Atlantic Monthly, 119–20, 179

Back Home (Cobb), 147
Ballard County, Ky., 65
Barlow, Anastasia, 162
Barlow, Florence, 162–64
Barlow, Milt, 167
Barlow, Milton, 162
Barnes, Sidney, 45–46
Barren County, Ky., 48
Barrymore, Lionel, 145–46
Barton, William E., 114–15, 121, 122
Beckham, J. C. W., 170
Bederman, Gail, 76
Bell, John, 2, 16–17, 37, 86
The Belle of the Blue Grass Country (Pittman), 153
Benevolent Society (Winchester), 47
Ben-Hur (Wallace), 155
Berea College, 13, 117–22
Berea Quarterly, 120–22
Big Sandy Valley, 116
Birth of a Nation, 170–71
Blair, James, 67
Blight, David, 6, 88, 94, 134
Bluegrass region, 11, 12, 58
Boone, Daniel, 73, 77
Booneville, Ky., 66
Boston Standard, 106

Bowling Green, Ky., 17, 102
Boyle, Jeremiah, 21
Boyle County, Ky., 68
Bragg, Braxton, 42, 86
Bramlette, Thomas, 27, 44, 68
Brandeis, Louis, 96
Breathitt County, Ky., 65, 131
Breckinridge, John C., 16, 85–86; monument to, 86–87
Breckinridge, Robert J., 14, 18, 19
Breckinridge, W. C. P., 52
Bridgewater, James, 65–66
Brisbin, J. S., 47
Bristow, Benjamin Helm, 96
Brown, John, 94
Brundage, W. Fitzhugh, 5, 85, 164
Buchanan, James, 86
Buckner, Benjamin, 24–25
Buckner, Simon Bolivar, 83, 88, 181
Buell, Don Carlos, 22
Burbridge, Stephen Gano, 23, 40, 87, 94
Burnside, Ambrose, 22
Burton, Thomas, 64
Butler, William, 47–48, 93

Camden (N.J.) Review, 105
Camp Dick Robinson, 81
Campfires of the Confederacy, 162
Camp Nelson, 26, 81, 185
Camp Nelson Civil War Heritage Site, 185, 187
Cavalier image, 73, 75–76
Century, 90, 112, 123, 130
Chase, Salmon P., 18, 23
Chicago Record, 106
Chicago Tribune, 44, 136
Children of the Confederacy, 161, 162
Cincinnati, Ohio, 11, 15, 50
Cincinnati Commercial, 39, 47, 73
Cincinnati Evening Times, 51
Cincinnati Gazette, 37, 39, 40, 41, 45, 54, 86
"Civilizing the Cumberland" (Fox), 131
The Clansman (Dixon), 169–70
Clark, Thomas D., 204–5 (n. 3)
Clark County, Ky., 81
Clay, Brutus, 18–19, 28–29, 31
Clay, Cassius, 13–14, 18, 20, 116, 117
Clay, Green, 22

Clay, Henry, 17, 18, 75, 85
Clay County, Ky., 115
Cleveland Gazette, 106
Cobb, Irvin, 134, 146–47
Cochran, Hattie, 139–40
Collier, Robert, 175
Colliers Weekly, 134, 174, 175
Colored Boosters Club, 170
Colored Ministers Alliance, 170
Colored State Central Committee, 46
"Comments on Kentucky" (Warner), 112
Confederacy, symbols of, 5, 183–84
Confederate Association of Kentucky, 157
Confederate Burial Memorial Association
Confederates: monuments to, 1, 84, 86–87, 155–56, 160–61, 163, 171–74, 181–82, 184–85, 204–5 (n. 3); postwar behavior of, in Kentucky, 39–40; leadership of, in Democratic Party, 39–40, 43–44, 64; as perpetrators of postwar violence, 56, 64–67
Confederates in the Attic (Horwitz), 184
Confederate Veteran, 109, 162, 181
Confederate Veterans Association of Kentucky, 157
Confederate Veterans Home (Kentucky), 144, 164, 171
"Confedrit X Roads," 49–50
Conservative Democrats. See Democratic Party
Conservative Union Party, 38, 47
Constitutional Union Party, 16, 37–39
Coppini, Pompeo, 172–74
Cosmopolitan, 112
Coulter, E. Merton, 2, 3, 14
Covington, Ky., 11, 107, 168
Cowan, Andrew, 176
Cox, Karen, 161
Cunningham, S. A., 181
Crime. See Violence
Crittenden, John, 18, 28
"The Cumberland Mountains and the Struggle for Freedom" (Barton), 121
"A Cumberland Vendetta" (Fox), 123
Cynthiana, Ky., 83, 172

Daily Kentucky Yeoman, 40, 68
Davidson, Hannah, 65

Daviess County, Ky., 59

Davis, Garrett, 23, 44

Davis, Jefferson, 33, 49, 83, 88, 147, 161,
175, 188; birthplace monument to, 181–
82, 184, 187, 188; controversy over
statue to, in Frankfort, 184

Davison, A. M., 93

Decoration Days. *See* Memorial days

Democratic Party, 4, 16, 37, 38; and postwar politics in Kentucky, 33–34; postwar
success of, 41–45, 50–52; ex-Confederate
leadership in, 39–40, 43–44; "Bourbon"
movement in, 194 (n. 46) "New Departure" movement within, 52–54; as spon-
sor of violence, 64–68

Dennett, Alfred, 175

Denver Post, 109

Dixie Outfitters, 184

Dixon, Susan Bullitt, 30, 31, 57

Dixon, Thomas, 169

Dodd, William O., 88

Dodge, Levant, 175

Douglass, Frederick, 99–101

Dueling, 75. *See also* Violence

Duke, Basil, 10, 52, 83, 88, 96, 158, 163, 172,
176; as editor of *Southern Bivouac*, 89–90,
97; opposition to organized labor, 96–97

Duke, Henrietta Morgan, 163–64

Dunbar, Paul Laurence, 148–53

Duvall, Alvin, 40–42

Early, Jubal, 86

Eastern Kentucky. *See* Appalachian
Kentucky

Edmonds, Richard, 51

Ekkoes from Kentucky (Locke), 49–50

Emancipation, 10, 23–24, 28, 34–38; as
cause of changing wartime loyalties in
Kentucky, 23–30, 31, 41; and compensation for slave owners, 24, 34–35, 41;
white reaction to in Kentucky, 35–37;
and Union war memory, 93–94

Emancipation Day Celebrations, 5, 46,
82, 92–93

Emancipation Proclamation, 26, 29, 92;
preliminary, 24, 41

Eminence, Ky., 87

Estill County, Ky., 59

Fairview, Ky., 181

"A Family Feud" (Dunbar), 150

Fayette County Justice Association

Fee, John, 13, 116, 117

Feuding, 127. *See also* Violence

Field, Henry, 78

Fields, John, 27

Fifteenth Amendment, 63, 93, 117

"The Finish of Patsy Barnes" (Dunbar),
151

Fitzhugh, R. H., 157

Flemingsburg, Ky., 165, 168

Floyd County, Ky., 116

Folks from Dixie (Dunbar), 149

Foner, Eric, 193 (n. 12)

Foster, Gaines, 84, 183, 205 (n. 14)

Foster, Stephen, 16

Fourteenth Amendment, 40, 42

Fourth of July celebrations, 5, 46, 81–82,
92–93

Fox, John, Jr., 123–30, 131

Frankfort, 58, 64, 78, 136

Frank Leslie's Illustrated Newspaper, 84

Freedmen's Bureau, 38–39, 49, 61–62

Freehling, William, 13

Free South, 14

Frost, William Goodell, 119–20, 121–22,
131, 132, 201 (n. 23)

Fry, Speed, 66, 185

Fugitive Slave Law, 19–20

Fulton, Ky., 168

Galt, Laura, 162

Gannon, Barbara, 198 (n. 23)

Garrard County, Ky., 68, 131

Gaston, Paul, 51, 144

Georgetown, Ky., 161

Godkin, E. L., 73

Goebel, William, 134

Grady, Henry, 51, 53

Grand Army of the Republic (GAR), 89,
122, 156, 157; 1895 encampment in
Louisville, 1, 103–10, 155, 171; difficulties of, in Kentucky, 90–91, 174–75;
racism in, 91–92, 106–8

Grand Rapids (Mich.) Democrat, 108

Grant, Ulysses S., 66, 70

Grayson, Ky., 169

"Great Hog Swindle," 23
Greeley, Horace, 54
Green, Lizzie E., 102
Green, Nancy Lewis, 162
Green Hill Cemetery (Frankfort), 182
Griffith, D. W., 170
Grinnell, Josiah, 44
Guerrant, Edward, 29, 88
Guerrilla warfare, 21, 22, 33, 57, 131
Gunlock, Nettie, 105
Guthrie, Ky., 135, 184

Hagood, L. M., 169
Haldeman, Walter, 40, 52
Halstead, Murat, 73
Hardin, Lizzie, 32–33, 35, 55, 81
Harkins, Anthony, 128
Harlan County, Ky., 66
Harlan, John Marshall, 66, 176
Harper's Weekly, 72, 74, 111, 112, 123–24
Harris, Joel Chandler, 134, 144, 153
Harrison, Alfred, 55
Harrison, Lowell, 42
Harrodsburg, Ky., 32
Hatfield-McCoy feud, 131
Hawes, Maria, 9, 30, 31
Hawes, Richard, 9
Hays, Will, 108
Helm, John L., 42, 43
Hemp, 12
Henderson, Ky., 57
Henry County, Ky., 59, 61, 69, 77, 131
*A Hero in Homespun: A Tale of the Loyal
   South* (Barton), 114–15
Hill, David, 29
History of Morgan's Cavalry (Duke), 88
History of the First Kentucky Brigade
   (Thompson), 87
Hobson, Edward, 40–42
Hogg, Hiram, 21
Holt, Joseph, 19–20, 46, 94
Home and Farm, 89
Homicide: North and South (Redfield), 73
Honor, concept of, 73–80
Hopkinsville Kentuckian, 105
Horwitz, Tony, 182, 184
Howard, Victor, 26
Howells, William Dean, 153

Hudson, Blaine, 185
Hunt, Lynn, 189 (n. 7)

Illustrated Confederate War Journal, 162

Jackson, Jordan, 176
Jackson County, Ky., 115
Jacob, Charles, 96
Jefferson Davis Memorial Association,
   181–82
Jeffersontown, Ky., 87
Jessamine County, Ky., 155–56
Jessamine County Memorial Association,
   155
Jim Crow laws, 143
Johnson, Andrew, 37
Johnson County, Ky., 116
Johnston, Annie Fellows, 133–34, 138–45,
   153, 154
Johnston, J. Stoddard, 40, 45, 68, 83, 176

Kemble, E. W., 152–53
"The Kentuckian" (Speed), 130
The Kentuckians (Fox), 123, 129–30
Kentucky: A Pioneer Commonwealth
   (Shaler), 177
Kentucky Colonel, image of, 54, 72, 135,
   136–37, 140, 145–46
Kentucky Historical Society, 188
Kentucky Lincoln Heritage Trail, 187
Kentucky Statesman, 42
Kentucky Women's Monument Association,
   155
Kinchloe, Jesse, 46
Klotter, James, 76
Knights of Labor, 97
Knott, Richard W., 89
Krock, Arthur, 146
Ku Klux Klan, 46, 58–60, 62, 63, 64–65, 66,
   67–69, 70, 71

Ladies Memorial and Monument Associa-
   tion (Lexington), 84
Ladies of the GAR, 105, 107, 200 (n. 62)
Lancaster, Ky., 81, 93
The Land of the Little Colonel (Johnston),
   138
Lawler, Thomas G., 104, 106–7

Lawlessness. *See* Violence

Lawrence County, Ky., 116

Leathers, John, 176–77

Lebanon, Ky., 59, 81

Lee, Robert E., 94–95, 157, 159, 161

Leslie, Preston, 68–69

Levering, Abraham, 105

Lewis County, Ky., 55

Lexington, 11, 12, 46, 58, 63, 70, 84, 87, 88, 157, 160, 161

Lexington Cemetery, 83, 84

Lexington Daily Transcript, 86

Lexington Gazette, 61

Lexington Leader, 153, 168, 174

Lexington Observer and Reporter, 14, 37, 52, 86

Lincoln, Abraham, 16–17, 20, 46, 86, 116, 120, 142, 147; administration of, 10, 22, 38; and relationship to Kentucky during Civil War, 22, 24–25; white Kentuckians views of, during Civil War, 27–28, 38; cast as Appalachian, 121–22; creation of birthplace monument for, 175–78, 207 (n. 57); in Civil War memory, 175–78, 183, 185–88; as Kentuckian, 185–87; bicentennial celebration of, 185–88

Lincoln, Nancy Hanks, 187

Lincoln, Sarah Bush Johnston, 187

Lincoln, Thomas, 187

Lincoln Centenary Committee, 176

Lincoln County, Ky., 65, 68

Lincoln Farm Association, 175–77, 178, 181

Lincoln Heritage Trail, 187, 208 (n. 8)

Lincoln Marriage Temple, 187

Literature, 2; historical memory of Kentucky in, 49–50, 111–12, 119–32, 133–54 passim; portrayal of Appalachian Kentucky in, 111–15, 119–21, 123–31; portrayal of Civil War loyalties in, 111–15, 123–27, 144–45, 147–48, 150–51; portrayal of African Americans in, 134, 137–38, 140–44, 147–53

The Little Colonel, 133, 140–46, 154

The Little Shepherd of Kingdom Come (Fox), 123–28

Lloyd, John Uri, 147–48

Locke, David Ross, 49–50

Logan, John A., 91

London, Ky., 116

Lost Cause, 5, 34, 54, 83–84, 85, 86, 127, 144, 156, 160, 164, 180, 183

Lost Cause, 162–64

Louisville, 1, 11, 16, 35, 46, 47, 48, 58, 94, 155, 157, 160, 162, 184; labor disturbances in, 96–97; as host of 1883 national African American convention, 99–102; as host of 1895 GAR encampment, 103–10; as host of 1900 UCV reunion, 158–60; as host of 1904 UCV reunion, 160

Louisville & Nashville Railroad, 88

Louisville Commercial, 71, 95, 104, 105, 108, 159–60

Louisville Courier, 40, 51, 62

Louisville Courier Journal, 1, 51–54, 61, 67, 70, 72, 130, 145, 155, 159–60; as mouthpiece of sectional reconciliation, 97–98; on 1883 African American national convention, 100–101

Louisville Journal, 18, 40, 51

Louisville Post, 107, 108

Louisville Times, 145

Loyal League, 63, 66, 68, 69

Lucas, Marion, 27

Lynching, 60–65, 151–52, 184

Lyrics of Lowly Life (Dunbar), 153

Madison County, Ky., 64, 66

Magoffin, Beriah, 2, 94

Magoffin County, Ky., 65

"Mammy" (freedwoman), 9

Manchester, Ky., 116

Marion County, Ky., 59

Marrs, Elijah, 63

Marshall, Humphrey, 88

McKee, Sam, 42–43

Memorial activities, 4, 81–110 passim, 122, 155–82 passim; African American, 47, 82; and political meaning, 82; women's role in, 84–86, 105, 107, 122, 160–73, 182, 200 (n. 62)

Memorial days: national, 82, 156, 197 (n. 3); Confederate, 84–87, 197 (n. 3)

Mercer County, Ky., 68

Midway, Ky., 87

Milward, H. K., 91

Minneapolis Journal, 109
"Miss Confederacy" pageant, 184
Mitchell, Robert, 102
Montgomery Mail, 51
Monticello, Ky., 60
Monuments, 183; Confederate, 1, 84, 86–
    87, 155–56, 160–61, 163, 171–74, 184–
    85, 204–5 (n. 3); to Confederate martyrs,
    87, 181–82; Union, 94, 117, 155–56, 179,
    182, 185, 204–5 (n. 3)
Morehead, Charles, 21
Morgan, John Hunt, 29, 40, 57, 81, 83, 127,
    161, 170, 172; monument to, 171–74
"Morgan's Men," 156–57
"A Mountain Europa" (Fox), 123
Mt. Sterling, Ky., 172
Murray, Eli, 96
Murray (Ky.) Ledger, 106
"My Old Kentucky Home" (Foster), 16

Nasby, Petroleum V. *See* Locke, David Ross
Nast, Thomas, 72, 74
Nation, 73
National Association for the Advance-
    ment of Colored People (NAACP), 170
National Collegiate Athletic Association
    (NCAA) basketball Championship
    (1966), 183–84
National Tribune, 157
"Nelse Hatton's Vengeance" (Dunbar), 150
Newport, Ky., 1
New South, 109; Kentucky as part of, 51–
    54, 109
New York Times, 39, 43, 44, 55, 86, 108–9;
    as critic of Kentucky violence, 58, 66, 67,
    70, 71, 76–79, 130
New York Tribune, 39, 50
Nicholasville, Ky., 155–56
Nightriders, 59. *See also* Ku Klux Klan;
    Regulators

"The Oddities of Southern Life" (Watter-
    son), 97
Ohio River, 11, 13
Oldham County, Ky., 59
Order No. 59, 23, 87
Orphan Brigade, 88, 179, 181

"Our Contemporary Ancestors in the
    Southern Mountains" (Frost), 119–20
Outlook, 119
Owen County, Ky., 65, 69, 131
Oxley, Jefferson, 155

Paducah, Ky., 146
Page, Thomas Nelson, 134, 144, 153
Page, Walter Hines, 51
Palmer, John, 35, 46, 47
Parades, 4, 5, 92
Paris, Ky., 60, 165
Parrish, Charles H., 176
Parson, E. Y., 72
Pewee Valley, Ky., 138, 140–44, 147, 154
Perry County, Ky., 65
Perryville, battle of, 159, 171, 185–86
Perryville Battlefield Historical Site, 187
Perryville Battlefield Preservation Associa-
    tion, 185–86
Philadelphia Inquirer, 136
Phillips, Andrew, 29
Phillips, D. C., 37
Pike County, Ky., 116
Pikeville, Ky., 116
Pinkerton, Allan, 96
Pirtle, Andrew, 25
Pittman, Hannah, 153
Pittsburgh Commercial, 71
Pittsburgh Gazette, 39
Pollard, Edward, 199 (n. 40)
Populist movement, 54
Porter, Rebecca, 140, 143
Power, Alice Bruce, 165
Preliminary Emancipation Proclamation,
    24, 41
Prentice, George, 18, 40, 51
Preston, William, 43, 83, 85, 88
Princeton Banner (Ky.), 77
Publisher's Weekly, 144
Pulitzer, Joseph, 72

Reconciliation, 94–99, 156–60, 171; and
    1895 GAR encampment, 103–10; and
    Lincoln's birthplace, 175–78
Reconstruction, federal, 2, 56, 79, 127;
    celebration of ending of, 95–96

Redfield, H. V., 73

Regulator groups, 58–60, 62, 66. *See also* Ku Klux Klan

Reid, Whitelaw, 35, 73

Reinterment, 82–83

Republican Party, 38, 40, 42; postwar weakness of, in Kentucky, 45–46; African American voters in, 46–48; as victims of postwar violence, 56, 63, 65–67; in Appalachian Kentucky, 116–17

Reynolds, Mrs. Dudley, 162

Riley, William E., 33

Robinson, Stuart, 21

Rogers, J. A. R., 121

Roosevelt, Theodore, 120, 123, 177

Ross, J. Allen, 102

Rosseau, Lovell, 44–45

Rowan County, Ky., 131

Rupp, Adolph, 184

Russellville, 17, 65

St. Joseph, Ky., 87

Saturday Evening Post, 146

Saufley, Micah, 30, 31

Scott, Anne Firor, 143

Scott, Charles, 165, 167–68

Scott County, Ky., 66

Scribner's, 112, 127

Sea, Sophie Fox, 164–65

Semmes, Raphael, 94

Semple, Ellen Churchill, 113–14, 115

Shaler, Nathaniel Southgate, 177–79

Shapiro, Henry, 112

Sherman, John, 70

Silber, Nina, 108, 201 (n. 23)

Simmons Band, 78

Simrall, Belle, 30

Singal, Daniel, 75

Skagg's Men, 59

Slavery, 1; in Kentucky, 10–16, 23–24, 34; in historical memory, 164–71, 177, 183, 187–88; in Appalachian Kentucky, 115–16

Sleettown, Ky., 185

Smith, E. Kirby, 83

Smith, George, 22

Smith, James, 92

Sons of Confederate Veterans (SCV), 158, 188

Southern Bivouac, 89–90, 162, 163; as voice of sectional reconciliation, 95; anti-labor messages in, 97; on 1883 national African American convention, 101

Southern Historical Society, 88

Southern Historical Society Papers, 88–89

"The Southern Mountaineer" (Fox), 123–24

"The Southern Mountaineer: Our Kindred of the Boone and Lincoln Type" (Barton), 122

Southern Relief Association, 83

Spanish-American War, 156, 160

Speed, James, 18, 39, 47

Speed, James Gilmer, 130

Speed, Joshua, 176

Speed, Thomas, 177, 179–81

Stamping Ground, Ky., 63

Stanley, A. O., 135

Stanton, Edwin, 22

Stevenson, John, 43, 68, 70

Steward, W. H., 102

Stowe, Harriet Beecher, 15–16, 165, 190 (n. 16)

Strikes, 96–97

Stringtown-on-the-Pike: A Tale of Northernmost Kentucky (Lloyd), 147–48

Syracuse Courier, 109

Tallant, Harold, 14

Taylor, William, 75

Temple, Shirley, 145

Texas Western University, 183–84

Thirteenth Amendment, 38, 40, 187

Thompson, Edwin Porter, 87

Thornton, J. R., 21

Tilden, Samuel, 72

Tobacco, 12; and violence in Kentucky, 134–36

Todd County, Ky., 181–82, 183–84

Tolliver-Martin feud, 131

Tompkins, Daniel, 51

"The Tragedy at Three Forks" (Dunbar), 151–52

Tri-weekly Commonwealth (Frankfort), 41, 42

Tri-weekly Yeoman (Frankfort), 83
The True American, 13
Tuttle, John, 57–58
12th United States Colored Heavy Artillery
   Regiment, 185
"Two Gentlemen of Kentucky" (Allen), 137
Tyler, Henry, 105
Tyler, Mary Creel, 105, 107

Uncle Charles (slave), 35
Uncle Tom's Cabin (Stowe), 15–16, 165
"Uncle Tom's Cabin" (traveling produc-
   tion), 165–71
Uncle Tom's Cabin Law, 170–71
Unconditional Union Party. *See* Union
   Party
Underwood, Edward E., 176
The Union Cause in Kentucky (Speed),
   180–81
Union of Benevolent Societies, 46
Unionists: in postwar Kentucky politics,
   44–45, 48–49; and wartime symbols, 48–
   49; as victims of postwar violence, 56,
   59, 63, 65–67; as perpetrators of postwar
   violence, 66; monuments to, 94, 117,
   155–56, 179, 182, 185, 204–5 (n. 3)
Union Party, 38, 46
Union Regiments of Kentucky (Speed),
   179–80
United Brothers of Friendship, 46
United Confederate Veterans (UCV),
   157–58, 168, 173; 1900 reunion in Louisville of, 158–60, 171; 1904 reunion in
   Louisville of, 160
United Daughters of the Confederacy
   (UDC), 160–73, 181; and campaign to
   ban *Uncle Tom's Cabin*, 165–71; and
   construction of Morgan monument,
   172–74
University of Kentucky, 183–84
University of Louisville, 184–85

Vanceburg, Ky., 117
Van Pelt, S. D., 174
Violence: and postwar elections, 41;
   against Republicans, 45; and restoration of prewar social order, 56, 58–69,
   70; and Kentucky's reputation, 56, 70–
   73, 76–80, 99, 134–37; and antebellum
   chivalry, 56, 73–76; committed by mobs,
   56–58, 68–69, 78; and Ku Klux Klan, 58–
   59; against African Americans, 58–70;
   and control over black labor, 59; and
   black emigration, 59–60; and lynching,
   60–65; caused by African American political activity, 62–64, 131; and African
   American postwar historical memory,
   64–65; northern critiques of, 65–73, 75–
   80; response of Kentucky's government
   to, 68–69; Kentucky's history of, 73–75;
   and ideas of civilization, 73–79; and
   concept of honor, 73–80; and gender,
   75–76; geography of, 78; and prevalence
   of firearms, 78; and Confederate identity, 79–80; in Appalachian Kentucky,
   127–32, 134; and tobacco wars, 134–36.
   See also Guerilla warfare

Wallace, Ellen, 21, 25–26, 28, 30
Waller, Altina, 129
Ward, Florence, 169
Warner, Charles Dudley, 112–13, 130–31
Warren, Robert Penn, 5, 135, 181, 183,
   184, 188
Warren County, Ky., 48
Washington, Booker T., 148
Washington Times, 136
Watterson, Henry, 1, 176, 185; and found-
   ing of *Louisville Courier-Journal*, 50–54;
   as New South spokesman, 50–54, 98–
   99; as opponent of violence, 68–71, 129–
   30; as symbol of violence, 72–74, 78–79;
   as voice of sectional reconciliation, 97–
   98, 199 (n. 40); on African Americans,
   98; as source of Kentucky's Confederate
   identity, 98–99; on 1883 African Ameri-
   can national convention, 100–101; and
   1895 national GAR encampment, 103
Wayne County, Ky., 57
Whig Party, 17, 37
Williams, John Alexander, 116
Williamsburg, Ky., 160
Willson, Augustus, 176
Wilson, Shannon, 120
Winchester, Ky., 93, 172
Woodson, Isaac T., 104

Wolfe County, Ky., 65

Wolford, Frank, 27–28, 45, 94

Woman's Christian Temperance Movement (WCTU), 171

Woman's Relief Corps (WRC), 107, 182, 200 (n. 62)

Woodford County, Ky., 63

Woodward, C. Vann, 34, 76, 113

Wright, George, 60

Wyatt-Brown, Bertram, 75

Young, Bennett, 52, 96, 158, 160, 162, 181